"Tanahashi's book on the *Heart Sutra* in its primarily Chinese and Japanese contexts covers a wide range of approaches to this most famous of all mahayana sutras. It brings the sutra to life through shedding light on it from many different angles, through presenting its historical background and traditional commentaries, evaluating modern scholarship, adapting the text to a contemporary readership, exploring its relationship to Western science, and relating personal anecdotes. The richness of the *Heart Sutra* and the many ways in which it can be understood and contemplated are further highlighted by his comparison of its versions in the major Asian languages in which it has been transmitted, as well as in a number of English translations. Highly recommended for all who wish to explore the profundity of this text in all its facets."
— Karl Brunnhölzl, author of *The Heart Attack Sutra: A New Commentary on the Heart Sutra*

"A masterwork of loving and meticulous scholarship, Kaz Tanahashi's *Heart Sutra* is a living, breathing, deeply personal celebration of a beloved text, which all readers—Buddhists and non-Buddhists, newcomers to the teaching and seasoned scholars alike—will cherish throughout time."
— Ruth Ozeki, author of *A Tale for the Time Being*

THE

Heart Sutra

A Comprehensive Guide to the Classic of Mahayana Buddhism

KAZUAKI TANAHASHI

SHAMBHALA
Boston & London
2014

Shambhala Publications, Inc.
Horticultural Hall
300 Massachusetts Avenue
Boston, Massachusetts 02115
www.shambhala.com

9 8 7 6 5 4 3 2 1

FIRST EDITION
Printed in the United States of America

♾ This edition is printed on acid-free paper that meets the
American National Standards Institute Z39.48 Standard.
♻ This book is printed on 30% postconsumer recycled paper.
For more information please visit www.shambhala.com.

Distributed in the United States by Random House, Inc.,
and in Canada by Random House of Canada Ltd

Designed by Steve Dyer

LIBRARY OF CONGRESS CATALOGING-IN-PUBLICATION DATA
Tanahashi, Kazuaki, 1933–
The Heart Sutra: a comprehensive guide to the classic of Mahayana Buddhism /
Kazuaki Tanahashi. — First edition.
pages   cm
Includes bibliographical references and index.
ISBN 978-1-61180-096-8 (hardcover: alk. paper) 1. Tripitaka. Sutrapitaka.
Prajñaparamita. Hrdaya — Criticism, interpretation, etc. I. Tripitaka.
Sutrapitaka. Prajñaparamita. Hrdaya. English. II. Title.
BQ1967.T35 2014
294.3'85 — dc23
2013026815

To Peter Levitt

POETRY
DHARMA
FRIENDSHIP

Contents

vii

Illustrations

Preface and Acknowledgments

THE *HEART SUTRA* is the most widely recited scripture in Mahayana Buddhism. It is a text revered by millions of people and regarded as the most succinct presentation of the dharma. In its short form, the text summarizes the selfless experience of reality in meditation, and how this transcends our usual way of thinking.

Edward Conze, an Anglo-German expert on *Prajna Paramita* scriptures, once characterized the *Heart Sutra* as "one of the sublimest spiritual documents of mankind."[1] Every Mahayana Buddhist practitioner will understand Conze's reverent words of adoration. At the same time, the widespread and everlasting reverence and enthusiasm for this text that is full of negations is, to me, an unceasing enigma.

While understanding the meaning of each word and the teachings of the sutra enhances one's meditation practice and life experience, it must also be said that chanting the sutra wholeheartedly, without cognitively thinking through its message, has been an important Buddhist practice throughout the centuries wherever this sutra has been encountered. Considering all of these factors, I believe it is highly useful to examine why we are chanting it today.

This book presents my own encounter with, and exploration of, the *Heart Sutra* — its message, its history, its significance. I hope your journey through these pages will widen and deepen your connection to this extraordinary scripture.

Part One, "The *Heart Sutra* Here and Now," presents a new translation of the text by Joan Halifax and myself. Our intention is to bring forth the sutra's essential teaching of transcendence and freedom, which is often obscured by seemingly pessimistic and nihilistic expressions. We use the word "boundlessness" instead of the more common translation "emptiness" for the Sanskrit word *shunyata*. We use "free of the eyes, ears, nose . . ." instead of the usual rendition "no eyes, no ears, no nose . . ." Because we want to make the sutra accessible to non-Buddhists as well as Buddhists, we have replaced such traditional technical terms as *bodhisattva* and *nirvana* with more easily understandable words. I hope those of you who are used to chanting the common English versions of the sutra will find our translation helpful and thought-provoking. This first part also includes stories of my own affinity with the scripture and its potential to inspire us all.

Part Two, "Story of the Sutra," introduces ancient recountings of its use as a living text, as well as descriptions of my visits to temples in Korea and Japan, where I conducted research on the historical impact of the sutra.

Parts Three and Four, "Modern Scholarship" and "Most Recent Scholarship," discuss scholarly findings over the course of two centuries about the formation and expansion of the text.

Part Five, "Globalizing the Sutra," discusses Chinese enthusiasm for and pan-Asian responses to the text, as well as examples of how the sutra has inspired modern scientists.

Part Six, "Terms and Concepts," includes semantic, etymological, and grammatical analyses of the Sanskrit and Chinese terms in the text. Most of the words in the sutra have Sanskrit origins, so looking at these terms is extremely fruitful. A Chinese version has become the standard text in East Asia, however, and was the basis for some of the translations of the sutra in European languages. Three English translations are also included here: the version by F. Max Müller from the late nineteenth century, as well as those by D. T. Suzuki and Edward Conze from the twentieth century. I believe these three have been the most influential renditions of the sutra in the Western world.

You may find this part helpful for learning the meaning and linguistic background of terms in the *Heart Sutra*. For your reference, I have endeavored to provide, wherever I could, the linguistic relationship between the Sanskrit terms and their English counterparts.

The appendices include "Texts for Comparison," which presents samples of the *Heart Sutra* in seven Asian languages (Sanskrit, Chinese, Korean, Japanese, Vietnamese, Tibetan, and Mongolian), followed by several of their English counterparts. Earlier texts in Sanskrit and Chinese that are regarded as the main sources of the *Heart Sutra* are also included. The texts of all versions of the sutra are each divided into as many as forty or more segments. These parallel divisions are designed to facilitate finding words and comparing them across versions. As all of the non-English texts are presented in or accompanied by romanized transliterations, it is possible to cross-reference the texts even without knowing the particular languages or ideographs. "Identical Expressions in the Chinese Texts" shows the influence of earlier translations on each version of the *Heart Sutra* text.

What a joyous experience it has been to write a lengthy thesis on such a short scripture! What I have learned through research and contemplation turned out to be beyond my wildest fantasy. I started to see — and have continued to draw upon — the invisible connections among bits of information scattered throughout Asia and beyond. A great number of my predecessors and colleagues have guided me:

First, I would like to express my deep gratitude to the scholars and dharma teachers — both Asian and Western — who have studied, clarified, and elucidated the *Heart Sutra's* textual form, background, and meaning over the centuries. I have particularly benefited from the works of Dr. F. Max Müller, Dr. Bunyiu Nanjio, Dr. Hajime Nakamura, Dr. Daisetz T. Suzuki, Dr. Edward Conze, Dr. Donald S. Lopez, Jr., Dr. Shuyo Takubo, Dr. Shuyu Kanaoka, Dr. John McRae, Bernie Glassman Roshi, Dr. Vesna Wallace, Red Pine, Karl Brunnhölzl, Dr. Sally Hovey Wriggins, Dr. Abdurishid Yakup, Chögyam Trungpa Rinpoche, Thich Nhat Hanh, and His Holiness the Dalai Lama.

The pioneering work of Dr. Jan Nattier has shaped my understanding on the origin of the sutra. Dr. Paul Harrison kindly offered me a revised and thorough reading of an archaic Sanskrit fragment of the *Prajna Paramita* literature that corresponds to the earliest known form of the *Hridaya* — the Sanskrit form of the *Heart Sutra*. Dr. Fumimasa-Bunga Fukui's extensive and complete philological study of the sutra has benefited me tremendously. Rev. Dongho, Rev. Quang Huyen, and Erdenebaatar Erdene-Ochir have provided me with transliterations of the Korean, Vietnamese, and Mongolian versions, respectively. I thank Dr. Christian P. B. Haskett for his transliteration and translation of the Tibetan version for this volume and for his advice on Sanskrit. My gratitude goes to Rev. M. H. Lahey, another Sanskrit advisor, as well as to Xiao Yongming and Andy Ferguson, my Chinese romanization advisors, for their thorough advice. Thanks go also to Ellen Marie Herbert for her research on subjects regarding Korea.

The Chinese Buddhist texts I have used were drawn from the website of the Chinese Buddhist Electronic Text Association in Taiwan.

Joan Halifax Roshi has been a marvelous collaborator for me in working out our new translation of the sutra. We have tried hard to create this rendering, have chanted it in a number of services, and have expounded the sutra together in our intensive meditation retreats at the Upaya Zen Center in Santa Fe. Joan and I thank Christoph Hatlapa Roshi, Rev. Heinz-Jürgen Metzger, and Dr. Friederike Boissevain for their translations of this version of the *Heart Sutra* into German. We also thank our friends who have translated it into other languages: Rev. Shinzan Jose M. Palma and Daniel Terragno Roshi (Spanish), Rev. Amy Hollowell and Joa Scetbon-Didi (French), Chiara Pandolfi and Guglielmo Capelli (Italian), Prof. Alexandre Avdoulov (Russian), Tenkei Coppens Roshi (Dutch), and Rev. Luc De Winter (Flemish). It was wonderful to sit in the large cathedral in Antwerp and hear the polyphonic singing of our English version, set to music by Luc De Winter.

I thank Dr. Jon Kabat-Zinn, Dr. Laurence Dorsey, Dr. Steven Heine, Dr. Taigen Dan Leighton, Robert Aitken Roshi, Shunryu Suzuki Roshi, Roko Shinge Chayat Roshi, Richard Baker Roshi, Mel Weitsman Roshi, Chozen Bays Roshi, Hogen Bays Roshi, Dr. William Johnston, Dr. Richard Levine, Acharya David Schneider, Dr. Eric Greene, Abbot Gaelyn Godwin, Dr. Roger S. Keyes, and Dr. Linda Hess for their expert advice. I appreciate Dr. Hideki Yukawa, Dr. Piet Hut, Dr. Neil D. Theise, and Dr. Alfred W. Kaszniak for sharing their knowledge and thoughts on recent studies in physics, biology, and neurology. Thanks to Wouter Schopman, Pat Enkyo O'Hara Roshi, Soichi Nakamura Roshi, Lewis Richmond Roshi, Dr. Osamu Ando, Christine Haggarty, Gary Gash, Kichung Lizee, Dr. Hanns Zykan, Dr. Eva Buchinger, Taijung Kim, Hyuntaik Jung, Rev. Peter Zieme, Dr. Anne Weisbrod, Trish Ellis, Arjia Rinpoche, Alexander Williamson, Lona Rothe-Jokisch, Joy C. Brennan, Michael Slouber, Liza Matthews, Sarah Cox, David Cox, Jessie Litven, Tae Shin Lee, Mitsue Nagase, Mahiru Watanabe, Lisa Senauke, Minette Mangahas, and Tempa Dukte Lama for their generous help. Rev. Alan Senauke, Dr. Susan O'Leary, Karuna Tanahashi, Josh Bartok, Rev. Roberta Werdinger, and Peter Levitt have given me most valuable editorial advice. Every time I examine Sanskrit terms and grammar, I remember fondly my private study as a young student with the late Dr. Hidenori Kitagawa.

It's always a great pleasure to work with the staff at Shambhala Publications, including Dave O'Neal, Nikko Odiseos, Hazel Bercholz, Jonathan Green, and Ben Gleason. I thank Karen Ready for her extraordinary copyediting. My gratitude goes to Victoria Shoemaker for representing me.

KAZUAKI TANAHASHI

Notes to the Reader

TITLE

Hridaya in this book refers to a Sanskrit version of the *Heart Sutra* or versions such as Tibetan that have derived from it; the word *sutra* is seldom used in its title.

SANSKRIT

When Sanskrit terms are treated as English words in the main text — that is, when they have been adopted by Webster's dictionary or are commonly familiar to American readers of Buddhist-related materials — they are anglicized so that diacritical marks are omitted (for example: *prajna* and *sutra*). The widely used IAST system (International Alphabet of Sanskrit Transliteration) is used in italics when the meanings of the words are examined (for example: *prajñā* and *sūtra*). IAST romanization is also used in the sutra texts presented in the section called "Texts for Comparison" in the appendices. Compounds are divided except when the original versions transcribed or quoted in "Texts for Comparison" present them in an undivided form.

No Sanskrit words except proper nouns (and Sanskrit words that appear at the beginning of English sentences) are capitalized in this book.

Diacritical marks are omitted in the Notes and Bibliography. *Gate* is spelled *gaté* in "Heart of Realizing Wisdom Beyond Wisdom" (translated by Kazuaki Tanahashi and Joan Halifax) so as not to be pronounced as in "gateway" by some readers who may not be familiar with the text.

CHINESE

The pinyin system of transliteration is used. In this book romanized Chinese words are spelled in two ways: When they represent the transliteration of lines or phrases following a text given in ideographs, they are divided by syllables (i.e., *bo re bo luo mi duo*). Otherwise, two or more syllables are put together as compounds (i.e., *bore boluomiduo*) that correspond to the original Sanskrit words.

In the following list, the right column gives approximate English pronunciations of potentially misread letters used in the pinyin system (shown in the left column):

c	ts
q	ch
x	sh
zh	j

For Chinese ideographs the unabridged form is used.

The ideographs of names indicated in the notes with asterisks (*) are listed in "Names in Ideography" in the appendices in order to assist readers of any East Asian languages.

JAPANESE

Macrons are omitted in the main text. For ideographs, the unabbreviated form is used.

DATES

This book follows the lunar calendar, used traditionally in East Asia. The first to third months correspond to spring, and the other seasons follow in three-month periods.

AGE

This book follows the traditional East Asian way of reckoning a person's age, where he or she is one year old at birth and gains a year on New Year's Day.

PART ONE

The Heart Sutra Here and Now

I

A New Translation

LET ME PRESENT the version of the *Heart Sutra* translated by Joan Halifax and myself in 2002. It is based on the seventh-century Chinese version by Xuanzang, with additional reference to its Sanskrit counterpart, the *Hridaya*. The texts we referred to, along with the best-known English translations, can be found in appendix 1; my thoughts behind the translation of each term can be found in Part Six, "Terms and Concepts."

The Sutra on the Heart of Realizing Wisdom Beyond Wisdom

Avalokiteshvara, who helps all to awaken,
moves in the deep course of
realizing wisdom beyond wisdom,
sees that all five streams of
body, heart, and mind are without boundary,
and frees all from anguish.
O Shariputra [who listens to the teachings of the Buddha],
form is not separate from boundlessness;
boundlessness is not separate from form.
Form is boundlessness; boundlessness is form.
Feelings, perceptions, inclinations, and discernment are also like this.
O Shariputra,
boundlessness is the nature of all things.
It neither arises nor perishes,
neither stains nor purifies,
neither increases nor decreases.

Boundlessness is not limited by form,
nor by feelings, perceptions, inclinations, or discernment.
It is free of the eyes, ears, nose, tongue, body, and mind;
free of sight, sound, smell, taste, touch, and any object of mind;
free of sensory realms, including the realm of the mind.
It is free of ignorance and the end of ignorance.
Boundlessness is free of old age and death,
and free of the end of old age and death.
It is free of suffering, arising, cessation, and path,
and free of wisdom and attainment.

Being free of attainment, those who help all to awaken
abide in the realization of wisdom beyond wisdom
and live with an unhindered mind.
Without hindrance, the mind has no fear.
Free from confusion, those who lead all to liberation
embody profound serenity.
All those in the past, present, and future,
who realize wisdom beyond wisdom,
manifest unsurpassable and thorough awakening.

Know that realizing wisdom beyond wisdom
is no other than this wondrous mantra,
luminous, unequalled, and supreme.
It relieves all suffering.
It is genuine, not illusory.

So set forth this mantra of realizing wisdom beyond wisdom.
Set forth this mantra that says:

GATÉ; GATÉ, PARAGATÉ, PARASAMGATÉ, BODHI! SVAHA!

2

Encountering the Enigma

THE FIRST TIME I chanted the *Heart Sutra* was during the morning service after Zen meditation at the Diamond Sangha in Honolulu. Robert Aitken and his wife Anne had a small meditation group there. They sat on the ground floor of their beautiful home, surrounded by lush tropical plants, in a residential area of the city. It was 1964, a few days after I had first ventured outside Japan at the age of thirty.

Reciting the *Heart Sutra* in Japanese and then in English, I was happy to harmonize with the American meditators' rhythmic chanting. I was also confused: "Emptiness . . . emptiness . . . no eyes, no ears . . ." What could this mean?

D. T. Suzuki put it succinctly:

> What superficially strikes us most while pursuing the text is that it is almost nothing else but a series of negations, and that what is known as Emptiness is pure negativism, which ultimately reduces all things into nothingness.[1]

Although at that time I was not aware of his comment, I had similar feelings about the sutra. I had come from a Shinto family and grown up attending a Protestant church. I had worked at a Buddhist temple, translating the writings of Dogen, a thirteenth-century Zen master, into modern Japanese. I had organized Zen meditation sessions led by my teacher and co-translator, Soichi Nakamura. When I asked him to teach me sutra chanting, my roshi smiled and dismissed me by saying, "You should chant the sutra of the universe." So I had never learned the *Heart Sutra*.

From Honolulu, I went to San Francisco, where I sat with Shunryu

Suzuki Roshi and his group. Abbot of Soko-ji, a Zen temple for Japanese-Americans, he was also teaching meditation to non-Japanese students. One of them, a relaxed young man with an unshaven face and long hair, who might then have been called a beatnik, showed me around the city in his old truck. The interior of his vehicle was ornately decorated; a small Buddha figure was glued onto the center of the dashboard. He would turn his ignition key, offer incense to the Buddha, and take off. While driving, he listened to a tape recording of a group chanting the *Heart Sutra*. I must admit that it sounded rather weird to my ears. This was my initiation into the sixties counterculture in the United States.

During my visit to North America over the next year and a half, I staged exhibitions of my paintings and got to know Zen and Aikido practitioners. Then I went back to Japan to finish my Dogen work with Soichi.

In 1977, I moved to the United States to be a scholar-in-residence at the San Francisco Zen Center. I sat regularly — but not as seriously as most of my fellow meditators. Chanting the *Heart Sutra* in Japanese and English was part of the center's daily routine. I would often go astray and think about the meaning of the words in the sutra, as well as their alternative translations, and usually I would get lost. At times I could not help being self-conscious: as the only native speaker in the crowd, I was supposed to recite the Japanese version fluently, but instead I was the one who kept stumbling.

When it came to the meanings of words in the sutra I had a slight advantage, as I had needed to study Buddhist terminology and philosophy in order to translate Dogen's writings from medieval Japanese and Chinese into modern Japanese and later into English. I fully understood, however, the initial responses of readers who were unfamiliar with the text. Karl Brunnhölzl expresses it clearly in his book *The Heart Attack Sutra:*

> In brief, what we can safely say about the *Heart Sutra* is that it is completely crazy. If we read it, it does not make any sense. Well, maybe the beginning and end make sense, but everything in the middle sounds like a sophisticated form of nonsense, which can be said to be the basic feature of the prajnaparamita sutras in general.[2]

I held the scholar-in-residence post at SFZC until 1984, but by then I had decided to settle in the United States. In 1986 in Ojai, California, I participated in a retreat for artists that was designed to envision the future of American Buddhism, led by Thich Nhat Hanh, the Vietnamese Zen master exiled in France. It was at the retreat that I met Joan Halifax, my collaborator-to-be on the translation of various chants including the *Heart Sutra*. I also met two outstanding poets, Peter Levitt and Rick Fields. Peter, Rick, and I agreed on the need for a new rendition of the *Heart Sutra*. Finding a way to retranslate it was a project we took on at the retreat. But the three of us got stuck on the word usually rendered as "suffering," and did not get any further.

Coincidentally, Nhat Hanh was giving talks on the *Heart Sutra* to the sixty or so retreat participants. Peter Levitt later edited Nhat Hanh's talks on the sutra, creating a book called *The Heart of Understanding*. In spite of his profound practice of buddha dharma, Nhat Hanh used simple words like "love" and "understanding," and clearly elucidated the teaching of the sutra. I believe his writings have been a breakthrough in conveying Buddhist teachings to the West.

From 1989 to 1990, while my wife, Linda, was doing research in India, we lived on the subcontinent for a year with our two young children. In addition to painting and writing, I translated Nhat Hanh's books *The Heart of Understanding* and *Being Peace* into Japanese. Living in India, translating into Japanese the books addressed to a U.S. audience by a Vietnamese master who lived in France — this reflected for me the cross-cultural nature of an emerging, socially engaged global Buddhism.

Since that time, when dharma centers in North America and Europe started to invite me to conduct calligraphy workshops, Dogen seminars, and art shows, my opportunities to chant the *Heart Sutra* have widened. I have heard the sutra chanted in Korean, Chinese, Tibetan, Vietnamese, and Japanese. Western people seem to like to chant the *Heart Sutra* in Asian languages; there is something magical about reciting without fully understanding the words. This may be similar to the experience of people who love praying in Latin at Roman Catholic churches. I have heard the sutra chanted in European languages, too: there is a Dutch version of the sutra, a German version, a French version, and so on. Even if you do not speak these languages, you are able to recognize words that sound like parts of the sutra you usually chant. Although I do not fully understand many foreign versions, I feel happy when I join a recitation. Meditating with a group of people, even strangers, and chanting in one voice feels like a kind of communion — a sacred act that penetrates mundane life. With it, we become part of a centuries-old tradition.

3

Inspiration of the Sutra

T HE *HEART SUTRA* resonates with meditation and a meditative way of life in a way that is as extraordinary as it is profound. Without doubt this is why it is often recited at meditation gatherings and at many Buddhist ceremonies. What, then, are the essential teachings of the *Heart Sutra?* What is its significance for practitioners of meditation today?

Innumerable teachers and scholars have drawn lessons from this text, based on their learning, experiences, and intentions to help others. Here are some of my own interpretations of the sutra, which I offer as a humble student centuries removed from my thirteenth-century Japanese Zen master Dogen — interpretations that are based on the new translation that Joan and I have made and the studies that I undertook.

The fuller title of the *Heart Sutra* is *Prajna Paramita Heart Sutra,* which, as presented earlier, Joan Halifax and I have translated as the "Sutra on the Heart of Realizing Wisdom Beyond Wisdom." It is often regarded as the essence of the enormous body of the Mahayana's *Prajna Paramita* scripture group. (*Prajna* is regarded as "transcendental wisdom." *Paramita* is often translated as "perfection." I will discuss these terms in Part Six, "Terms and Concepts.")

The main purpose of the *Heart Sutra* is to explain the core practice in Mahayana Buddhism, which is, as its title suggests, realization of wisdom beyond wisdom. "Realization," which is none other than actualization, suggests that everything about the sutra is not mere intellectual investigation but practice — practice of meditation. The sutra touches upon three basic themes: the invocation of the bodhisattva Avalokiteshvara; an examination of all things in the light of *shunyata;* and the recitation of the mantra. This approach to dividing the text, which I will refer to later in this book, has been suggested by the U.S. scholar in Buddhist studies, Jan Nattier.

THE INVOCATION OF AVALOKITESHVARA

Avalokiteshvara, a mythological being central to a great number of Buddhist practitioners as the personification of loving-kindness, is mentioned only once in this brief scripture. It is important, however, that this bodhisattva is described in the first line as the one who moves through the deep course of realizing wisdom beyond wisdom. Thus, this line implies that wisdom beyond wisdom is not separate from loving-kindness. (I will further discuss the relationship between these two crucial aspects of human consciousness later in this chapter.)

According to the *Heart Sutra,* it is through practicing wisdom beyond wisdom that Avalokiteshvara becomes free of *duhkha.* The Sanskrit word *duhkha* is usually translated as "suffering," which can refer to a persisting physical pain or loss caused by disease, injury, violence, attack, social injustice or disorder.

Recent scientific studies show that mindful meditation can help reduce stress and provide healing from physical difficulties and psychological disorders.[1] So it is conceivable that a practice like Avalokiteshvara's meditation can at times help to remove the suffering caused by injury or disease.

Suffering can also consist of existential pain and distress brought about by fear of death, actual separation, lack of satisfaction, or failure to fulfill desire. In such instances, the emotional impact of such suffering might be characterized as anguish. Meditation calms one's mind and helps one to see beyond immediate problems or desires. It can lead to a paradigm shift toward a less materialistic and competitive way of life. Thus, meditation can be effective in reducing the "pain" caused by fear, sadness, and desire.

Avalokiteshvara's freedom from anguish is a model presented in this sutra. In understanding, reciting, and practicing this principle of freedom, many others can also experience liberation. So we can interpret the end of the first line of the sutra as "(Avalokiteshvara) frees all (those who practice likewise) from anguish."

CONSIDERING EVERYTHING AS *SHUNYA*

The second theme of the *Heart Sutra* is *shunyata*, which is commonly translated as "emptiness" and can be interpreted as "zeroness." The sutra proclaims that all phenomena are *shunya*, or zero.

True to the joke "Christians love God while Buddhists love lists," the *Heart Sutra* takes up various lists of terms and concepts. The lists included in this sutra are the five *skandhas* (streams of body, heart, and mind); the six modes of change (arising, perishing, staining, purifying, increasing, and decreasing); the six sense organs; the objects of the six senses; the six sense-consciousnesses; certain elements from the twelvefold chain of causation; and the Four Noble Truths.

What does the sutra mean by stating that "all five streams of body, heart, and mind" — forms, feelings, perceptions, inclinations, and discernment — are *shunya*? "Form" means matter or phenomena in most cases. But in the context of the five streams, this word seems to indicate one's physical body. So, "the five streams of body, heart, and mind" can be interpreted as aspects or activities of one's body, heart, and mind. With regard to human beings, it is these aspects and activities that the sutra tells us are *shunya*.

Modern science confirms a close interconnection between body and mind. Where, then, does heart fit in this category? Mind does not exist without heart. And heart does not exist without body. In fact, the heart as an instrument of feeling is inseparable from the heart as an organ. For this reason, these two aspects of human beings — mind and heart — are represented by the same word in some languages. Furthermore, the mind is a part of the body, and vice versa. So it may be good to say "mind, heart, and body." After all, it doesn't make sense to exclude heart from the *Heart Sutra*.

When we feel healthy, we are healthy. When we feel sick, we are sick or become sick. There are a great number of factors (such as genes, age, social and cultural conditioning) that exist or arise out of our control. Within all these limitations, however, we can influence our bodies with our hearts and minds in positive or negative ways.

The "five streams of body, heart, and mind" in the *Heart Sutra* is an analytical description of human existence and its activity. The five streams are body, feelings, perceptions, inclinations, and discernment. ("Inclination" refers to a voluntary or involuntary movement of our mind and heart toward action; "discernment" is the distinguishing of differences.) We perceive, feel, act; we are drawn to something and make distinctions with our mind, heart, and body. We keep receiving information and responding to it through these constantly changing aspects of our existence. At each moment, these five streams work simultaneously, and no individual stream can be isolated from the rest. Thus, none of the five streams exists within a solid set of boundaries. Since this is the case, we can say that every stream is *shunya*, and understand this to mean that each is *shunya* in itself and, at the same time, a functioning part of the others.

When we see an apple, we perceive and recognize it as an apple, enjoy its shape, color, smell, and touch. We desire to eat it, consider whether it's all right to do so, pick it up, and possibly decide to take a bite. Alternatively, we may not eat it because we see a bruise or remember that it is the last remaining fruit and want to leave it for someone else. This is an example of how the five streams of body, heart, and mind work. We make countless decisions and take numerous actions by means of the entwining five streams at any given time.

Although the five streams work as an inseparable entity, it is useful in meditation to see them as streams of five distinct elements. Sometimes in meditation, as in life, we are dominated by one stream. For example, it might be pain in our body, sleepiness, a certain emotion or thought. During this time, our entire being is occupied by a single overpowering physical or emotional sensation. We temporarily lose sight of our existence as an entity composed of the dynamic activities of the five streams.

But when this happens, we can utilize the five streams by consciously shifting our attention from a feeling in the physical body to a focused perception — of the sound of birds chirping, for example, or of our breath as it moves in and out. This method can lead us to serenity and ease, and remedy our self-destructive tendency. Of course, there is a danger of ignoring pain to the point of injury, or diverting emotion to the point of indifference. Dealing with any of the five streams of our body, heart, and mind has to be done with care and moderation. The more conscious we become of the five streams, the more we realize that all these streams are closely intertwined, and that a person is a manifestation of their combined activity.

Once we accept the fact that body, heart, and mind are inseparable, we can become free of the struggle to make the mind, spirit, or soul remain active after the body stops working. Everything is interconnected, and after death no part of us stays as it was. You may go to heaven, paradise, or hell, or be reborn into this world with the deepest, unknowable part of your-self, but it is extremely unlikely that any part of your body or mind will be brought with you as it now is. This realization, of course, may initially cause a great deal of angst. However, we all need to start with the acceptance of its truth. Only after we fully face, take up our abode in, and make peace with this existential reality, can we become liberated. As the sutra says, "Avalokiteshvara . . . frees all from anguish."

This awareness also applies to the moment-to-moment cycles of life. Every moment of our lives, things are both perishing and arising. Some of our cells are dying while others are revitalized or reborn. We get old, and at the same time we get young. We get polluted physically, emotionally, and mentally, and simultaneously we get purified. Things decrease and increase. We forget, learn, and remember many things.

We tend to be more aware of the aspects of decay such as aging or de-clining health, but this is an example of limited perception since we also experience revitalization after we exercise, dance and sing, or sleep. We age and de-age simultaneously, and to a certain degree we have the option to age or de-age at each moment. And in other areas of our lives, we can also choose to stay ignorant or to learn, to be destructive or loving.

Things happen and do not happen at the same time. Although the *Heart Sutra* seems to emphasize the side of things not happening ("neither arises nor perishes . . . neither increases nor decreases"), we also need to under-stand and see through to the side of things happening. Movements for war and peace are constantly taking place, and we are called to choose one over the other every moment of every day.

The *Heart Sutra* claims that in the midst of phenomena where all things are changing, the reality of boundless interactions continues, and that this fact itself will not change. After all, the ultimate reality both encompasses and is free of change in all manifestations.

The notion of the five streams of body, heart, and mind interacting with one another as a single entity can also be applied to our six sense organs — eyes, ears, nose, tongue, body, and mind. There are no eyes separate from ears, nose, and the rest of the body (such as skin, flesh, and bones) as well as the mind. The entire body is a single entity.

The objects of our senses — what is seen, heard, smelled, tasted, touched, and perceived — are also all interactive and inseparable. The shape of an apple, its sound or lack of sound, its smell, taste, and our perception of it are indivisibly interconnected. Likewise, various aspects of our consciousness that make eyes, ears, nose, tongue, body, and mind function are all connected and intertwined.

The *Heart Sutra* states that our ultimate experience goes beyond all these types of consciousness. The sutra leads us to a full experience of our senses, their objects, and our consciousness, and in doing so demonstrates a glimpse of complete freedom from all these distinctions. You might call it a higher state of consciousness that can be discovered in meditation.

There is an ancient Buddhist teaching of the twelvefold causation — the chain of dependent origin. It goes in the following sequence: Ignorance causes formative forces. Formative forces cause consciousness. Consciousness causes name-and-form. Name-and-form causes sense fields. Sense fields cause contact. Contact causes feeling. Feeling causes craving. Craving causes grasping. Grasping causes becoming. Becoming causes birth. Birth causes decay and death.

This sequence explains how our angst develops. Roughly speaking, ignorance causes recognition, which causes desire and becoming conscious of the emergence of noticing. And where there are desires and the emergence of noticing, there are old age and death. This is the fundamental human condition.

The *Heart Sutra* declares that we can become free from each stage and even from freedom itself. What, then, is freedom from freedom? Is it a restriction, or a higher level of freedom?

A human being is a compound of innumerable causes and effects. Each one of us is here in this world because of many decisions made by our parents and their parents, all the way back to the beginning of time. Our upbringing is the result of biological elements, history, culture, social conditions, personality, education, and many other events that happened in the past and are happening in the present. We are the visible and invisible effect of limitless karma — individual and collective social actions.

Thus, we are influenced by a tremendous amount of forces that are completely out of our control. Even with these limitations, however, there are also a great number of elements we can control and change. Changing one's gender, nationality, religion, or legal name is not easy, but such changes are not impossible, either. Changing one's partner, career, diet, exercise, tastes, habits, behavior, way of thinking, way of speaking, lifestyle, and daily schedule are all possible. We are in the midst of changeable and unchangeable karma in each moment. We are bound by cause and effect, but at the same time we are partly free of cause and effect. This is the case during meditation, when we can be completely free from the chain of causation. It is a state in which we can be anybody and anywhere. We are what we meditate. We are also the source of cause and effect. The teaching of the Four Noble Truths addresses our ability to be engaged in cause and effect.

The Four Noble Truths are described as suffering, arising, cessation, and path. They point us to the prevailing existence of suffering, the cause of suffering, the potential of freedom from suffering, and ways for this freedom to be learned, which are characterized as the eightfold noble path. The eightfold noble path is wholesome view, wholesome thought, wholesome speech, wholesome conduct, wholesome livelihood, wholesome effort, wholesome mindfulness, and wholesome meditation. Thus, the four noble truths can be seen as a formula to understand the dynamics of suffering and a remedy for becoming free from it.

To give you a simple example: You slander someone, who may be either present or absent. The person gets angry and strikes back at you. This negative reaction causes you pain, which creates multiple problems for your state of mind, health, relationships, or social standing. You may realize that the initial cause of these problems was your own insensitive act of slandering the person. You may then decide not to repeat the same mistake, and thus become liberated from this type of suffering.

The inclusion of the Four Noble Truths in the *Heart Sutra* ("free of suffering, arising, cessation, and path"), reminds us that this sutra is part of the long line of Buddhist scriptures, going back to the early texts in Pali.

Despite the importance of the four noble truths in the history of Buddhism, however, the *Heart Sutra* calls for freedom from them. At a glance it may even appear that the text is "anti" four noble truths. Is this so? Does it mean we can ignore or violate this most fundamental teaching in Buddhism?

The word "freedom" often suggests that we can do anything we want, including being unethical and destructive. But there is also another kind of freedom, one that may prove to be more truly free. If we fully follow rules and ethics, we no longer need to think or worry about them. Thus, we are completely free from rules and ethics.

Banging on a piano keyboard without practicing is one kind of freedom that doesn't get us anywhere. By diligently practicing the piano, however, we come to play beautifully and improvise freely. That is the kind of freedom the *Heart Sutra* calls for.

Until now, I have reviewed with you the sutra's point of seeing all elements of human existence and activities through the filter of *shunya,* or zeroness. What, then, does *shunya* exactly mean? Does it mean that nothing exists and nothing matters?

An earlier English translation of the sutra states, "In emptiness there are no eyes, no ears, no nose . . ." It does not at all state that eyes, ears, and nose do not exist. It is not nihilism. It means that when we experience emptiness, we see no difference between eyes, ears, nose, and so on. It suggests that an experience of emptiness is that of nonduality. Nonduality sees no boundary or distinction among various aspects and values of things. This is why I suggest that we understand *shunyata* as boundlessness and use this term as a translation of *shunyata.*

In meditation we experience distinctions in feelings and thoughts. We feel comfort and pain. We qualify actions as right or wrong. We identify some things as good and others as bad. At times, however, we experience a state where the differences among all things become obscure. In this realm, the distinction between small and large, near and far, momentary and timeless, self and other, and even life and death fades away. Whether we notice it or not, meditation is selfless and nondiscriminatory.

It is not that beginning meditators only experience distinctions and seasoned meditators only experience that which is beyond distinctions. All levels of practitioners experience both at the same time. The difference between beginning and seasoned practitioners may be that the latter are more aware of the nondual experience.

Joan and I loosely translated *nirvana* as "profound serenity" in our translation of the *Heart Sutra.* But there are many other ways of understanding the Sanskrit word *nirvana.* Some Buddhists may say it is a complete state of calmness only buddhas can experience. Others may say that it is a state of annihilating the chain of birth and rebirth. Zen master Dogen seems to indicate that it is a nondual experience. Thus, for him nirvana is an experience of *shunyata* — zeroness or boundlessness. He says:

> On the great road of buddha ancestors there is always unsurpassable
> practice, continuous and sustained. It forms the circle of the way and
> is never cut off. Between aspiration, practice, enlightenment, and *nir-*
> *vana,* there is not a moment's gap; continuous practice is the circle of
> the way.[2]

Thus, each moment of our practice encompasses these four aspects of
experience — aspiration for enlightenment, practice, enlightenment, and
nirvana. I call it a micro-circle. Dogen further suggests:

> Accordingly, by the continuous practice of all buddhas and ancestors,
> your practice is actualized and your great road opens up. By your con-
> tinuous practice, the continuous practice of all buddhas is actualized
> and the great road of all buddhas opens up. Your continuous practice
> creates the circle of the way.[3]

This is a macro-circle. We do not practice meditation alone. We practice
together with all the awakened ones everywhere in the past, present, and
future. Indeed, do we not meditate together with all the awakened ones and
their helpers throughout space? Do we not identify ourselves with the great
realization of wisdom beyond wisdom in the past, present, and future?

This experience of all-embracing meditation is not limited to seasoned
practitioners but is open even to those who are at the very first moment of
practice. Dogen says: "When even for a moment you sit upright in *samadhi*
expressing the buddha mudra in the three activities (body, speech, and
thought), the whole world of phenomena becomes the buddha's mudra
and the entire sky turns into enlightenment."[4]

Some of those who are familiar with the term "emptiness" might say that
the Buddhist understanding of "emptiness" has become common in English usage and there is no need for a new translation of *shunyata*. It is true
that many Buddhist teachers have elucidated the profound meaning of this
term, and a great number of people understand it.

I would argue, however, that "empty" or "emptiness" nevertheless has
rather negative connotations in English. For example, the *American Her-*
itage Dictionary defines the word *empty* thus: holding or containing nothing; having no occupants or inhabitants (vacant); lacking force or power;
lacking purpose or substance (meaningless); not put to use (idle); needing
nourishment (hungry); and devoid (destitute).

Let me give you a sobering example in which I imagine my own situation. When I come to face death, somebody might say, "Don't worry. All is empty. You will simply return to emptiness." Hearing this, I might be discouraged and depressed. Someone else might say, "When you die, your body, heart, and mind perish. You part from all your beloved ones and all your possessions. But you are not limited to your body, heart, and mind. Your love, aspiration, vision, and service to others are also part of yourself. They will continue to be active and help others. You are without boundary. Losing your body, heart, and mind is only losing a part of yourself." Offered this understanding, I believe I would be encouraged, and my fear of death might be radically reduced. This could be how I want to die, which in turn may determine how I want to live.

As you see in this example, the translation of a word is not only a matter of choosing one word instead of another. It can be a choice between negativity and positivity, between nihilism and a vision of expansiveness in life.

Here is another example of how we understand a word. Zero can be merely nothing or the state of being empty, but it can also transcend both. An addition of one zero increases a number by a factor of 10. How about an addition of five zeros? Zero is powerful.

Only two numbers — one and zero — form a binary system. The number one is an active number, the beginning of all numbers, and an element of most numbers. One plus one is two. Two divided by three is 0.666 . . . On the other hand, zero is a passive number. Zero has nothing in itself. But once it is combined with one or any other numbers, it brings forth a magical effect. For example, one divided by zero is infinity.

As we see in computer programming, combinations of one and zero are the basis for sets of numbers, letters, languages, and concepts. These numbers can create shapes, colors, images, sounds, movements, and scenes. The computer-program mind mimics our biological and neurological system. Understanding computer programming, in turn, helps us to understand various phenomena in natural and human-made systems. Thus, zero and one are key elements not only in computer code, but in all systems of the universe.

There are two major types of worldview: I call them pluralism and singularism. Pluralism, or dualism, is a common way of seeing phenomena according to their difference from one another. It is a practical and intellectual mode of perception. Discerning differences of shapes, colors, and sizes, and recognizing the appropriateness and rightfulness of actions are how common sense and an ordinary type of wisdom manifest.

Singularism, on the other hand, can be seen as monism or nondualism. It does not deny the pluralistic worldview, but sees reality as a unified whole that transcends all relative, dualistic phenomena. In this sense, singularism may be seen as similar to absolutism, where existence is ultimately understood as an all-inclusive whole. Although Buddhists do not monopolize it, singularism is a major foundation for Buddhist thinking and practice.

The *Heart Sutra* appears to present a monistic view in which all things can be reduced to zeroness. (It's ironic that *mono* in the word *monistic* means one as opposed to zero in the binary system. Yet here the Buddhist monism or philosophy of oneness regards all things as zero.) This wholeness is the intersection of one and zero.

The view that all things are equal and not different runs counter to our ordinary worldview, which is confined by hierarchy, degrees of values, and judgments of right and wrong. Singularism is often seen as being based on the deepest part of our consciousness, which is non-conceptually experienced in meditation. It is an unworldly, spiritual paradigm, one that can be characterized as nothing short of mystical.

There is great merit in singularism. If we see what is large as no different from what is small, and what is many as no different from what is few, we may become less greedy. If we see enemies as friends, we may fight less. If we see people in the future not apart from those in the present, we may act more considerately. If we see nonhumans as intimate with humans, we may respect animal rights. If we see nonsentient beings as not different from sentient beings, we become more conscious of the environment. When we transcend distinctions and boundaries, we become more compassionate. This is the realization of all things beyond boundaries. This is wisdom beyond wisdom.

Is there a division between pluralism and singularism? If so, is there a pluralistic or dualistic contrast between pluralism and singularism? This certainly poses a dilemma.

I don't think the *Heart Sutra* is totally on the side of singularism to the extent of excluding pluralism. On one hand, the sutra says, "[Boundlessness] is free of ignorance. . . . Boundlessness is free of old age and death." On the other hand, the sutra says, "[Boundlessness is] free of the end of ignorance . . . and free of the end of old age and death." This passage on the twofold freedom from singularism and pluralism suggests that the scripture is pointing to the transcendence of these seemingly opposing views.

This notion of freedom from the end of ignorance and from the end of old age and death reminds us of the three stages of our experience: recognizing the existence of ignorance, old age and death; becoming free from ignorance, old age, and death; and becoming free from freedom from ignorance, old age, and death.

These three stages of meditative experience can be compared with Dogen's famous statement in his brief essay "Actualizing the Fundamental Point."[5]

First Dogen says, "As all things are buddha dharma, there are delusion, realization, practice, birth [i.e., life] and death, buddhas and sentient beings." This is a beginning stage of meditation. As we see the difference between awakened ones and those who are not, we are inspired to practice.

Dogen then describes the second stage: "As myriad things are without an abiding self, there is no delusion, no realization, no buddha, no sentient being, no birth and death." In meditation we come to realize the singularity of all things, where at times we experience freedom from discriminatory views. We free ourselves from trying to be awakened when we realize that we already are awakened. And yet, as Dogen explains, there still is practice, for we manifest this awareness in practice.

Finally, Dogen explains the third stage in the following way: "The buddha way, in essence, is leaping clear of abundance and lack; thus there are birth and death, delusion and realization, sentient beings and buddhas." When we push through the distinction between pluralism and singularism, we go back to pluralism. However, the pluralism in this stage is quite different from the beginning stage. The freedom found here transcends the opposition of these two modes, for within pluralism there is singularism, and within singularism pluralism is found.

We need pluralism to be able to conduct even the simplest tasks in life, such as distinguishing a dime from a quarter, getting somewhere on time, or staying within necessary social boundaries. On the other hand, we need singularism to see that ultimately all people are one. Pluralism or singularism alone confines our views and actions. From moment to moment in our everyday lives, both of these are required.

Our life may be seen as a dance with pluralism represented by one foot and singularism by the other. At one moment, a single foot touches the ground. By making a stiff step we become rigidly isolated. The next moment we use both feet. The moment after that, the other foot is on the ground by itself. If there is the slightest misstep, boundaries are violated and there is a chance that through some action our integrity will be lost. Each step is a challenge.

However, can we not also see our dance in life and meditation as something other than the constant switching between the opposites? When the dancing becomes natural and fluid, singularism and pluralism are no longer in opposition. They become one and inseparable, which allows us to keep dancing with integrity and grace.

I think it is important to understand the message of the *Heart Sutra* literally from the text, but, in addition we should understand what its message implies in the larger context of Mahayana Buddhist teaching. For example, the *Heart Sutra* doesn't mention ethics, but if we see it as belonging to the lineage of Buddhist scriptures in which ethics based on observing precepts is essential, we know that a call for the integrity of practitioners through ethical actions is invisible but present in the sutra. In fact, Mahayana Buddhism calls for six *paramitas,* or six realizations: generosity, keeping precepts, patience, vigor, meditation, and wisdom beyond wisdom. Thus, it is clear that the realization of wisdom beyond wisdom goes hand-in-hand with the realization of the other five practices.

I encourage you to develop your own definition of the realization of wisdom beyond wisdom. Speaking for myself, it is a continuous, wholesome experience of freedom from and integrity in pluralistic and singularistic understanding and action. All the Zen koans point to this. Dogen calls it "actualizing the koan (*genjo koan*)," which I translate as "actualizing the fundamental point."[6]

THE MANTRA

The third and final teaching of the *Heart Sutra* is the mantra. A mantra is a specially combined sacred formula of sounds often used as a magical spell. Over the centuries, mantras have been used in attempts to invoke supernatural effects, most commonly to avert disaster and bring forth healing and happiness.

You may regard a mantra as a preset prayer in which the literal meaning is unknown or insignificant. Because the sounds of a mantra are not easily comprehensible, they do not appeal to the intellect but instead reverberate within our whole body, heart, and mind. Instead of making us think, the sounds help us to just be, in a way that includes reverence.

The recitation of a mantra can help us to gather together our body, heart, and mind. Sometimes, in meditation and in life, we get lost, confused, or panicked. Chanting the *Heart Sutra* can help us become focused and fearless. This happened to the monk-scholar Xuanzang when he was alone crossing the Gobi Desert toward India. It also helped Hokiichi Hanawa in his singlehearted drive to compile major ancient Japanese literary works. (I will introduce these stories later in this book.)

Humans are inclined to pray. We may pray to God, the Buddha, a bodhisattva, a god or goddess with whom we feel a sacred connection, or any object of worship. Or we may just pray without having anyone to pray to. When our friends are sick, we send them our prayers. I have even known atheists who prayed, in their own way, when their children were sick. When all medical and health-care procedures are exhausted, often we cannot help but pray.

As long as we feel healthy and strong, we may not feel the need to pray. But someday, should we become fragile and hopeless, it will be helpful to have a good incantation available, especially one like the *Heart Sutra* mantra that has been recited by uncounted people for centuries. The accumulated power of the mantra must be enormous.

Although science does not explain exactly how it is possible, recent scientific studies suggest that prayers have the power to heal.[7] We have known since ancient times that our hearts and minds are so powerful that concentrated direction of our attention in prayers or incantations at times can work.

Dogen calls such a supernatural effect of the concentrated use of our hearts and minds a "minor miracle." For him, each moment of practice and each breath we take is a "great miracle." He says, "Miracles are practiced three thousand times in the morning and eight hundred times in the evening."[8]

Minor miracles created by magic were not needed by Dogen, who was a fully committed strong practitioner of Zen meditation. Perhaps this is why he did not mention the mantra in his commentary on the *Heart Sutra*, "Manifestation of *Prajna Paramita*."[9] But since most of us can be fragile, the mantra can be extremely helpful.

As I will discuss later, the *Heart Sutra* mantra — Gaté, gaté, paragaté, parasamgaté, Bodhi! Svaha! — can be interpreted as "Arriving, arriving, arriving all the way, arriving all the way together: awakening. Joy!" This is a marvelous reminder for our meditation practice that each moment of our practice is, as Dogen suggests, not separate from awakening or enlightenment. Each moment of our practice and of our life is blessed.

I see the *Heart Sutra* mantra as a powerful tool for meditation, a double-edged sword of human consciousness. One edge reminds us of the joy of practice and life. The other protects us from the confusion and fragmentation of our consciousness. Thus, you may see the *Heart Sutra* mantra as a constant reminder of our awakened nature that keeps wisdom beyond wisdom working effectively.

LOVING-KINDNESS

Because wisdom beyond wisdom is not separate from loving-kindness, we may also need a reminder and reinforcement for loving-kindness. For that purpose, the incantation of a short text called the *Ten-Line Life-Affirming Sutra of Avalokiteshvara* (Emmei Jukku Kannon Gyo) is often used. The Japanese version goes like this:

> *Kanzeon*
> *namu butsu*
> *yo butsu u in*
> *yo butsu u en*
> *bupposo en*
> *jo raki ga jo*
> *cho nen Kanzeon*
> *bo nen Kanzeon*
> *nen nen ju shin ki*
> *nen nen fu ri shin.*

This sutra is usually chanted aloud many times, each time with increased speed and volume. Joan Halifax and I translated this scripture as follows:

> Avalokiteshvara, perceiver of the cries of the world,
> takes refuge in Buddha,

will be a buddha,
helps all to be buddhas,
is not separate from buddha, dharma, sangha—
being eternal, intimate, pure, and joyful.
In the morning, be one with Avalokiteshvara,
In the evening, be one with Avalokiteshvara,
whose heart, moment by moment, arises,
whose heart, moment by moment, remains!

Hakuin, the eighteenth-century Japanese Zen master, regarded as the restorer of the Rinzai Zen School, encouraged his students to chant this verse. As a result, this extra short scripture has been chanted, in the main, on a daily basis in Rinzai Zen monasteries and centers since his admonition. I hope it will be chanted in other schools of Buddhism as well.

It is a Chinese-originated text. According to the *Chronology of Buddha Ancestors* (Fuzu Tongji) compiled by Zhipan in 1269 C.E., the defeated and imprisoned general Wang Xuanmo received this sutra in a dream in 450 C.E., and the vigorous chanting of it saved him from execution.

The bodhisattva Avalokiteshvara, who is invoked at the beginning of the *Heart Sutra,* is usually regarded as a female in East Asia (though the Indo-Tibetan world still sees Avalokiteshvara as a male). So, we can say in a limited manner that "she" is a goddess of loving-kindness. In fact, she *is* loving-kindness personified.

Bodhisattva has already become an English word. And yet, as it is such a rich word, it is not always easy to understand what it means in different contexts. Joan and I translated this word in our version of the *Heart Sutra* as one "who helps all to awaken." I would personally like to see Avalokiteshvara as a goddess, partly because the concept of a "goddess" is not confined to Buddhism. It is my hope that people will take up an interfaith view of this bodhisattva.

We all need an ideal image of loving-kindness that is central to wisdom beyond wisdom. When faced with the choice to be indifferent, insensitive, and violent, or to be kind and loving, our role model could help us to make a positive and life-affirming decision. Thus, holding Avalokiteshvara in our consciousness and invoking the name of the goddess is potentially a powerful practice.

We may ask ourselves: "Are you a goddess of loving-kindness?" You might say, "No, no. I am a human being," or, "I am a man. How can I be a goddess?"

But the *Ten-Line Life-Affirming Sutra of Avalokiteshvara* calls us to be "one with Avalokiteshvara." Why not imagine, then, no matter how else we may define ourselves, that we are also one with the goddess?

Let me ask you again, then: "Are you a goddess of loving-kindness?"

PART TWO

Story of the Sutra

4

Pilgrimage to the West

THE *HEART SUTRA* has two versions: a shorter text and one that is longer. The shorter text, which came to be known first, has been chanted in regions where Chinese ideographs are used. The longer text has been chanted in Tibet, Nepal, Bhutan, and Mongolia.

Although there is a Sanskrit version of the shorter text, it is seldom chanted. The principal Chinese version that corresponds to the Sanskrit version is a translation by Xuanzang (604–664). His name is also spelled Hsüan-tsang, Hiuen-tsiang, Yüan-tsang, and Xuanzhuang.

The Xuanzang version is the shortest of all extant Chinese renditions of the sutra, with the main part consisting of only two hundred seventy-six ideographs. It is regarded as supreme in its clarity, economy, and poetic beauty. It is commonly chanted in China, Korea, Japan, and Vietnam. Consequently, East Asian teachers who have founded Buddhist groups in the West rely primarily on the Xuanzang version.

The *Heart Sutra's* story weaves its way through the life and work of this ancient Chinese monk. My source is a biography by Huili, a disciple who edited many of Xuanzang's translations. After Huili's death, Yancong, another student, completed the biography in 688. Titled *Biography of the Tripitaka Dharma Master of the Da Ci'en Monastery of the Great Tang Dynasty* (Datang Da Ci'en-si Cancang Fashi Chuan), it is regarded as the most detailed and accurate biography of Xuanzang available.[1] Here, in brief, is his story:

In the autumn of 629, twenty-six-year-old Xuanzang broke the Chinese imperial prohibition on traveling abroad and set off on a journey westward for

India in search of authentic dharma.[2] After diligently seeking out the best scholars in Buddhist philosophy and extensively studying Mahayana as well as earlier scriptures in Shu (Sichuan in western China) and Chang'an — the capital city of the newly formed Tang Empire — he realized something crucial was lacking. He particularly wanted to obtain scriptures not available in China at that time, and find solutions to unanswered questions on the "Consciousness Only" theory in the Yogachara (Meditation Practice) School — the most advanced Mahayana philosophy.

After his fellow travel companions had given up and his local guide attempted to stab him, Xuanzang continued alone on a skinny, aged horse. He traversed the vast, flowing sand dunes on Central Asia's caravan path in

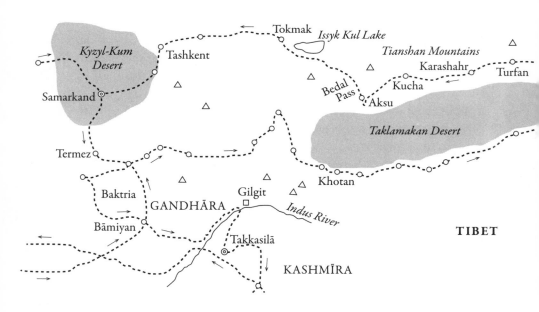

FIG. 1. *Xuanzang's routes: China–India.*

the southwestern tip of the Gobi Desert. (This intercontinental route was named the Silk Road by the German geologist Ferdinand von Richthofen in 1877.)

Xuanzang slipped through the five watchtowers of the Yumen Barrier, the furthest western outpost of China, on his way to Hami. He walked for days, getting lost under the brutally scorching sun. Thirsty and exhausted (probably to the point of hallucination), Xuanzang found himself surrounded by grotesque evil spirits. Again and again, he invoked the name of his guardian deity, Avalokiteshvara Bodhisattva, but the spirits persisted. As he fervently chanted the *Heart Sutra*, they were finally driven away.

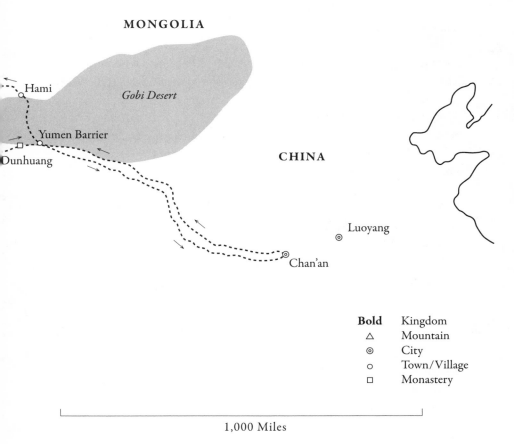

Bold	Kingdom
△	Mountain
◎	City
○	Town/Village
□	Monastery

1,000 Miles

The scripture Xuanzang chanted had a special personal meaning. When he was studying in Shu, he came upon a poor monk who had festering sores all over his body. Pitying his sickness and stained clothes, the young Xuanzang took him to a local temple where he found money with which the monk might purchase food and clothes. As a token of his gratitude, the sick monk taught Xuanzang the *Heart Sutra*. Xuanzang continued to study and chant it for years.

When Xuanzang reached the temple in Hami, the king of the oasis state invited him to the palace and made offerings. The envoy of Turfan, who was also present, noticed Xuanzang's profound personality and reported back to his king about the monk who had just started a long pilgrimage. Xuanzang was unable to resist a cordial invitation sent by the Buddhist king of Turfan, so he made a detour to visit Turfan, crossing the northeastern end of the Taklamakan Desert through the southern foot of the snow-capped Tianshan Mountains.

The king, overjoyed and impressed, asked Xuanzang to be the preceptor of the nation. Although he politely declined, the king forcibly insisted. Xuanzang fasted to show his determination to continue his search. Three days passed. When the king saw that Xuanzang was already becoming emaciated, he withdrew his command and asked Xuanzang to stay for one month and give dharma discourses to his subjects. Upon the monk's departure, the king made an offering of clothing suitable for his travel ahead, a large amount of gold and silver, and hundreds of rolls of silk — enough to sustain his journey for twenty years — along with letters of introduction to twenty-four kings and khans in the Eastern and Western Turkestan regions. He also provided thirty horses and twenty-four helpers.

When Xuanzang and his large caravan were on their way to the next oasis kingdom of Karashahr, they were stopped by a group of bandits who had just killed all the Iranian merchants traveling ahead of his caravan. Fortunately, the guide of Xuanzang's expedition gave the bandits money and everyone got through. In the flourishing kingdom of Kucha, the king, with a great many Theravada home-leavers, welcomed him with music and feasting. After a three-month sojourn, Xuanzang pushed westward to Aksu in an attempt to cross the Bedal Pass through the high and steep Tianshan Mountain range covered with glaciers. During an arduous climb in a snowstorm, the pilgrim lost one-third of his crew as well as many oxen and horses, which succumbed to freezing and starvation.

Reorganized at the southern side of the huge Lake of No Freezing, Issyk Kul, the shattered caravan made it to Tokmak. There Xuanzang was greeted by the Great Khan of the Western Turks, who reigned over most of Central Asia and beyond. The Khan also tried to persuade him to stay, but eventually Xuanzang had him write notices of safe passage to the rulers of nations on the path of the monk's impending journey. It was the summer of 630. Almost a year had now passed.

After stopping in a forest with a number of small lakes, Xuanzang visited villages and kingdoms on the northwestern side of the Tianshan Mountains, meticulously recording their names and locations. He journeyed through more kingdoms west of Tashkent until he crossed the Desert of Red Sands, Kyzl-Kum. Finally he arrived in Samarkand, a prosperous trading kingdom of Sogdians, most of whom were Zoroastrians. Its king was unfriendly to the pilgrim at first but soon changed his attitude, not only taking the precepts from the monk but asking him to ordain other monks as well.

From Samarkand, Xuanzang turned south, visiting ancient Buddhist sites in Termez, Kunduz, Balkh, and Bamiyan. He then set out to the southeast, passing the Gandhara and Kashmir regions. Entering the subcontinent of India, he visited sacred sites in Mathura, Shravasti, Lumbini, Kushinagara, Sarnath, Vaisali, and Buddhagaya (present-day Bodh Gaya).

In the autumn of 632, after a three-year journey in which he miraculously escaped myriad dangers, Xuanzang arrived at the Nalanda University Monastery in the kingdom of Magadha in northeastern India. Buddhism was flourishing, and Nalanda, with over ten thousand students, was the center of Buddhist studies. Xuanzang met the abbot Shilabhadra, a renowned master of Yogachara, said to have been one hundred and six years old. Three years before, Shilabhadra had had unbearable pains in his limbs and wanted to end his life by fasting. But Manjushri Bodhisattva, deity of wisdom, and two other bodhisattvas appeared to him and said that a Chinese monk was on his way to study with him. From that moment, Shilabhadra's pains went away. The old master recognized Xuanzang as the monk he had awaited.

Shilabhadra (circa 529–645) came from a royal family based in Samatata in eastern India. After traveling in search of a master, he arrived at Nalanda, where he met Dharmapala (530–561). Dharmapala was a young and brilliant leader of the monastery, as well as a theorist in the Yogachara School, which practiced a succession of stages of bodhisattvas' yogic meditation. This school had been established by Asanga and his brother Vasubandhu

FIG. 2. *Xuanzang's routes: India.*

in the fourth century, based on the philosophy that all existences are representations of the mind and no external objects have substantial reality. Dharmapala was the compiler of the *Treatise on Realization of Consciousness Only*, in which he included ten other thinkers' commentaries.[3] At age thirty, Shilabhadra represented his master, Dharmapala, and established a reputation by defeating a non-Buddhist thinker in a debate. He later became Dharmapala's successor.

In the company of thousands of other students, Xuanzang listened to Shilabhadra's lectures. For five years, he studied various Buddhist texts, the Sanskrit language, logic, musicology, medicine, and mathematics. He also conducted an in-depth investigation of the Consciousness Only theory under the tutelage of Shilabhadra. Xuanzang then proceeded to write a three-thousand-line treatise in Sanskrit entitled *Harmonizing the Essential Teachings* in an attempt to transcend differences between the major Mahayana theories: Nagarjuna's Madhiyamika and Asanga's Yogachara. It was highly praised by Shilabhadra as well as other scholarly practitioners, and came to be widely studied. Xuanzang also wrote a sixteen-hundred-line treatise entitled *Crushing Crooked Views*, advocating Mahayana theories.

After collecting scriptures, visiting various Buddhist sites, and giving discourses in the eastern, southern, and western kingdoms of India, Xuanzang continued to study with dharma masters in and out of Nalanda. When Xuanzang received permission from Shilabhadra to return to China, King Harshavardhana — ruler of the western part of northern India — eagerly invited Xuanzang to his court in Kanykubja on the Ganges. He was a supporter of Hinduism and Jainism, as well as various schools of Buddhism. In the twelfth month of 642, the monarch invited spiritual leaders from all over India to participate in an exceedingly extravagant philosophical debate contest. Representing Nalanda, Xuanzang (whose Indian name was Mahayanadeva) crushed all his opponents' arguments and was announced the winner by the king. Harshavardhana then provided the homebound pilgrim with his best elephant as well as gold and silver, and organized a relayed escort for Xuanzang's caravan all the way up to China.

In an early part of his journey home, one box of scriptures carried on horseback was washed away in the crossing of the Indus River. Xuanzang spent some months waiting for its replacement. From Kashmir, he and his party climbed through the Hindu Kush and Pamir mountains. They stopped at the great Buddhist kingdom of Khotan, then toiled through the

southern end of Taklamakan Desert. From there, they made a brief stop at
Dunhuang before going back to the Yumen Barrier, where they waited for
imperial permission for Xuanzang to finally reenter his homeland. Bearing
relics and images as well as 657 Sanskrit sutras and commentaries, all carried
by twenty-two horses, Xuanzang returned to Chang'an at the beginning of
645. It had been a sixteen-year journey. Hundreds of thousands of people
greeted him.

5

A Tiny Text by a Giant Translator

CHANG'AN, SITUATED on the southern bank of the river Wei in the Guanzhong Basin (present-day Shaanxi Province), was an orderly gridded megalopolis guarded by massive dirt walls. In the first part of the eighth century, this powerful capital city had a population of more than one million people, as well as a prospering culture and commerce. Chang'an was on its way to being the largest city in the world.

At that time, Chang'an was under the rule of Emperor Tai (599–649), originally named Li Shimin. The ruler of the preceding Sui Dynasty, Emperor Yang, was a vicious tyrant whose corrupt rule induced a revolt of farmers all over China. Foreseeing a collapse of the Sui Dynasty, Shimin had urged his father — the grand lord Li Yuan (566–635) — to raise an army against the emperor. Following the overthrow in 617, the young Shimin successfully led diplomatic and military campaigns, abolished the Sui Dynasty, and initiated the Tang Dynasty in 618, installing his father as the founding emperor. After pacifying revolts and surviving his jealous brothers' attempt to kill him, Shimin asked his father to retire, thus becoming the second emperor of the Tang Dynasty in 626 at age twenty-eight. The entire nation was united again. He also succeeded in swallowing neighboring states in North and West Asia and subordinating southern nations, thus making China's domain larger than ever.

When Emperor Tai gave his first audience to Xuanzang in 645, Tai was forty-seven years old and Xuanzang forty-two. Instead of punishing him for disobeying his edict proscribing foreign travel, Tai praised him for his courage and achievement. That same year, the emperor assisted Xuanzang in launching a national project to translate a great number of Sanskrit scriptures into Chinese. Tai gave Xuanzang a temple called Hongfu Monastery in Chang'an. He also hired many editing assistants, including twelve monk-scholars from all over China, to check the accuracy of the renditions. Xuanzang dictated his translations directly from the original texts.

Many prominent scholars and artists, including the calligraphers Yu Shinan and Chu Suiliang, served at Tai's court. An admirer of the fourth-century calligrapher Wang Xizhi, Emperor Tai made an extensive effort to collect and study Xizhi's masterpieces. Tai himself started a custom of writing inscriptions in cursive style, moving away from the customary formal script. He went on to become one of the most renowned calligraphy masters of the classical period.

What made Tai one of the greatest monarchs in Chinese history was that he knew his own shortcomings and accepted others' advice. (Later he wrote a four-fascicle book, *Imperial Model* [Di Fan], mentioning his own failures, as an admonition for his crown prince.) Tai reduced tax rates and eased punishment. He perfected the examination system for hiring different levels of government officials, which was open to anyone of any background — the system that had been initiated by Emperor Wen, the first monarch of the Sui Dynasty (r. 581–604).

In 646, upon imperial request, Xuanzang completed a report about the topography, history, customs, and politics of the places he had visited in Central Asia and India. His twelve-scroll work, *Records of the Western Regions Compiled during the Great Tang Dynasty* (Datang Xiyu Ji), was the most extensive and detailed book of geographical descriptions that had ever been written.[1] The popular sixteenth-century epic *Journey to the West* (Xiyu Ji), by Wu Chengen — stories of a monk guarded by a powerful monkey, boar warriors, and a river monster — is based on Xuanzang's writing.

In 648, Xuanzang completed his one-hundred-fascicle translation of Asanga's *Stages of Yogachara* (Yogacharabhumi). (A scroll, or fascicle, is a chapter-length text assembled in a separate volume.) In the same year, Emperor Tai asked Xuanzang to take an official position at the court. Xuanzang declined, declaring that his life's mission was to clarify the Buddha's dharma. Tai was impressed with Xuanzang's determination, and soon after, the emperor wrote an introduction to Xuanzang's translation of the sutras under the title "Great Tang's Three-Basket Sacred Teaching."[2] (The Buddhist canon is called the Tripitaka, or Three Baskets. The "baskets" — or "collections" — consist of sutras, precepts, and later scholars' treatises. One who has mastered the entire scripture is called a Tripitaka dharma teacher, or simply Tripitaka. This was our translator Xuanzang's title.)

Also in 648, the Crown Prince — a close disciple of Xuanzang — became a senior monk at the Da Ci'en Monastery in Chang'an. The translation academy built on the northwestern side of the great monastery compound was then the center for national translation work. Soon after that, according to Huili's biography of Xuanzang, Emperor Tai became gravely ill and asked Xuanzang to be near him at the Cuiwei Palace on Zhongnan Mountain, in the south of the capital city. Although Huili did not mention it, a later record says that Xuanzang translated the *Heart Sutra* at the palace on the twenty-fourth day of the fifth month of 649. It was transcribed by Monk Zhiren.[3] Three days later, Emperor Tai passed away, and the Crown Prince ascended the throne as Emperor Gao.

In 659, Xuanzang and his foremost disciple, Kuiji (632–682), made a ten-fascicle summary of Dharmapala's *Treatise on Realization of Consciousness Only* that was to become the fundamental text for understanding the Yogachara philosophy.

Afterward, Xuanzang spent two years translating the most comprehensive collection of the *Prajna Paramita* scriptures. From the original two hundred thousand Sanskrit lines, he created six hundred scrolls, which made this work the largest Buddhist scripture ever.[4] (A "line," or *shloka*, when used to measure the length of a Buddhist text, consists of thirty-two syllables.) On completing the translation of the *Maha Prajna Paramita Sutra* in 663, he exclaimed: "This sutra pacifies the nation. It is a great treasure to the world. This completion is to be celebrated by everyone in the sangha!" He was sixty-two years old.

Xuanzang then asked one of his students to count the texts he had translated. The result was seventy-four texts in 1,338 scrolls. This surpassed his great predecessor Kumarajiva's seventy-three texts in 383 scrolls.

Although Xuanzang limited his role to that of master translator and did not write commentaries of his own, he was the most influential Buddhist of his time and had thousands of students. He encouraged his senior disciples to write commentaries. His cotranslator Kuiji — who became known as the author of one hundred treatises — founded the Faxiang (Dharma Characteristics) School. This school provided a most advanced theoretical ground for the development of the Tiantai School as well as for the formation of the Huayuan (Avatamsaka) School in the seventh and eighth centuries. Other students of Xuanzang—the monks Dosho, Chitsu, and Chitatsu—developed the Hosso School, the Japanese form of the Faxiang School. Xuanzang also helped three monks, Puguang, Fabao, and Shentai, to form the Jushe School, which is based on the *Treatise on the Treasury of Dharma Studies* (Abhidharma Kosha Shastra) by Vasubandhu—a compilation of pre-Mahayana ontological theories. The Jushe School developed into the Kusha School in Japan. Xuanzang's fresh use of words in translation, combined with his high degree of accuracy, stimulated a surge of Buddhist studies and thought, resulting in the rise of a golden age of Buddhism in China and beyond.

Xuanzang passed away in 664. It is said that over one million people bowed at his coffin and over thirty thousand people stayed overnight at his tomb. Emperor Gao said in grief, "We have lost our national treasure."

6

Talisman of Talismans

Buddhism was introduced from China to Korea in the fourth century, and from the southern Korean state of Baekje to Japan in 538. Some brief fragments of stories about the *Heart Sutra* have been attributed to this period. (I will examine the authenticity of these stories later in chapter 16, "Emergence and Expansion of the *Heart Sutra*.")

The *Japanese Book of Miraculous Stories* (Nihon Ryoi Ki), compiled in 822, includes a story of the monk Gikaku from Baekje, Korea, who moved to Japan after his country was destroyed in war in 663. At midnight, one of his fellow monks noticed a shining light in Gikaku's room, so he peeked in. Gikaku was sitting upright and chanting the *Heart Sutra*, and while he was doing so light shot out from his mouth. The monk was frightened and the next morning he told the whole assembly what he had seen.

Gikaku explained: "After reciting the sutra one hundred times, I opened my eyes. The walls in my room had disappeared, and I was in the midst of the garden. I made a walking meditation in it and looked at my room. The walls and doors were all closed. So I stayed outside and went back to chanting. This is a wonder of the *Heart Sutra*."[1]

Here is another story from the same book: A drunken beggar was asleep on a street. As a joke, someone shaved his head and put a rope around his neck. A wealthy man brought him home, dressed him in a Buddhist robe, and asked him to expound the *Lotus Sutra*. The man said, "I only chant the *Heart Sutra* mantra while begging for food. I don't know anything about the *Lotus Sutra*." Nevertheless, the wealthy man insisted.

That night, a brown cow appeared in the beggar's dream and said, "I am the mother of the owner of this house. Because I stole money from him, I have been turned into a cow as punishment. If you have any doubt, set up a seat for me at your dharma talk, and see what happens." The next morning, the man said to the audience, "I know nothing. I sit here because my host wants me to. Let me just tell you about my dream."

Hearing the beggar's dream, the rich man prepared a seat for his mother, and called her. A brown cow came into the room and sat on the seat. The man said, "Indeed, you are my mother. I forgive you now." Hearing him, the cow made a gasp and died. All those present began to weep.

The book's author comments that this miracle was a result of the man's love for his mother and the beggar's power, accumulated from chanting the *Heart Sutra* mantra.[2]

According to the *Documents of the Shoso-in Treasury* (Shoso In Monjo), the earliest known recitation practice of the *Heart Sutra* in Japan took place in 732 and the earliest known copying practice in 757. Emperors ordered public recitation of the sutra in the years 759, 774, 808, 837, and 875.[3]

In a related way, as Buddhism in Japan had merged with indigenous Shintoism since the eighth century, it was not uncommon that the *Heart Sutra* was recited in Shinto shrines for rituals of healing or exorcism. In 1549, Japan was hit by a widespread epidemic. Emperor Gonara (r. 1526–1557) asked Buddhist monks to intensify their recitation of the *Heart Sutra*, which was believed to be the most effective remedy. The emperor made many copies of the sutra with gold ink on indigo paper and offered them to the head Shinto shrines of all provinces. It took him five years to complete his dedication. Seven copies remain among Japan's important cultural properties.[4]

Emperor Gonara had his court ladies offer one thousand recitations of the sutra for his longevity every year on his birthday. Such recitations became customary in the palace. There is a record that during the reign of Emperor Gomizuno'o (r. 1621–1629), ladies in higher positions copied and read the sutra fifty times each, and those in lower positions twenty-five times, for a total of one thousand recitations. The ladies burned the copies in a sacred fire as part of the ritual. This custom of performing "the *Heart Sutra* ceremony" to remove calamity and invite happiness lasted until the Meiji Reformation of 1868, when Shintoism was separated from Buddhism and established as the national religion.[5]

. . .

Countless monks and nuns have chanted the *Heart Sutra* throughout their lives. Hokiichi Hanawa (1746–1821), a scholar in literature, however, seems to hold the record for quantity of recitations. Although he lost his sight at age seven, Hokiichi became an outstanding expert in studies of historical documents. He wanted to collect and publish the best books, as well as materials from the past. In 1779, he vowed to create an unprecedented publication project called the *Collection of Classified Books* (Gunsho Ruiju). For success, Hokiichi chanted the sutra over one hundred times a day, until he had recited it one million times. According to his journal, he had chanted the *Heart Sutra* 1.9 million times by 1819, when he finished publication of the five-hundred-and-thirty-fascicle book. He continued his recitation until 1822, when a one-thousand-fascicle sequel was completed.[6]

Nowadays, Zen temples like the Gold Pavilion, the Silver Pavilion, and the famous rock gardens in Kyoto attract huge numbers of tourists. In their souvenir shops, you can find a copy of the *Heart Sutra* printed on many different objects, including round fans, folding fans, candles, miniature screens, calligraphy scrolls, handkerchiefs, neckties, wrapping cloths, hand towels, and teacups. At a subtemple of Mount Koya, the head monastery of the Shingon School, a friend was offered a blanket with the *Heart Sutra* printed on it. You can even buy a two-by-three-inch pocket-sized protector called "the *Heart Sutra* Talisman" at bookstores anywhere in Japan. (See the Selected Bibliography for a variety of Japanese publications on the sutra.)

7

In Print for One Thousand Years

JOHANNES GUTENBERG'S invention of the printing press in the mid-fifteenth century led to a wide circulation of the Bible and other books in Europe and eventually throughout the world. The earliest known printed sheet, however, is that of the *Sutra of Great Incantations.* Discovered in Korea, it is dated 751, preceding Gutenberg by seven centuries.[1] The earliest surviving copy of a printed book is that of the *Diamond Sutra,* dated 868, which was brought to England from one of the caves in Dunhuang on the Silk Road by a Hungarian archaeologist named Aurel Stein, who was leading the British Expeditionary Party in 1907.[2]

Founding Emperor Tai of China's Song Dynasty sent his messenger to the lord of the western region of Shu in 971, and ordered the carving of printing blocks for the Tripitaka. Printing technology had already been developing in this region. By 983, the carving of the canon was completed, and over 130,000 woodblocks were transported to the capital city of Kaifeng in central China. Printing started in the following year. This epoch-making edition of the Tripitaka is known as the Shu version.[3]

Members of the Tartar tribes of Manchuria, the Khitan, completed printing of a Chinese-language Buddhist canon in 1054. The print has been lost, but its table of contents still exists and shows that the *Heart Sutra* was included in this printing.[4] This version of the canon became the basis for the stone-carved sutra on Mount Fang (present-day Mount Danjing, Henan Province). A stone rubbing of the *Heart Sutra* shows that it has a Chinese title, but the text is a Chinese transliteration of the shorter *Hridaya* text written out by Maitribhadra, a northeastern Indian monk who came to Khitan in the early tenth century.[5]

Following the publication of the Shu version of the Tripitaka, versions of the Tripitaka in Chinese-originated ideographs were printed in China, Korea, and Japan. (Presumably Xuanzang's version of the *Heart Sutra* was included in all versions of the printed Mahayana Tripitaka.)[6] As one of the most widely demanded scriptures in the ideographic canon, the *Heart Sutra* has been independently printed quite frequently, using the woodblock of the sutra taken from the entire set of printing plates. This makes it a text that has been in print for more than a thousand years — one of the longest living texts in the history of printing.

The woodblocks of the Shu version of the Tripitaka, however, were destroyed during an invasion by the armies of the northeastern Chinese kingdom of Jin in 1126. That leaves the woodblocks of the Korean Tripitaka as the oldest existing plates of the Buddhist canon.

In 1011, Emperor Hyeon of the northern Korean kingdom of Goryeo initiated the reprinting of the Shu version of the Tripitaka with the intention of protecting the nation from invasions by the Khitan. The printing was concluded decades later, but the woodblocks were destroyed in war. Additional sutras were subsequently collected, and printing of an expanded edition of the Goryeo Tripitaka was completed in 1087. The plates for this later version were burned during the Mongol invasion of 1232. But in 1236, under imperial order, monk-scholars led by one named Suki started comparing all available versions of the scriptures in order to establish an entire text for the expanded Goryeo Tripitaka. (Suki later published his team's comparative annotations in thirty fascicles.) In 1251, the printing was complete. Among the 52,382,960 engraved characters in this version, not a single mistake has been found.[7] After being moved twice by imperial edicts, the 81,137 woodblocks of the Goryeo Tripitaka — carved on both sides, and including 1,511 scriptures — found their home at the Haein Monastery in South Korea. They have been there since 1398.[8]

This Tripitaka became the basis for three versions of the ideographic canons published in Japan, the last of which is the one-hundred-volume *Taisho* Canon (Taisho Shinshu Daizokyo), edited by Junjiro Takakusu and others, published between 1923 and 1934. The *Taisho* Canon, which with over 120,000,000 characters is the world's largest printed book, is an invaluable source and the one most frequently referred to by Buddhist scholars today.

· · ·

As part of my research for the present book, I wanted to see the *Heart Sutra* as it appears in the Goryeo Tripitaka, in its living environment. In late October of 2004, I flew to Busan, a southeastern port city of the Korean Peninsula. Taijung Kim, a renowned calligraphy and painting teacher, met me with one of his students, Hyuntaik Jung, at a hotel in Busan. It was about a three-hour drive, and much of our communication was done with an improvisational mixture of spoken languages and written ideographs.

In a guest facility of the monastery, I was given an unfurnished room of traditional hermitage size — roughly ten by ten feet, in a large building called the Authentic Practice Hall, now being used as an office and residence quarters.

That afternoon, my new calligrapher friends and I had less than one hour to visit the large, modern-style museum of the monastery. There, a printing plate for the forty-fifth fascicle of the *Avatamsaka* (Flower Splendor) *Sutra* was displayed behind a glass case. It was dated 1098, so it must have been a surviving block from the second Goryeo Tripitaka. The size of the board, oriented vertically, is seventy by twenty-four centimeters. In the center of the relief surface, a column of characters indicates the title and the fascicle number of the sutra. Such a column is usually shown at the front spine of a book as a quick reference for the title of the sutra. A print from this slab must have therefore been folded in half and intended to be a book. Thus, we can guess that the second Goryeo version was in book format as opposed to scroll format.

The writing on the printing plate is engraved in reverse, of course. The printed text in Chinese reads vertically, progressing from right to left. Though there is no punctuation, there are paragraph changes. The prose has no character spaces, but in the poems, each verse is followed by a blank space the size of a single ideograph. If the plates I saw were typical, I estimated one plate to have a maximum of twenty-six columns, with twenty-two characters per column.

Next to the *Avatamsaka* plate was a display of the *Heart Sutra*. Unfortunately, it was a blackened copper replica. I had wanted to know how worn out it was, compared with the blocks of other sutras. This "woodblock" made of copper had almost no signs of wear. Nevertheless, the replica shows us the format of the *Heart Sutra* plate in the later Goryeo edition. Metal tabs, nailed to the edges, keep the plates from sticking to each other and allow airflow between the plates.

FIG. 3. *Later Goryeo version of the* Heart Sutra. *Chinese. Print.*

There is no extra column for the title of the sutra in the center. This means that the later Goryeo version prints must have been mounted on scrolls. Fourteen characters each are carved on twenty-five columns per plate, making it smaller than the earliest version.

I had previously seen a photographic reproduction of the *Heart Sutra* in this later version of the Goryeo Tripitaka. It showed that the title of the sutra was *Prajna Paramita Heart Sutra,* without the first word, *Maha.* Underneath this title was the single symbol *yu* ("feather"), an ideograph from the *One Thousand Character Text* by Zou Xingsi (d. 521) of the southern kingdom of Liang, composed of unrepeated symbols. Here, *yu* served as a library index code for the sutra.

The colophon of the scripture read as follows: "In the senior-water dog year, the Director of the Tripitaka Bureau engraved this under imperial command." The Chinese cyclical calendar combines the ten elements — five (wood, fire, earth, metal, and water) times two ("senior" and "junior") — and the twelve zoological signs. These symbols collectively cover the span of sixty years, which represents a complete calendar cycle. This cyclical calendar is a common system in East Asia, where the calendar based on imperial eras changes frequently in accordance with the monarchic reigns. Here we can determine that the "senior-water dog year" corresponds to 1238 C.E.

As in the prints of other sutras in the later Goryeo version, each character of the *Heart Sutra* is exquisitely written and engraved. Most characters are

tall, and what makes this edition calligraphically unique is that the characters are slightly tilted toward the left. Tilting is generally avoided in East
Asian calligraphy. In this case, however, it works mysteriously well, creating
a kind of hypnotic effect.

Each line seems to have been carved quickly but very precisely, often with
beginning or ending pressure points, which loosely correspond to serifs in
Western calligraphy. Seeing these meticulously carved characters, I could
believe the legend that the wood carvers made three full prostrations after
carving each ideograph. Looking at each one of these printed characters, I
too felt like making three bows.

The aesthetic supremacy of the Goryeo version of the Tripitaka is widely
accepted. And because of its consistent calligraphic style, it is believed that a
single (now unknown) calligrapher wrote over fifty-two million characters
before a team of carvers engraved them.

Soon after this, I went to the museum bookstore and asked a woman behind
the counter, who seemed to be the manager, if she had a print of the *Heart
Sutra* for sale. She took out a folded print from her file and showed it to me.
It was printed in light gray with an attachment in Hangul — the Korean
phonetic script — mixed with a small number of ideographs.

Evidently, this print was made for tracing the sutra. The attachment is a
prayer with blank columns for the devotee's name and address as well as the
date. At the end, it says in ideographs, "To be enshrined inside the stomach
of the Shakyamuni Buddha image."

I gestured to the woman that I wanted to buy it. She wordlessly indicated
that she would simply give it to me. I accepted it, bowing with my hands
together, at which time she signaled that the attachment was not useful to
me and quickly cut it off with a knife. She was about to throw it away when
I stopped her and said I needed it. (Later, when I took time to examine it,
I found four ideographs in the middle of the Hangul prayer: "my diseased
father and mother." Perhaps she sensed that I was not going to offer a prayer
in Korean for my parents.)

Shamelessly I motioned to her that I would very much like to see more
prints of the sutra. She searched her file once again, showed me a print in
dark black ink, and gestured that it was the last piece she had. When I asked
her how much it was, she indicated again that it was a gift to me. Over-
whelmed, I bowed deeply once again.

That night I rested well in my tiny room in the ancient compound of Haein-sa, until the bells and drums started sounding at three o'clock in the morning, followed by chanting voices from the Avalokiteshvara Hall right next door.

Haein-sa means "monastery of ocean-mudra *samadhi*." As described in the *Avatamsaka Sutra*, this *samadhi* represents a state of absorption in meditation like a calm ocean that reflects all beings and all teachings. One of the three major temples in Korea, this monastery, as the keeper of the Tripitaka woodblocks, represents the dharma treasure. It is the largest Buddhist training center in the country, with about two hundred resident monks. My visit to the monastery coincided with an interim period, so I saw only thirty or so monks, along with some lay workers in residence. (An American Zen teacher in a Korean Buddhist order later described this monastery as "the Oxford University of Korean Buddhism.")

The next morning I saw Weonjo Sunim, a young attendant monk of the abbot and my host. I asked him if it would be possible for me to enter the sutra storehouse and take some pictures, to which he replied, "It's not allowed to go inside, but I will show you the buildings."

That afternoon, we climbed up the steep granite stairs in the back of the Buddha Hall. I told him that I was doing research on the *Heart Sutra*.

He smiled and said, "Oh, the *Heart Sutra* is the most important sutra in Korea. Do you understand the sutra?"

"I hope so."

"My teacher says if you understand the *Heart Sutra*, you understand the entire buddha dharma."

Quickly recalling my previous statement, I said, "In that case I must say I don't understand the *Heart Sutra*." We laughed.

Right behind the flight of the stairs, there stood a wide building of plain wood with a slightly arched roof. Weonjo pointed to the sign above the front entrance, which read "Sutra Hall." We went through the short hallway into a courtyard and entered the central altar room of the storehouse building—the Dharma Treasure Hall. A dozen laypeople were sitting inside. They noticed my monk friend in his gray robe and bowed to him. After he returned their bows, we made nine full prostrations to the golden image of Vairochana Buddha.

We then went out from the Sutra Hall for worship into the courtyard, sandwiched by the storehouses. Each storehouse is fifteen *kan* long and two *kan* wide. (One *kan* in Korean, or one *ken* in Japanese, is roughly ten feet.) On each end of the courtyard stands a building of a similar structure, two *kan* in length. These buildings have vertically latticed, glassless windows all the way around.

Weonjo took me to one of the windows, through which we could see black-lacquered printing slabs stacked sideways like books, showing their vertical ends with engraving of the categories, sutra titles, and fascicle numbers. There were ten levels of plain wooden shelves, supported by bare pillars standing on square stone bases on the earthen ground.

Weonjo and I went around the building to the end, where we could see the central walkways through the building. It is said that each step in the process of manufacturing these printing slabs alone — cutting the white birch wood to size, submerging it in seawater, boiling it in fresh water, and drying it in the shade — takes three years to complete. The slabs are then cut exactly to size and engraved on both sides, which takes a number of years, and are finished with a coat of black lacquer. Indeed, the production of these blocks took a total of sixteen years. They have survived wars, fires, weather, and insects. Only a few blocks were found missing in 1915, and they were replaced some years later.[9]

"We haven't found a better way to store them," Weonjo said. In fact, some years prior to my visit, the monastery had constructed a multimillion-dollar building with the latest facilities, but found it inadequate to store the national treasure. So they decided to keep the woodblocks in the old way and use the new building as a study hall.

In response to the story of my research on the *Heart Sutra* and my lifelong admiration of the Goryeo Tripitaka, Weonjo said, "You might like to have a piece of the sutra. I will bring it to your room at four o'clock this afternoon."

I thanked him, assuming that he would bring me another print of the *Heart Sutra*. But instead he brought a copper replica of the printing block of the sutra, placed in a beautiful cardboard box and wrapped in cloth.

How marvelous!

8

An Ancient Tower Resurrected

THE DEVOTIONAL POWER of the *Heart Sutra* can be seen even today in the story of Yakushi-ji, the Temple of Medicine Buddha, in Nara. This temple was built in 698, at the peak of early Japanese Buddhism. Now it serves as one of the head temples of the Hosso School, along with Kofuku-ji.

At the center of the temple compound, inside the double hallways, was a two-storied Golden Hall facing south. Like other temples in Nara, when it was constructed Yakushi-ji had a main hall made of white plaster walls and wooden structures painted in bright green and vermilion. In front of this hall — which enshrined the Medicine Buddha — stood a pair of magnificent three-storied pagodas with lean-tos or additional roofs in between, so the pagodas would appear to have five stories.

A chronicle of Yakushi-ji provides a long list of buildings lost to fire, war, storm, and earthquake. It also documents the efforts to repair and rebuild the temple. The only building that has survived from the beginning is the East Pagoda.

By the time Gyoin Hashimoto was abbot of the temple and spiritual head of the Hosso School during and after World War II, the Golden Hall was in disrepair and the West Pagoda was gone. He wanted to restore the temple to its original form, but his dream required great funds, which were not available. Tourists and schoolchildren nevertheless continued to visit.

Gyoin noticed that one young novice mesmerized people when he showed them around the temple and explained the dharma to visitors. Gyoin trained this novice, Koin Takada, entrusting the abbacy to him in 1967 and asking him to continue the effort to restore the temple's buildings.

Koin launched an ambitious drive to gather one million handwritten copies of the *Heart Sutra*, along with other short sutras. He traveled all over Japan and invited the public to make brush-written copies of the sutras and send them to Yakushi-ji with a donation. This request captured the imagination of a great number of people. The initial goal of collecting one million copies was achieved, and the sutra dedication kept growing.

Repair of the Golden Hall was completed in 1976. A new West Pagoda was erected in 1981, based on an old plan, with the highest quality carpentry and related crafts.[1] It is amazing to look up at the resurrected pagoda's complex geometry of gently upturned tile roofs, crowned with its decorated gold and silver spire. The fresh green copper and vermilion painted on wooden surfaces brings back the glory of the Nara Period (710–784). Walking up scores of steps, you cross the span of twelve hundred years between the weathered East Pagoda and the youthful West Pagoda. They stand side by side in harmonious contrast.

The West Pagoda is not only a restoration of an architectural masterpiece after four hundred and fifty years. It is also the embodiment of Koin Takada's vision and passion, which initiated a mass religious movement and revitalized the essential Buddhist practice of handwriting sutras.[2]

Today at this Medicine Buddha temple, there is a new octagonal building commemorating Xuanzang. Above the front entrance of the shrine is a large horizontal sign. The board is inscribed with the two paradoxical characters "Not East." This represents the traveling monk's vow not to take even one step backward to China until he reached India and acquired the dharma. Indeed, this determination enabled him to bring countless Buddhist teachings eastward back home.

The honorary founder of this temple, Kuiji, who participated in Xuanzang's translation of texts on Yogachara, completed a systematic summary of the Consciousness Only doctrine, and eventually founded the Faxiang School. The Hosso (the Japanese form of Faxiang) School became the most prominent of the six scholastic traditions of Buddhism that flourished in the Nara Period.

In the compound of Yakushi-ji, there is also a public *dojo* — a practice place — for copying sutras, to which everyone is welcome. In 2002, I had the good fortune to visit this hall. At the front office, I made a donation and received a model calligraphic print of the Xuanzang version of the *Heart Sutra*, an instruction sheet, and a blank sheet of high-quality rice paper. The man at the office also let me borrow a purple strip of cloth — a simplified Buddhist robe — to wear around my neck while copying the sutra.

A young woman led me through a hallway by a quiet garden, to the front of a room sheltered by an impressive number of *shoji* doors. She asked me to sit at a small table in front of the entrance, and showed me the procedure. I put a pinch of cloves into my mouth for purification and went into a large room, which was set up with many tables and chairs — perhaps enough for three hundred people. It was early in the morning, and only a few people were there, all immersed in calligraphy. At each section of the table was a piece of black felt on which to place the paper, a metal weight, an ink stone, a block of sumi ink, a small water container, and a brush.

Following the instructions, I stepped over the white jade icon of an elephant set on the floor. This signified the entry into a sacred domain. Then I took a seat, bowed, put the simplified robe around my neck, poured drops of water on the ink stone, and started to grind ink.

The model print had lines at the top and bottom as well as vertical lines that divided the columns of ideographs. The writing paper was strong but thin and semitransparent, making it well suited for tracing. I looked around and saw my neighbors tracing the printed models. To a lifetime student of East Asian calligraphy, tracing feels like cheating — it was the last thing I would want to do. But I realized that this system would be an expedient way for most people to engage in the practice of sutra copying. I decided to give up my pride as a calligrapher and do as others were doing.

I knew that my handwritten copy of the sutra would never be seen by anyone as a piece of art. This was a practice of copying simply for the sake of copying. I was there to make a small gift to the temple, but the temple was giving me far more — the gift of allowing me to join the vast spiritual practice of brush-writing the *Heart Sutra* in this sublime environment.

I started writing the characters, growing more and more joyful with each new moment, each new stroke. Time dropped away. Soon the ending came, with the complex Chinese spelling of *"gaté, gaté . . ."* Then, on the designated spot on the sheet, I wrote my name, address, and age, the date, the sequential number of the copy I had just made (in my case the number one), and a brief prayer. As I saw some others do, I went to the central Buddha figure, dedicated my work to the altar, and walked away, having joined the ranks of countless sutra scribes.

PART THREE

Modern Scholarship
(19th and 20th Centuries)

9

The Earliest Mahayana Scripture

ACCORDING TO recent Indian and Western scholarship, Shakya-muni Buddha lived around 566 to 486 B.C.E.[1] His first dharma discourse took place in Deer Park in Sarnath, near present-day Varanasi, and is referred to as the first turning of the dharma wheel. The Buddha's teachings over his lifetime include that of *anatman*, or "no self"— the realization that there is no independent and everlasting self such as the soul; this understanding ultimately liberates individuals from self-clinging.

The emergence of the enormous body of *Prajna Paramita* (Realization of Wisdom Beyond Wisdom) scriptures four hundred or more years after the Buddha's time functioned as a catalyst for the rise of Mahayana Buddhism. These scriptures served as a huge step whereby the early notion of *anatman* evolved into *shunyata*—an interrelated nonexistence of substantial individual entities, as well as of all phenomena. The rise of Mahayana is often characterized as the second turning of the dharma wheel.

Sutras created in ancient India take the form of teachings given by Shakyamuni Buddha, so none of them have the compilers' names, nor are they dated, except in rare cases such as the *One Hundred Parable Sutra*.[2] Historically, most Buddhists believed that all sutras were the actual words of the Buddha, spoken during his forty-five years of teaching. Only when a body of European critical scholarship emerged in the nineteenth century was evidence revealed that sutras had developed over time in response to the understanding and needs of people in later periods.

It was customary for translators of Sanskrit texts into Chinese to record their names along with the titles of the translated works, often with the year of completion noted as well. Ten comprehensive catalogs of translated texts were compiled between the late fourth century and the ninth century, of which the most recent nine are extant. The catalogs include not only these texts, but also known records of translations that are no longer available, as well as scriptures whose authenticity is doubtful or that have been determined as forged. This is why we can retrace the rise, survival, and fall of translated texts in the Chinese language.

The translation in 179 C.E. of the *8,000-line Prajna Paramita* into Chinese by Lokakshema — from Bactria in western Central Asia — marked the first translation of this large body of Sanskrit *Prajna Paramita* literature.

Kumarajiva's translations of the *8,000-line* and *25,000-line Prajna Paramita* in the early fifth century were widely studied and recited. He also translated a 100-fascicle summary of the *Treatise on Great Wisdom* (Dazhidu Lun), an extensive *Prajna Paramita* commentary, one of three major works attributed to Nagarjuna that was extant in Chinese only and that is often used as a Buddhist encyclopedia.

Xuanzang made a translation of all available scriptures belonging to this category, a total of forty. He classified them as presented by the Buddha in sixteen assemblies, compiling them as the *Great Prajna Paramita Sutra* in 663. (In China the word "sutra" was added to the title. Thus, these enormous texts are referred to in the ideographic world as "Great Prajna Paramita Sutra" or "Great Sutra.")

According to Edward Conze, among the many versions of the *Prajna Paramita* scriptures, the *8,000-line Prajna Paramita* can be considered the earliest. This text was started in India in the first century B.C.E. and completed in the first century C.E. Later, a huge number of lines were added to form the *18,000-line, 25,000-line,* and *100,000-line Prajna Paramita* scriptures.[3]

The *8,000-line Prajna Paramita* text is the first known sutra that contains the word "Mahayana." It also advocates the ideal image of Buddhist practitioners as bodhisattvas. Bodhisattvas are beings who vow to be reborn many times, dedicating themselves to the awakening of others by way of appropriate moral conduct and skillful means, free of earthly attachment. They themselves do not become buddhas until all others do.

10

Prajna Paramita as the Basis for the *Heart Sutra*

CONSIDERED AN EXPRESSION of the highest experience of nonduality, the *Prajna Paramita* scriptures have been transmitted, recited, explained, and commented upon with great devotion in China, Korea, Japan, and Vietnam, as well as in Tibet, Nepal, and Mongolia. They are used as texts for philosophical studies and as tools for repetitive recitation in meditation. But the books themselves are also often placed on altars and worshipped as sacred objects. Flowers and incense as well as prayers to remove negative influences are frequently offered to them.

In Japan, this massive sutra is called by various names: *Dai Hannya* (Great Prajna), *Hannya* (Prajna), or *Hannya-sama* (Revered Prajna). Since ancient times, Xuanzang's 600-fascicle version has been recited for repentance, protection, and healing.

In the Noh play *Aoi no Ue* (Lady Aoi), based on a character in the *Tale of Genji,* written in the Heian Period (794–1185), the shining prince's young wife, Aoi, is haunted by the wraith of Genji's former wife, Rokujo. Pushed away by monks' chanting voices, the wraith exclaims: "O how frightful is the voice of Hannya! Enough! I, the vengeful spirit, will never appear again."

Traditionally, it takes days and days to chant the entire sutra. Thus, a ritualized way of "reciting" the sutra came into being. This method of recitation — also known as "turning the sutra" — has been in existence since the Nara Period. In this ritual, monks flap accordion-like folded books, opening and closing them with a flourish while chanting the title of each

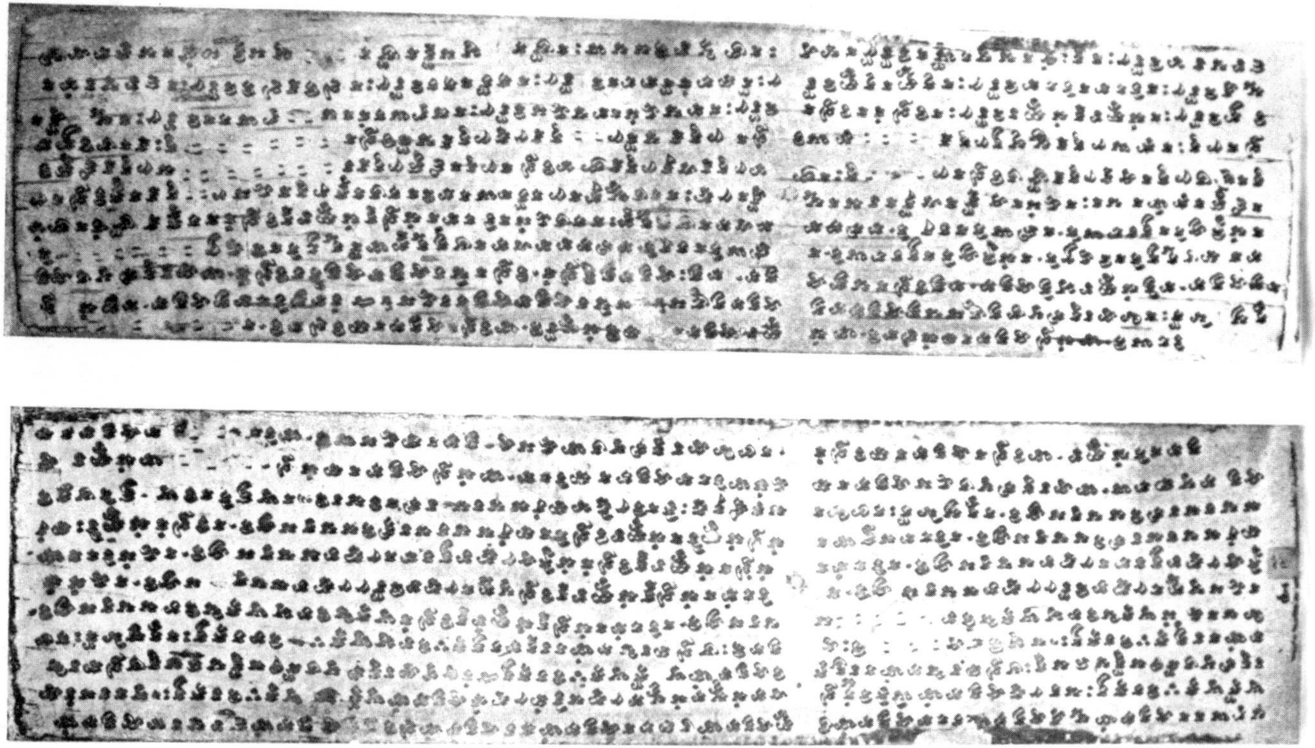

FIG. 4. Prajna Paramita scripture, *Gilgit fragment. Sanskrit.*

chapter. It is said to bring a benefit equivalent to that earned by reading the book in its entirety.

By way of contrast, "The Essential Meaning of Prajna" — the 578th chapter of the *Great Sutra* — is often recited in full. This chapter explains how the power of hearing, maintaining, and spreading the sutra subdues evil spirits and helps devotees to attain the highest state of being. The custom of worshipping the *Prajna Paramita* scripture in China laid ground for use of the *Heart Sutra* as a magical incantation.

Xuanzang did not include the *Hridaya* in his comprehensive *Maha Prajna Paramita Sutra*. This presumably means that the *Hridaya* was not in the collection of the Sanskrit *Prajna Paramita* literature he had acquired.

The section of the Chinese *Heart Sutra* inserted between the passages "O Shariputra, form is not different from *shunyata*" and "All those in the past, present, and future who realize wisdom beyond wisdom manifest unsurpassable and thorough awakening" largely corresponds to a part of the first chapter of the Chinese version of the *25,000-line Maha Prajna Paramita Sutra* (see p. 205). From this fact, we can easily infer that the great *Prajna Paramita Sutra* was the main basis for the *Heart Sutra*.

Early manuscripts of Buddhist scriptures almost completely disappeared from India because of destruction by natural or human activity. A small number of fragments of the *25,000-line Prajna Paramita* along with other manuscripts were excavated from a temple site of Gilgit, in present-day northeastern Pakistan, in 1931. Written in Brahmi script — one the oldest styles of writing in India — these documents are thought to date from no later than the eighth century, and some are considered to date from the sixth century, which is over five hundred years earlier than the Nepalese versions of the sutra Edward Conze introduced.

Remarkably, among the fragments found in Gilgit was the part that corresponds to the core section of the *Hridaya*. Raghu Vira and Lokesh Chandra edited and published a facsimile edition of the excavated Buddhist manuscripts; the originals are supposed to be held by the National Archives of India.[1] I wanted to obtain a higher quality photo of this precious document and contacted the Archives, but they replied that they didn't have the document. Thus the sample shown in figure 4 is an unfortunately blurry reproduction of the facsimile.

Later, Gregory Schopen supplied his transcription of the text to Jan Nattier, whose analysis of this part of the *Prajna Paramita* will be discussed below in the chapter on "Most Recent Scholarship."[2] Paul Harrison, a specialist in Buddhist literature and history, kindly provided his own revised reading of the text, which I have included in the section "Texts for Comparison" in appendix 1.

I I

Versions of the Chinese *Heart Sutra*

CONTEMPORARY JAPANESE scholars list seven extant Chinese translations of the *Heart Sutra*.[1] They are all included in the *Taisho* Canon. (The authenticity of some of the following texts has been challenged by Jan Nattier, a U.S. scholar, whose theory will be introduced in chapter 12.) Each entry of the following list begins with the translator's name. For ideographs of these names, see appendix 3 (p. 235).

Kumarajiva (arrived in China 401), "Maha Prajna Paramita Great Dharani Sutra," shorter text.[2]

Xuanzang (translation 649), "Prajna Paramita Heart Sutra," shorter text.[3]

Yijing (631–713), "Prajna Paramita Heart Sutra," shorter text. (Questionable, as its text is nearly identical with the Xuanzang version.)[4]

Dharmachandra (arrived in China 732), "Treasury of Universal Wisdom Prajna Paramita Heart Sutra," longer text.[5]

Prajna and Liyan (translation 790 or 792), "Prajna Paramita Heart Sutra," longer text.[6]

Chosgrub (760?–860), "Prajna Paramita Heart Sutra," longer text.[7]

Prajnachakra (ninth century), "Prajna Paramita Heart Sutra," longer text.[8]

Danapala (arrived in China 980), "Sacred Mother of Buddhas Prajna Paramita Heart Sutra," longer text.[9]

(The first, second, and fifth texts are included in "Texts for Comparison," pp. 208, 210, and 221.)

Among these extant versions of the *Heart Sutra*, the majority of scholars believe the oldest text to be Kumarajiva's translation, *Maha Prajna Paramita Great Bright Mantra Sutra*. On the other hand, the most widely circulated version in East Asia is the *Prajna Paramita Heart Sutra* in Xuanzang's translation.

In addition, there are three "lost" translations, as ancient Chinese scholars listed the titles of scriptures whose contents were no longer available:[10]

> Zhiqian (ca. 223), "Prajna Paramita Mantra Sutra," shorter text.
> Bodhiruchi, translator (arrived 693), "Prajna Paramita Namas Sutra," shorter text?
> Shikshananda (652–710), "Maha Prajna Essential Heart Sutra," longer text?

Among these vanished texts, the most noteworthy is the rendition by Zhiqian of the third century. Traditionally regarded as the oldest Chinese translation of the *Heart Sutra*, this text was reportedly included in a catalog called *Record of the Translated Tripitaka,* compiled by Sengyou (ca. 515).[11]

You may remember the pioneering comparative philology of the twelfth-century Korean monk Suki (p. 43). Since his time, printed Tripitakas in the Chinese language have retained a high degree of accuracy.

On the other hand, manuscripts hand-copied in China before printing started have been lost. That is why the forgotten documents recovered from a cave in Dunhuang, a key station on the Silk Road on a northwestern edge of China, have become extremely valuable sources for Buddhist studies. Some of these documents, which I will address further in chapters 11 and 14, shed light on the *Heart Sutra* as it existed more than one thousand years ago.

During the period between 1898 and 1915, Russia sent a series of expeditionary parties led by D. Clementz and S. Oldenburg to Central Asia, resulting in the publication of reports on uncovered centuries-old manuscripts. Stimulated by these intriguing findings, Great Britain, Germany, France, and Japan sent their own teams to Central Asia in the first part of the twentieth century. The biography of Xuanzang by Huili and *Records of the Western Regions Compiled during the Great Tang Dynasty* by Xuanzang charted their courses.

In the south of the desert city of Dunhuang, three clusters of caves are spread on the cliffs of barren sand-covered mountains and large boulders.

FIG. 5. *A stupa-shaped* Heart Sutra. *Chinese. Discovered at Dunhuang Cave. The writing starts beneath the bodhisattva image, moves diagonally, horizontally, or vertically in different directions, forming a stupa shape, and ends at the lower right section.*

Among them is the West Thousand Buddha Cave group, consisting of nineteen caves that are decorated with frescoes and enshrine painted stucco sculptures of Buddhas and bodhisattvas. The east cluster is the Yulin Cave group, consisting of forty-two caves filled with murals. The central and largest cluster, the Mogao Cave group, nearly a mile long, encompasses over one thousand caves, many of which are magnificently adorned, reflecting a variety of styles of Buddhist art from different eras.

In 1900, Wang Yuanlu, a Daoist hermit who was living in what would later be called Cave 16 of the Mogao Cave group, saw huge stacks of seemingly worthless, bruised writings and books rolled up inside the adjacent cave (later called Cave 17). In 1907, the archaeologist Aurel Stein heard about him and went to meet him. Stein told Wang of his devotion to Xuanzang: "I have followed his footsteps from India across inhospitable mountains and deserts and have traced the ruined sites of many sanctuaries he visited." Successful in impressing Wang, Stein indiscriminatedly acquired a great many rolls of writings in utmost secrecy.[12] Thus, his team carried the bundles on camelback and by ship to Great Britain.

In 1908, a year after Stein's quest, a French team, led by the sinologist Paul Pelliot in an expedition dating from 1906 to 1909, arrived at the Magao Caves. The 40,000 religious and secular documents from this cave that were brought to daylight by Stein and Pelliot, written in Chinese, Tibetan, and Central Asian languages, date from 405 to the eleventh century, when the Mogao Caves were closed to protect them from robbery during the reign of the Xixia Dynasty of the Tibeto-Burmese Tanguts. The Dunhuang findings are now regarded as one of the greatest discoveries of the twentieth century.

Fumimasa-Bunga Fukui lists 180 copies of the *Heart Sutra* transcript found in Dunhuang.[13] Most of them are in the collections of the British Museum, the British Library, and the National Library of Paris.

12

Versions of the *Hridaya*

WHILE MANY of the Chinese translations of Buddhist scriptures have survived in printed form, the majority of Sanskrit scriptures have been lost. None of the Sanskrit manuscripts of the Xuanzang translation of the canon, for example, remain. The only extant manuscript from close to his time seems to be that of the *Hridaya* (or the *Heart Sutra* in Sanskrit). A handwritten copy of the shorter *Hridaya* was housed in one of the oldest temples of Japan, the Horyu Monastery near Nara. This manuscript now resides at the Tokyo National Museum.

The Horyu-ji manuscript follows the general format of ancient Sanskrit manuscripts — handwritten horizontally with lines drawn close to the top of the letters on two fan palm leaves.[1] Georg Bühler, a German scholar who established Indian paleography, suggests that the Horyu-ji *Hridaya* was copied in India in the beginning of the eighth century.[2] The Japanese Buddhist scholar Ryusho Hikata later noted that it was more likely copied in the later half of the eighth century.[3]

In either case, this makes it the oldest hand-copied manuscript of the *Hridaya*. Shoko Kanayama, a Japanese Sanskritist, says that the Horyu-ji *Hridaya* is one of the two extant representative manuscripts written in Gupta scripts, the other being a manuscript discovered by Captain H. Bower in Kucha, Central Asia.[4] (I will discuss Sanskrit scripts in chapter 20, "Scriptwise.")

Kanayama, however, notes that the surface of the material and format of writing of the Horyu-ji manuscript differ from those of Indian palm leaf manuscripts. Also, it seems to have been written with a soft brush instead of sharpened bamboo, or wood. Consequently, he suggests that this particular

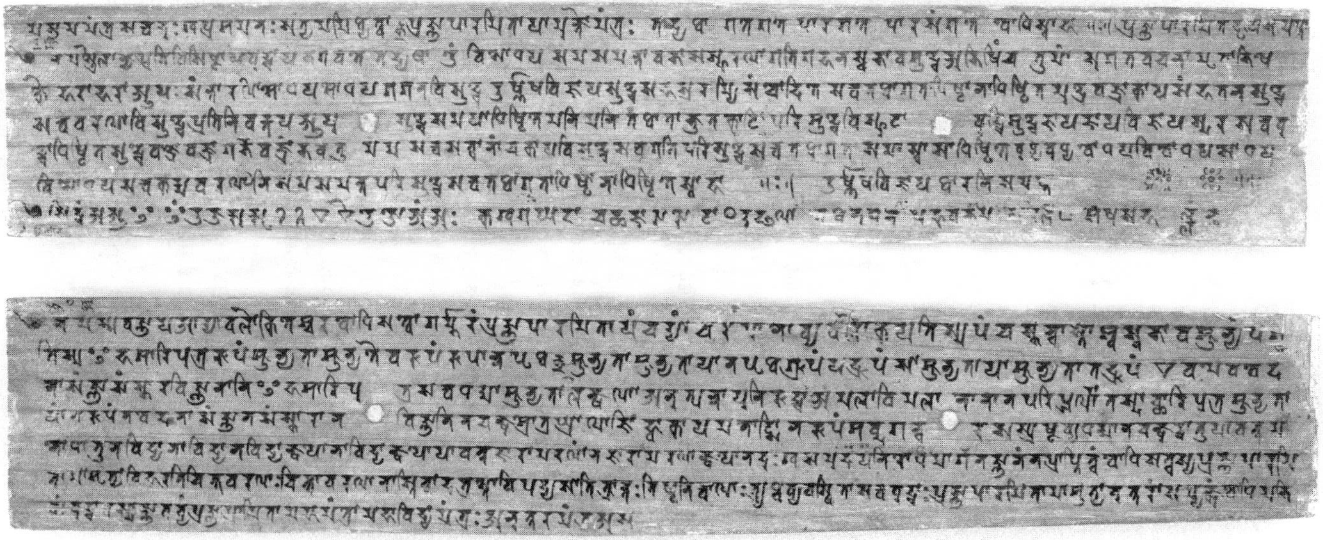

FIG. 6. *Horyu-ji version of the* Hridaya. *Sanskrit.*

version was created in China.[5] I agree with him, as it is clear that the brush movements in the Horyu-ji *Hridaya* reflect skills in ideographic calligraphy.

If we observe the manuscript closely, we see two square holes in the middle of each leaf. This indicates that strings were threaded through the holes and tied to make loops — the oldest known way of "binding" a book. The wearing of the surface on the bottom and lower right corner of each leaf suggests that the leaves were frequently flapped open for recitation. In the Horyu-ji manuscript, the *Hridaya* (from the seven lines on the first leaf to the first line of the second leaf) is followed by the *Ushnisha vijaya dharani*, also known as "Honored Victorious Dharani" (the second to the sixth line of the second leaf), and the Sanskrit alphabet (the last line).[6] Thus, it can be assumed that this "book" was used for chanting in esoteric rituals and for reviewing this particular writing system.

The height of Sanskrit study in Japan was marked by Kukai (774–835), who had mastered Vajrayana Buddhism in China under the guidance of Huiguo (746–805), a dharma successor of Amoghavajra. Kukai was followed by a number of scholar monks during the Heian Period (794–1185), when esoteric Buddhist rites with the use of Sanskrit dharanis were enthusiastically practiced. Interest in Sanskrit declined, however, when the Pure Land, Zen, and Lotus schools became the mainstream schools of Buddhism in the Kamakura Period (1185–1333).

Centuries later, a monk of the Shingon (Mantra) School, Jogon (1639–1702), deplored the fact that there was no one who could teach Sanskrit in Japan at that time. He systematized his own understanding of its grammar and made a word-to-word translation of the Horyu-ji version of the *Hridaya*.[7]

F. Max Müller (1823–1900), a German pioneer of scientific comparative studies in linguistics, mythology, and religion who taught at Oxford University, published an annotated Horyu-ji manuscript of the shorter *Hridaya* text in collaboration with Bunyu Nanjo in 1884.[8] (See p. 216 for the text.) Müller compiled translated texts by experts in Oriental studies from all over the world and inaugurated the publication of the epoch-making collection *The Sacred Books of the East* (1879–1910). Some of his pupils, including Nanjo and Junjiro Takakusu, initiated critical Buddhist and Indian studies in Japan.

Archaic Sanskrit texts are often corrupted by scribes' mistakes and damages incurred over time. Much of the contemporary Sanskritists' work consists of making hypothetical critical editions of these texts, while trying to maintain their original expressions. (Readers can see an excellent example of such Sanskrit studies in Paul Harrison's work presented on p. 205 in the appendices.) The Horyu-ji version of the *Hridaya* has been edited, after the early work by Müller and Nanjo, by generations of leading Japanese Sanskritists: Ryosaburo Sakaki, Unrai Ogiwara, Shindo Shiraishi, and Shuyu Kanaoka.[9]

There is also a text from Dunhuang called the "Sino-Sanskrit version *Prajna Paramita Heart Sutra*."[10] It is a Chinese transliteration of the shorter *Hridaya* and was at first regarded as a version made by an anonymous editor. In 1985, Fumimasa-Bunga Fukui studied the Sino-Sanskrit materials and found one manuscript (fig. 7; Stein #5648, British Museum) that is identified as follows:

> Sanskrit *Prajna Paramita Heart Sutra*. Translated, under the imperial command, by Bukong, whose posthumous name given by the Emperor is Dabian Zhengguanzhi. Avalokiteshvara Bodhisattva had personally taught and bestowed this Sanskrit text to Tripitaka Dharma Master Xuanzang; Bukong has edited it.[11]

Fukui was thus the first scholar to point out that this transliteration had been done by Bukong (705–774), whose Indian name was Amoghavajra.

A Vajrayana teacher and translator, Amoghavajra from Simha (present-day Sri Lanka) was one of the outstanding figures in the Chinese Buddhist world. He perfected an accurate system to transliterate Sanskrit texts in Chinese by using Chinese ideographs alone. This particular text of the *Heart Sutra* is a combination of his Chinese transliteration of the Sanskrit original and his word-by-word Chinese translation.

Fukui also, as I mentioned earlier (p. 42), has introduced a Chinese transliteration of the shorter version of *Prajna Paramita Hridaya* by Maitribhadra, a monk from central India who arrived in China in the tenth century.

Edward Conze collected a number of Sanskrit copies of the shorter and longer *Hridaya* and included a painstaking and concise critical comparative study of twelve extant manuscripts in his acclaimed essay collection *Thirty Years of Buddhist Studies*. One manuscript—the Cambridge Text—has a suggested date of around the twelfth century. Five others are presumed to date from the seventeenth to nineteenth century.[12]

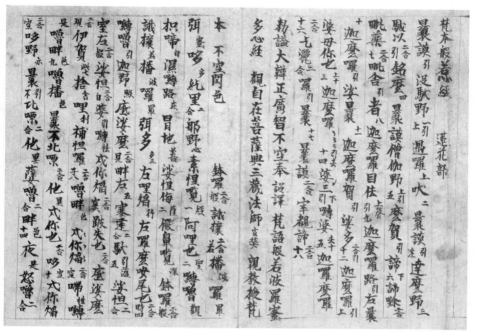

FIG. 7. *A Chinese transliteration of* Hridaya. *Discovered at Dunhuang Cave. The two center columns represent the text quoted in this chapter—"Avalokiteshvara Bodhisattva personally..." Following the line is the Sanskrit text transliterated in Chinese, with a number of small ideographs indicating pronunciation details.*

Thus, there are three texts available for studying the shorter *Hridaya*—the Horyu-ji version transmitted in Japan, the Amoghavajra version obtained in Dunhuang by Stein and identified by Fukui, and the Nepalese version presented by Conze. I introduce all of these texts below in Part Six, "Terms and Concepts," and appendix 1, "Texts for Comparison." Comparing these texts may give the reader some ideas about Sanskrit textual transformation over centuries.

The National Library of Paris houses seventy manuscripts of the *Hridaya* in Tibetan, discovered and brought to France by Paul Pelliot,[13] while the British Museum and the British Library house eleven manuscripts in Tibetan brought to England by Aurel Stein.[14]

The Tibetan and Mongolian renditions of the *Hridaya* exist only within the longer text, which includes a prologue that begins with "Thus have I heard" and a conclusion that describes the Buddha's praise of Avalokite-shvara. (The present book is primarily based on the shorter text, but I provide the Sanskrit, Chinese, Tibetan, and Mongolian versions of the longer text in appendix 1.)

The *Hridaya* is often regarded as a condensation of the enormous *Maha Prajna Paramita* scripture, as it contains the entire teachings and the magic of this vast document. This reduction of the scripture was taken even further in a sutra called "The Prajna Paramita in One Letter, the Mother of All Tathagatas." It contains but the single syllable *A* and exists only in the Tibetan canon.

PART FOUR

Most Recent Scholarship
(1992–Present)

13

A Chinese Apocryphal Text?

I N 1992, JAN NATTIER, a professor at Indiana University, published
a startling paper entitled "The *Heart Sutra*: A Chinese Apocryphal
Text?"[1] in which she presented a revolutionary view on the formation of
the sutra. Her paper is of great significance for anyone who is interested in
the history of the sutra. Her theory, in brief, is this:

Nattier lists five peculiar features of the shorter text of the sutra: its brev-
ity; the lack of a sutra's traditional opening ("Thus have I heard . . ."); the lack
of the Buddha's appearance; the role of Avalokiteshvara as the main speaker
(Avalokiteshvara generally plays no role in the *Prajna Paramita* literature);
and the placement of the mantra at the end. She points out that these features suggest that the circumstances of its composition may have differed
notably from those that led to the more extensive *Prajna Paramita* texts.

She divides the sutra into two major parts. The core section begins with
the first appearance of "O Shariputra" and ends with the line "no knowledge and no attainment." The frame section consists of the introduction
and conclusion.

The core section is virtually identical to a passage in Kumarajiva's trans-
lation into Chinese of the *25,000-line Prajna Paramita* (Pancavimshati
Sahasrika Prajna Paramita).[2] The Sanskrit version of the *25,000-line
Prajna Paramita* corresponds to Kumarajiva's Chinese *Maha Prajna
Paramita Sutra*. Thus, it is possible to establish a sequence of formation:
Sanskrit *25,000-line Prajna Paramita* → Chinese *Maha Prajna Paramita
Sutra* → Chinese *Heart Sutra*.

According to Nattier's comparative analysis of the *Hridaya* and the
corresponding part of the Sanskrit *25,000-line Prajna Paramita*, a general

similarity in the content of their ideas as well as their sequence is evident. Yet their styles are different: the former is concise, the latter repetitive. Also, there is a notable difference in grammar and vocabulary. Nattier thus argues that the *Hridaya* did not derive from the Sanskrit *25,000-line Prajna Paramita*, or vice versa.[3] Rather, she suggests that the *Hridaya* is a back-translation (a reconstruction of Sanskrit texts) from the Chinese *Heart Sutra*. "Such a striking similarity in content, combined with an equally striking difference in vocabulary, can only be explained as the result of a back-translation."[4]

Avalokiteshvara's following among Chinese Buddhists over the centuries had far exceeded his popularity in India. Thus, the choice of Avalokiteshvara as the central figure in a newly created Buddhist recitation text would be perfectly plausible in a Chinese milieu.

The mantra that concludes the *Heart Sutra* was also seen in other texts in the Chinese Buddhist canon by the time the sutra was created. It is therefore arguable that the composer of the original Chinese *Heart Sutra* adopted the mantra from an existing work and inserted it into the sutra.[5]

A biography of Xuanzang states that he received the sutra from a sick man and used it for protection on the road to India. "This account provides concrete evidence, then, both of Xuanzang's love for the text and his transport of its content (at least in oral form) to India," says Nattier.

According to Huili's biography of Xuanzang, during his stay at Nalanda University he discovered that the *Awakening of Faith in Mahayana* was unknown to his Indian co-religionists. His response was to translate the text into Sanskrit.[6] Nattier suggests: "Under the circumstances he may have done just what we would expect him to do: quietly re-translate the text back into Sanskrit. . . . The first Indian commentaries on the text appear roughly a century and a half after Xuanzang's visit. . . . Until further evidence of other possibilities should surface, Xuanzang must remain the most likely candidate for the transmission of this Chinese creation to India."

Based on the findings of John McRae, Nattier suggests that the two versions of the *Heart Sutra* — considered to represent the lost Chinese translations — are known to us only through their inclusion in Daoan's catalog, *Complete Catalog of Sutras* (Zongli Zhongjing Mulu). This list by Daoan was itself lost but was largely reproduced in Sengyou's *Record of the Translated Tripitaka* (Chu Sanzang Jiji), completed around 515 C.E.[7] Both titles are listed here as the work of anonymous translators. The attributions of these translations to Zhiqian and Kumarajiva, respectively, in later scripture catalogues were clearly added after the fact and can easily be discounted.[8] The likelihood that these titles are genuine references to early versions of the *Heart Sutra* is doubtful.

The earliest extant version of the *Heart Sutra* attributed to Kumarajiva is not found in the earliest catalogs of his work. Indeed, the first attribution to Kumarajiva is in the *Kaiyuan Era Catalog of Shakyamuni's Teachings* (Kaiyuan Shijiao Lu), completed in 730.[9]

The line "Form is not different from emptiness. Emptiness is not different from form" in the so-called Kumarajiva version does not appear in the same way as it does in his translation of the *25,000-line Prajna Paramita*. Instead, it appears exactly as it does in his translation of the *Dazhidu Lun* (Treatise on Realization of Great Wisdom), now attributed to Nagarjuna, which includes citations from Kumarajiva's own *Maha Prajna Paramita Sutra*.[10] Nattier thus suggests that the so-called Kumarajiva version of the *Heart Sutra* is not the work of Kumarajiva himself or an independent translation from the Sanskrit but rather is the creation of a third party: a Chinese author who was more familiar with the *Large Sutra* as presented in the widely popular commentary of *Dazhidu Lun* than he was with the text of the sutra itself. The new work would likely have been created after the completion of the *Dazhidu Lun* in 406 C.E.[11]

Regarding the Chinese version of the *Heart Sutra* attributed to Xuanzang, Nattier suggests that we can no longer use the term "translation," for there is every indication that it was fabricated in China. She writes, "Moreover, Xuanzang's biography speaks not of his translation of the text, but of his initial encounter with the sutra in Szechwan."[12]

The *Heart Sutra*, according to her, "does not appear where we would expect it to be: as part" of the huge *Prajna Paramita* scripture Xuanzang translated. In this scripture, "the various sutras are not treated as separate texts, but as chapters in a single work, a rather unusual arrangement that may well go back to Xuanzang himself."[13]

"The most likely possibility, it would seem, is that Xuanzang encountered the [Chinese] text in its full form and made only minor editorial changes, in all likelihood after his extended study of Sanskrit terms in India."[14] "He may have 'corrected' the text, probably after his travels in India."[15] "It was certainly Xuanzang ... who was responsible for the widespread popularity of the sutra in China, and in all probability for its initial circulation (and perhaps its translation into Sanskrit) in India as well."[16]

Nattier reminds us that the longer text of the *Hridaya* consists of a sutra's proper introductory section. The core section that follows is nearly identical to the shorter text (the Sanskrit version), which corresponds to the Chinese version attributed to Xuanzang. And the longer text ends with a conclusion, which includes the audience's response.

Nattier makes an additional remark: "Even if we accept the idea that the sutra is 'apocryphal' in the technical sense, this in no way undermines the value that the text has held for Buddhist practitioners." Then she concludes: "The *Heart Sutra* is indeed — in every sense of the word — a Chinese text."[17]

14

Thoughts on the Apocryphon Theory

FUMIMASA-BUNGA FUKUI, a leading Japanese scholar on the *Heart Sutra*, wrote in his book that the Nattier theory "shook the Japanese academic world."[1] He also remarked: "As the *Prajna Heart Sutra* is one of the most revered sutras in Japan, it would be a matter of grave concern if this were proved to be an apocyrphon produced in China."[2]

Fukui outlines the Nattier theory, saying that her way of dividing the sutra into three sections is her own invention and does not accord with traditional scholarly divisions. He insists that it is a mistake to assume that the mantra was added to the main scriptural text.

According to Fukui, there has not been a single record or argument in Chinese history that suggests that the *Heart Sutra* is an apocryphal text. On the other hand, there are many documents acknowledging translation by Xuanzang, so Nattier would need to prove all of these documents to be apocrypha. He claims her paper is "driven by theory and not convincing." Finally, he poses the question: Does Nattier's hypothesis, based on a very small number of materials comparing the three texts — the *Hridaya*, the Sanskrit *25,000-line Prajna Paramita*, and the Chinese *Heart Sutra* — prove that it is an apocryphal text?[3]

The U.S. translator and writer Red Pine also doubts Nattier's theory:[4]

> Despite the brilliance and depth of scholarship involved in Nattier's presentation of this thesis, we are shown no proof that the *Heart Sutra* was originally composed or compiled in Chinese, that any part of the first half was extracted from the *Large Sutra* or any other Chinese text, or that the mantra was added later. Instead, we are asked

to believe that this is what must have happened because certain lines in the two Chinese texts agree and those in the two corresponding extant Sanskrit texts don't, and it should be the other way around, with the Sanskrit texts agreeing and the Chinese texts diverging in the usual course of translation.

My own solution to this apparent inconsistency is to assume that the lines in question in the Sanskrit texts of the *Heart Sutra* and the *Large Sutra* used by Kumarajiva and Xuanzang were identical. Thus, there was no need, nor any basis, for divergence in the Chinese. In fact, there is no evidence, only speculation, that the two Sanskrit texts used by Kumarajiva and Xuanzang differed at the time they made their renderings of this passage in these two sutras. The differences we see today in the two Sanskrit texts, I would suggest, were the result of subsequent corruption or simply reflect the existence of variant editions.

I myself believe that Nattier presents a revolutionary finding in the origination of the *Heart Sutra* by her careful and thorough argument. Because of her work, scholarly understanding about the history of the *Heart Sutra* will never be the same.

In summary, I agree with Nattier that the *Heart Sutra* was compiled in China. We can further argue that the so-called Kumarajiva Chinese translation is likely the original version of the sutra. Xuanzang seems to have played a key role in the formation of the *Hridaya*. It does not, however, mean that he literally back-translated the sutra from Chinese to Sanskrit, as Nattier indicates. A later record suggests that he received the Sanskrit version "from Avalokiteshvara."[5] Thus it is possible to regard the emergence of the *Hridaya* as Xuanzang's mystical experience during meditation. Below is the reasoning behind my thoughts on the Nattier theory.

For your reference, all the *Hridaya* and *Heart Sutra* texts, as well as earlier texts quoted by Nattier and myself, are presented in "Texts for Comparison" in appendix 1. (If the following arguments seem too cumbersome, you are welcome to skip to chapter 15, "Roles of Ancient Chinese Translators.")

Comparing the two Sanskrit texts — the *25,000-line Prajna Paramita* and the *Hridaya* — I endorse Nattier's suggestion that the *Hridaya* did not come directly from the Sanskrit *25,000-line Prajna Paramita*, or vice versa.

Her hypothesis is a new finding: that the core section of the so-called Kumarajiva translation of the *Heart Sutra* is a composition of extracts from *Dazhidu Lun*, a popular commentary containing parts of the Kumarajiva translation of the *Maha Prajna Paramita Sutra*. After examining the original Chinese texts included in the *Taisho* Canon, I verify Nattier's theory in this regard. In other words, we can no longer call that version of the *Heart Sutra* Kumarajiva's own translation, although its core section comes from the *Maha Prajna Paramita Sutra* translated by him through *Dazhidu Lun*.

For all scholars of the *Heart Sutra* who had believed this version to be Kumarajiva's actual translation, this finding was a big blow. In addition, Nattier's denial of the prior existence of the third-century Zhiqian translation pushes the formation of the *Heart Sutra* two to four centuries later.[6] I myself was astounded by this new understanding.

We can now say that an unidentifiable person in China compiled the shorter text *Heart Sutra*. This compilation was an assemblage of three parts — an introductory part starting at "Avalokiteshvara," a core section from the *Dazhidu Lun* that quotes Kumarajiva's *Maha Prajna Paramita Sutra,* and the mantra.

Nattier points out that the so-called Xuanzang version of the Chinese *Heart Sutra* lacks two sections that are contained in both the *Large Sutra* and the so-called Kumarajiva version.[7] This means that the so-called Kumarajiva version of the Chinese *Heart Sutra* is closer to the earlier *Maha Prajna Paramita Sutra* than the "so-called Xuanzang version."[8] Nattier's observation leads me to believe that the so-called Kumarajiva version of the *Heart Sutra* preceded the Chinese Xuanzang version. I therefore propose to rename the so-called Kumarajiva version of the Chinese *Heart Sutra* the "α version" (alpha version).

In this way, the philological flow of the text can be presented this way:

Sanskrit *25,000-line Prajna Paramita* → Kumarajiva's Chinese *Maha Prajna Paramita Sutra / Dazhidu Lun* → α version

Which text, then, came next — the *Hridaya* or the Chinese version "attributed to" Xuanzang? In other words, which text — the α version or the Xuanzang version — became the basis for the Sanskrit version?

Let us compare these three texts: What is unique in the Sanskrit text and lacking in the Chinese versions is the dedication in the first line.

What is lacking in the Sanskrit version and common in the Chinese texts is the title at the beginning and a phrase in the first line, "becoming free from suffering." These discrepancies, however, do not provide clues to the chronological sequence of the texts.

What is lacking in the α version but existent in the Sanskrit version is the phrase "a great mantra."[9] The "Xuanzang" version reads "a great spirit mantra." It seems there is a progression from the absence of the phrase to "a great mantra," and then to "a great spirit mantra."

What seems to be a deciding factor, however, in determining the order is the section right before "Form is no other than *shunyata. Shunyata* is no other than form."[10] This section is identical in Kumarajiva's *Maha Prajna Paramita Sutra, Dazhidu Lun*, and the α version. It can be translated as follows: "Form is *shunyata,* therefore (it has) no mark of angst and destruction. Perception is *shunyata,* therefore there is no mark of perception. Feeling is *shunyata,* therefore there is no mark of knowing. Inclination is *shunyata,* therefore there is no mark of doing. Discernment is *shunyata,* therefore there is no mark of awakening. Therefore, Shariputra . . ."

In the corresponding section, the Sanskrit version says, "Form is *shunyata.* The very *shunyata* is form." The so-called Xuanzang version has no part corresponding to either of these Chinese or Sanskrit passages. Do we not see a direction toward simplification from the earlier Chinese texts, then via the Sanskrit version, and finally up to the "Xuanzang" version? It would be odd if the α version were immediately followed by the "Xuanzang" version and then evolved to the Sanskrit version. It would, in effect, mean that these passages from the earlier Chinese versions were erased in the "Xuanzang" Chinese version and were brought back in the Sanskrit version. Thus I believe it is logical to assume that the α version became the basis for the Sanskrit version.

At this point I will diverge from Nattier's argument that Xuanzang did not translate the *Heart Sutra;* I do not think she has presented sufficient evidence to discredit Xuanzang as translator of the *Heart Sutra.* Although Xuanzang's biography does not mention his translation of the sutra, his successor Kuiji's introduction to the *Sino-Sanskrit Heart Sutra* says, "This Sanskrit text of the *Prajna Paramita Sutra* has been transliterated (i.e., into Chinese) by the Tripitaka Master of Great Tang."[11]

It is true that Xuanzang's most comprehensive *Maha Prajna Paramita Sutra* does not include his translation of the *Heart Sutra.* For centuries, this monumental text was considered to be of Indian origin. If it is indeed an Indian text, is it not natural that the *Heart Sutra,* which is of Chinese origin, is not found in it?

As Fukui points out in his review of Nattier's paper, Xuanzang's *Heart Sutra* was carved on the monument erected by Emperor Gao in 672 at the Gaofu Monastery, Chang'an[12] (fig. 8). Those who endorsed Xuanzang's translation of the *Heart Sutra* — Emperor Gao, along with his officials whose names were carved on the monument — were all contemporaries of Xuanzang.

It is theoretically possible that the translation of the *Heart Sutra* "came to be attributed" to Xuanzang later, as Nattier suggests.[13] Were this indeed the case, it must have been done by one or more of his students during the eight years between Xuanzang's death in 664 and the dedication of the monument. I must say that this is highly unlikely.

I do believe that Xuanzang did not make a completely new translation of the *Heart Sutra.* However, in discussing whether he "translated" the sutra or not, we should not use the contemporary Western concept of "translation," which calls for unique interpretations and innovative renderings throughout the text. We need to understand what "translation" meant for olden-time Chinese Buddhists, including Xuanzang himself. As I demonstrate in the chapter, "Roles of Ancient Chinese Translators," those "translators" who followed in later times — Prajna and Liyan, Dharmachandra, and Zhihuilun — did not make more than "minor editorial changes," in Nattier's terminology.

From this perspective, it seems impossible to deny Xuanzang's role as the translator of the *Heart Sutra.* As a matter of simple logic, acknowledging Xuanzang's translation presupposes the existence of a Sanskrit original. (Without an original text, no "translation" would have been possible.)

What, then, was the original Sanskrit text? Was the *Hridaya* not the original for Xuanzang's Chinese *Heart Sutra?* As I suggested earlier, if we compare these two texts, it is clear that the former preceded the latter; it is therefore reasonable to assume that the *Hridaya* was not translated from Xuanzang's Chinese version. In summary, I suggest that the logical chronological sequence of the texts would read this way:

Kumarajiva's *Maha Prajna Paramita Sutra/Dazhidu Lun* →
α version → *Hridaya* → Chinese Xuanzang version

Assuming that we can accept this sequence of texts, where did the Sanskrit *Hridaya* come from? Nattier says, "Xuanzang may have quietly re-translated the text back into Sanskrit." By saying so, and with her use elsewhere in her article of the word "forgery," is she hinting that Xuanzang might have deliberately deceived or at least misled people of his time and later generations by composing and presenting the *Hridaya* as an authentic scripture? Wondering about this point led me to ask if any reputable translator would "quietly re-translate" a text into its source language and translate it back to his or her language. If I reflect on myself, although I sit on the lowest (and perhaps the newest) seat among translators, is there any chance that I would "create" or "forge" an "original" text and translate it back to another language? Never.

What may lead us to a conjecture on the initial emergence of the *Hridaya* is a passage in the Sino-Sanskrit edition of the sutra by Amoghavajra (see p. 213): "Avalokiteshvara Bodhisattva had personally taught and bestowed this Sanskrit text to Tripitaka Dharma Master Xuanzang." Although this manuscript was copied after Amoghavajra's death — over one hundred years after Xuanzang's death — it may give us a clue to the "transmission" of the *Hridaya* to Xuanzang.[14] How?

Consider this: What do meditators do when they need to know something of deepest importance? Do they not meditate on it, or pray to a guardian deity for it? When Xuanzang wanted to have the original *Hridaya* and could not get it, would he not have meditated and prayed to Avalokiteshvara, his guardian deity, to bestow the sutra upon him? (We know Avalokiteshvara was his guardian from Huili's account that Xuanzang invoked this deity when he was in danger in the Gobi Desert.) Did he not then in truth "receive" it from the bodhisattva? Is this not the implication of the passage in the Amoghavajra manuscript stating that the bodhisattva personally gave the sutra to him?

Meditation is, at times, described as a nondual experience, and some meditators say that giver and receiver become one in meditation. We could then say that the distinction between Avalokiteshvara and Xuanzang himself disappeared in his state of absorption, and thus Xuanzang received the *Hridaya* from the bodhisattva.

"Receiving" sutras from the Buddha or a bodhisattva, as Xuanzang's followers — including Amoghavajra — claimed to do, is traditionally how the origins of Mahayana sutras were accounted for. From a contemporary academic perspective, the process of a Chinese monk conceiving a sutra during meditation may well be defined as "creation," "composition," "production," "fabrication," "back-translation," "forgery," or writing "an apocryphal text," as Nattier suggests. However, one can equally well view the emergence of the Sanskrit version, according to Amoghavajra's edition, as a result of the monk Xuanzang's mystical experience.

These two views, scholarly and legendary, may not be mutually exclusive. Even if Xuanzang felt that he had been given the Sanskrit version by Avalokiteshvara, its contents were filtered through his knowledge of the earlier Chinese version. Of course, there would also have been an editing process, outside of nondual meditation.

The reader may get the impression that I have been making the case that Xuanzang did back-translate the *Heart Sutra*. However, I would not put it that way. In this particular case, the word *back-translation* can have the following implications:

1. The normal flow of Buddhist texts at that time in China was from Sanskrit to Chinese. If the Chinese text comes first and then the Sanskrit version emerges from it, some scholars may say this is a back-translation.

2. Xuanzang seemed to have had full knowledge of the α version, and at some point he had in his hand a Sanskrit version that corresponded to the α version. No one else seemed to have been responsible for the emergence of this new version. Again, some scholars may say Xuanzang must have back-translated the α version.

3. If Xuanzang had had the intention and plan to translate the Chinese text into Sanskrit, I would say that he back-translated the *Heart Sutra* into Sanskrit. However, we cannot prove this. It is unlikely for an established and respected translator like Xuanzang to intentionally "create" an "original" text. For some scholars, the point may be too subtle, but in this case I personally would not use the term "back-translation."

Suppose Xuanzang did feel that he had received the *Hridaya* from the bodhisattva, and then wrote it down (composed it), what was the probable date of his "transmission"? The reader may remember that according to a later account he completed the translation of the *Hridaya* into Chinese three days before the death of Emperor Tai. It might have been a moment when Xuanzang would have done anything to get the Sanskrit sutra for recitation, in order to acquire a higher magical power for healing the emperor than its earlier Chinese version carried. In this case, the sutra was conceived in China, so it deserves to be called an apocryphal text in the traditional Chinese sense. As Nattier reminds us, for a Buddhist scripture to be regarded as authentic in China, it had to be of Indian origin.[15]

The possibility that Xuanzang "received" the *Hridaya* in India cannot be entirely ruled out. Kuiji reported to the emperor that at Nalanda Xuanzang met again the sick monk who had given the sutra to him, whereupon the monk revealed that he was in fact Avalokiteshvara and blessed him for his safe journey home.[16] Thus, Xuanzang may have had contact with Avalokiteshvara in India. He may even have consulted with Indian monks on vocabulary and grammar. This could explain why, in spite of Nattier's observation that some lines in the *Hridaya* are not idiomatic, this text stood nearly uncorrected when it was expanded into the longer *Hridaya*.

Now we run into a peculiar dilemma: If Xuanzang had "received" the text in India, it would have to be seen as a scripture of Indian origin! Therefore, technically speaking, by the traditional Chinese standard that regards all sutras created in India as authentic, Xuanzang's Sanskrit version could be accepted as an authentic scripture.

15

Roles of Ancient Chinese Translators

KUMARAJIVA WAS a monk of the fourth to fifth century from the eastern Turkistan region of Central Asia. His father, an Indian Buddhist monk, married a younger sister of the king of Kucha while he was visiting the kingdom.[1] His mother, who later became a nun, took Kumarajiva, who had been ordained at age seven, to Kashmir to study Theravada Buddhism, then to Kashgar to study Mahayana Buddhism. His reputation as a great Sanskritist and invincible debater reached northern China, even to the point of becoming a cause for war. Hejian of the small kingdom of Zou dispatched his general Lu Guang, crossing the Gobi and Taklamakan deserts, to attack Kucha and capture Kumarajiva, who was thirty-two years old. Lu Guang took him to China, but the kingdom of Zou had been destroyed and the kingdom of Liang had meanwhile been established. Kumarajiva mastered Chinese while he was held there for fifteen years.

In 413, at age fifty-eight, Kumarajiva was invited to become national teacher by Yaoxing, who had established the kingdom of Later Zou, and was entrusted with the translation academy at the Xiaoyao Garden of the Ximing Villa in Chang'an. Kumarajiva gave lectures to hundreds of students and conducted the translation of Sanskrit scriptures into Chinese with a small number of assistants. During the last twelve years of his life, he was a prolific scholar, producing 73 texts in 383 fascicles. His style was so fluent and magnificent that it has captivated the widest number of readers in the ideographic world ever since; he also established a great number of Buddhist technical terms, most of which are still used. Kumarajiva educated three thousand students including eighty masters, and his translations provided the basis for the creation of the Chengshi (Satyasiddhi) and San-lun (Three Treatises) schools.[2]

On the other hand, Xuanzang of the seventh century was from Luo-yang, the capital of the declining Sui Dynasty, central China. These two great translators lived roughly two and a half centuries apart.

Both translators shaped the dharma and civilization of their times and ever after. Kumarajiva worked intuitively, being sensitive to his native-speaker students' responses. His adaptational and mesmerizing renditions were an invaluable contribution to the popularization of Buddhism and its scriptures. Xuanzang delegated specific tasks to his assistants to cross-check the translated texts against their originals. The accuracy of his trans-lations helped to greatly elevate the academic and philosophical standard of Buddhist studies. These two master translators' distinct ways of working remind us that a great translation is not merely a matter of interpretation and expression, but also requires an outstanding procedural system to carry out the task.

If we compare the texts that preceded the *Heart Sutra* (the Sanskrit *25,000-line Prajna Paramita* and the Kumarajiva translation of it) with the earliest *Heart Sutra* texts (the α version, the *Hridaya*, and the Xuanzang version), we can see the steps of continual simplification. The Xuanzang version is the final point of this line of textual condensation.[3]

The contrast in the receptions in later times of the two Chinese versions of the *Heart Sutra* translations is remarkable. All commentaries on the sutra were made regarding the Xuanzang version. We see no record of any stud-ies made on the α version, nor do we find any records of this version being recited before the emergence of the Xuanzang version. (Centuries later, the α version was included in the Chinese Buddhist canon, with Kumarajiva listed as the translator. This is how it survived and how we come to have access to it today.)

If we compare the α version and Xuanzang's Chinese version with the corresponding section of the *Maha Prajna Paramita Sutra* translated by Kumarajiva, we notice a distinct and overwhelming influence of the Kumarajiva text on the other two versions. Although the α version of the *Heart Sutra* can no longer be regarded as Kumarajiva's translation, his influence on these two versions is evident.

In the texts offered for comparison in appendix 1 and their analyses in

Part Six, I divide each of the various versions of the *Heart Sutra* into forty-four segments. According to this division, twelve out of sixteen segments of the core section of Xuanzang's Chinese sutra are identical to the corresponding part of Kumarajiva's *Maha Prajna Paramita Sutra*.[4]

Recall the early biographical account stating that Xuanzang first received the sutra from a sick monk in Shu. Since Huili's record does not indicate that what Xuanzang received was in Sanskrit, we may assume that he received it in Chinese. Indeed, it was likely the α version, since the translation Xuanzang made after his return from India is quite similar to this version, and there was no other known version of the shorter text of the sutra at that time. Xuanzang must have related intimately to the *Heart Sutra* he had been given, having chanted it countless times. According to the biography by Huili, Xuanzang expounded the dharma of the sutra on his way to India.

We do not know whether Xuanzang was aware at the time that the version he had received from the sick monk was the text attributed to Kumarajiva. However, when Xuanzang translated the *Hridaya* into Chinese, there is no doubt that he referred to the α version, which he might have believed to be the Kumarajiva translation. It is likely that he and his translation team also referred to the *Maha Prajna Paramita Sutra* in the Kumarajiva translation. Otherwise there is no explanation for the word-for-word adaptation of the passage *"Shunyata* does not differ from form, form does not differ from *shunyata,"* which existed only in the *Maha Prajna Paramita Sutra* before Xuanzang.[5]

The changes Xuanzang made to the α version are indeed small. He retitled it, called Avalokiteshvara by a new Chinese name, substituted a few words, and left out some lines.[6] The α version already had a beautiful rhythm suitable for chanting. Xuanzang strengthened the style by adding an ideograph here and there.

Let us compare some of the forty-four segments in the Xuanzang versions with those of the α version: Twenty-three of them are identical.[7] In four other segments, the commonly shared words are represented by different ideographs.[8] In four other segments, the word *paramita* is transliterated differently.[9] From the α version, Xuanzang eliminated fifty-one characters and added eight.[10] Xuanzang's artistry lay in the fact that he changed the earlier version as little as possible, making the text clearer and more concise.

Significantly, the first known Chinese title of this sutra was not *Bore boluomida xin jing* (Prajna Paramita Heart Sutra), but *Mohe bore boluomi da mingzhong jing* (Maha Prajna Paramita Great Dharani Sutra.)[11] Clearly, this short text was primarily used for magical incantation. Xuanzang translated the word *hridaya* in the title as "heart" rather than using the word "dharani" (magical spell), so that he left it open for interpretation, to be understood as either "essential point" or "dharani."[12] His poetic ambiguity has likely contributed to the later popularity of the sutra.

In the modern sense, Xuanzang's contribution to the Chinese text of the *Heart Sutra* may be regarded as a moderate revision of the earlier Chinese text, a form not deserving to be categorized as a "translation." However, the broad adaptation of terms that are found in Xuanzang's text is not an isolated case. If we compare the longer text of the *Heart Sutra* in the eighth-century translation by Prajna, Liyan, and others (*Taisho,* no. 253) with Xuanzang's Chinese text, there are notable overlaps: out of forty-two segments in the corresponding parts, thirty-four segments are identical and three contain the same words with different ideographs.[13] Today, this kind of adaptation would be seen as theft or plagiarism.

How do we explain such consistent similarity among these Chinese texts? Here is my suggestion: When we look at works by Xuanzang as well as those by later translators, it seems that the translators' intentions were not to create a unique or new text, but to maintain the expressions of earlier texts—to ensure that they be both faithful to the original and workable as texts. The translators introduced new renditions only of those passages that they felt were in need of change. They operated with the Buddhist principle of selflessness rather than self-expression. What they aimed for was not to express their individuality but rather to revere and authenticate the work of their predecessors in order to secure the continuous heritage of passing down sacred texts. This made translation a very sacred act.

The practice of making minimal changes to an earlier version of a text may also have had to do with the fact that people often chanted sutras together, in addition to reading them individually. Important passages were embedded in their consciousness, and it would not have been easy—or even appropriate—to make any all-encompassing changes.

We can find an important insight in a term used to describe translations: In the early Chinese catalogs of scriptures, second or third translations were listed as *chongyi. Yi* means "translation," and *chong* means "added," "repeated," or "overlapped." Thus, the later works were regarded as "overlapped" translations, rather than "new" translations.

Although he worked with a larger team than any translator of Buddhist texts before his time, Xuanzang made minimal changes to the *Heart Sutra*, one of the smallest texts. By doing so, he gave us a gift that still inspires us thirteen hundred years later.

16

Emergence and Expansion
of the *Heart Sutra*

I WOULD LIKE TO present a scenario about the formation and development of the *Heart Sutra*. My view is based in part on Jan Nattier's
compelling theory, in part on my own observations of textual and circum-
stantial evidence.

An unknown person, most likely a Chinese monk, compiled the *Heart
Sutra*. In this case, "to compile" means to put together different elements
that already exist, edit them, and then create an independent text.

Perhaps during the process of meditation, this person envisioned the
merging of three major Mahayana elements — the figure of Avalokiteshvara; a portion of a *Prajna Paramita Sutra;* and the mantra that already
existed.[1] It was a brilliant notion, as these three elements represented the
main pillars of Buddhism in China at that time:

1. Avalokiteshvara was then the most widely worshiped bodhisattva
   in China.
2. A small portion of Kumarajiva's Chinese translation of the Indian
   text, the *25,000-line Prajna Paramita*, quoted in the Chinese translation of the *Dazhidu Lun* (Treatise on Great Wisdom) — mentioned
   above on p. 85 — was presented as the essence of this enormous
   scripture.
3. With the spread of Esoteric Buddhism, the chanting of magical formulas had become increasingly important.

This earliest version of the sutra — the α version — was possibly used as a tantric chanting text, as its title, "Maha Prajna Paramita Great Dharani Sutra," suggests. Its compilation likely took place not so long before Xuanzang encountered it, possibly in western China. The fact that Xuanzang received it in such a remote area suggests that the sutra had not been well known in central China, and that the original compilation of the *Heart Sutra* in China possibly took place in the mid-seventh century.

As his biographers noted, Xuanzang received the α version from a sick monk in western China while he was studying. Having received the sutra in this manner, he made it his practice to chant the sutra, and he also taught it when he traveled to India. During his Indian journey, he endeavored to collect Sanskrit Buddhist scriptures, but he was unable to find a *Hridaya* text in Sanskrit. Finally, he prayed to Avalokiteshvara for a Sanskrit version, "received" it from the bodhisattva during meditation, and translated it into Chinese. The year was possibly 649, shortly before the death of his major patron, Emperor Tai.

When translating the sutra, Xuanzang and his research team referred to the α version of the *Heart Sutra*, as well as to the Kumarajiva translation of the *Maha Prajna Paramita Sutra*. With reverence for Kumarajiva's text, Xuanzang preserved in the core section of his translation most of the corresponding part of the *Maha Prajna Paramita Sutra* text. Thereafter, Xuanzang's Chinese version of the *Heart Sutra* completely overshadowed the α version, spreading to Korea, Japan, and Vietnam.

If we accept it as likely that the first appearance of the sutra did indeed take place in China in or around the mid-seventh century, all accounts alleging that the *Heart Sutra* originated at an earlier time can be seen as groundless legends. The Gikaku story is within our chronological range, but the notion that the *Heart Sutra* reached a country that distant fifteen years after its translation is rather unlikely. A stone rubbing of the writing in formal script is attributed to Ouyang Xun (557–641), a renowned calligrapher who also served in Emperor Tai's court. However, his dates are earlier than Xuanzang's translation of the *Heart Sutra,* so it is impossible that Xun actually created the artwork.

While Xuanzang's *Hridaya* spread throughout Central Asia and India, it did not yet possess a sutra's proper form, lacking the prologue "Thus have I heard . . ." as well as the epilogue. Before or in the eighth century, an unknown person added these sections and compiled a longer text.[2] Once Indian dharma teachers encountered this text, they commented on it, and the text was also translated into Tibetan. Thereafter, it was chanted by Tibetan Buddhists.

We may thus see the *Heart Sutra* as a vehicle made of Indian parts, assembled in China. The older model is widely circulated in East Asia, while the new larger model is popular in Tibet. Several types of this "vehicle" are now exported all over the world.

PART FIVE

Globalizing the Sutra

17

Chinese Enthusiasm

THE COURT OF Emperor Gao (r. 649–683) — the third monarch of the Tang Dynasty — inaugurated the globalization of the *Heart Sutra,* a process that would take thirteen hundred years. On the Buddha's enlightenment day — the eighth day of the twelfth month — of 672, eight years after Xuanzang's death, the court erected a monument at Hongfu Monastery in the capital city of Chang'an. The monument was engraved with the late Emperor Tai's introduction to the Xuanzang translation of the enormous Buddhist canon, and with Xuanzang's translation of the *Heart Sutra* itself. (See fig. 8.)

Monk Huairen had spent over twenty years assembling samples of handwritten ideographs by Wang Xizhi — considered the Sage of Calligraphy — to represent the text of the emperor's introduction, as well as Xuanzang's translation. He patched together brushwork of the Calligraphy Sage, then had the texts carved onto the stone.[1] This compilation of characters in semicursive script for the monument reflected Emperor Tai's taste, and is still regarded as one of the best samples of classical Chinese calligraphy in existence.

Emperor Gao himself might have been a driving force for this promotion of the sutra. He had, after all, as crown prince been Xuanzang's senior monk, and this version of the sutra was probably translated into Chinese while his father was gravely ill. The fact that Gao's court gave the *Heart Sutra* a status almost as important as the entire canon provided great prestige and helped to build a solid foundation for the widespread admiration and recitation of the sutra in the years and centuries to come.

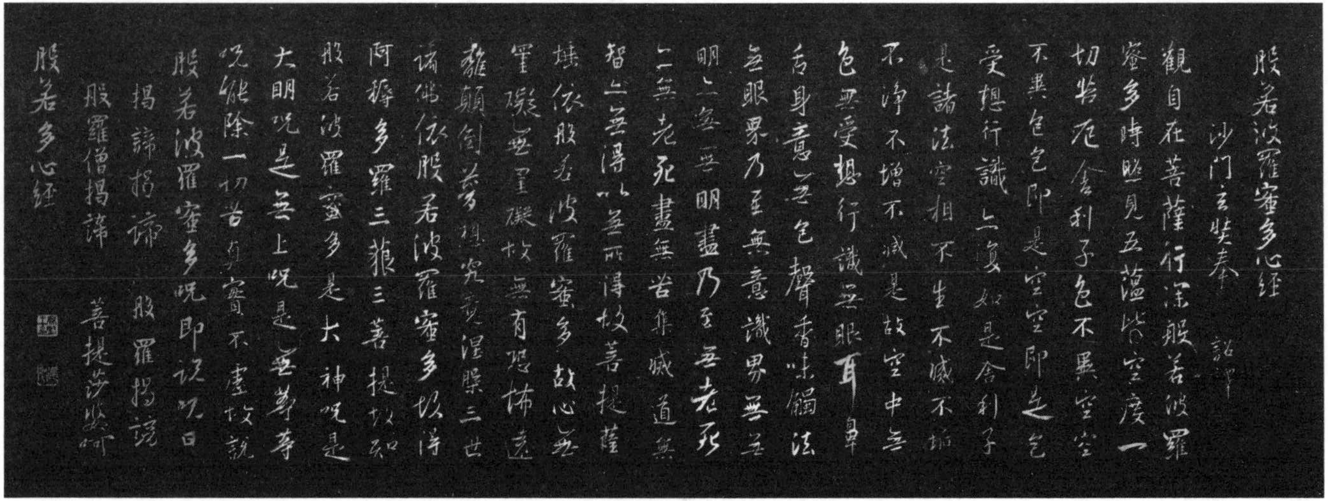

FIG. 8. *The earliest known rendering of the Heart Sutra. Carved in 672. Stone rubbing.*

Huijing (578–653) of the Jiguo Monastery in Chang'an seems to be the first monk to have written a commentary on the Xuanzang version while the translator was still alive. His *Rough Notes on the Prajna Paramita Heart Sutra* (Bore Boluo Miduo Xin Jing Shu) was compiled during the span of four years between 649 — the year of Xuanzang's translation — and Huijing's death.[2] Huijing divides the sutra into ten sections and presents paradoxical interpretations.

Xuanzang's leading student, Kuiji (K'uei-chi), who was fifty-four years younger than Huijing, wrote a two-fascicle commentary entitled *Subtle Praise to the Prajna Paramita Heart Sutra*.[3] In the introductory section, Kuiji points out: "A dharma-transmitting sage recorded the solid and most excellent teaching [of the *Maha Prajna Paramita*] by separately bringing out this sutra."[4] Extensively quoting the *Great Sutra, Unfolding the Secret Sutra* (Samdhi Nirmochana), and other sutras, he elucidated Buddhist doctrines including Yogachara (regarded as the third turning of the dharma wheel of the Buddha) and compiled many numerical lists of Buddhist concepts. Some of Kuiji's dharma descendants wrote commentaries on his commentary.

In the formative period of the Zen (Chan) School, Zhizou Zhishen (609–702) — who studied with Xuanzang and later with the Fifth Ancestor Daman Hongren — became the first Zen master to write a commentary on the *Heart Sutra*.[5] He was followed by Anguo Jingjiao (683–750?), as well as by Nanyang Huizhong (d. 775) — a successor of the Sixth Ancestor Dajan Huineng — who taught emperors Su and Dai, the seventh and eighth monarchs of the Tang Dynasty.[6] Zhishen, Jingjiao, and Huizhong were all masters of the Northern School of Zen, which emphasized scriptural studies and gradual enlightenment. By the tenth century, one school alone flourished: the Southern School of Zen, derived from the teachings of Huineng, which emphasized not depending on scriptures but instead achieving sudden enlightenment. Because of this, significant commentaries on the sutra by Zen practitioners were not again written until the twelfth century.[7] In the meantime, ironically, the *Heart Sutra* became the single most important text for daily recitation in Zen schools.

According to *Showa Catalog of Dharma Treasures* (Showa Hoho Somokuroku, 1934), there are seventy-seven known Chinese commentaries (all on the Xuanzang version), including those by such well-known Zen masters as Dadian Fatong (ca. twelfth century), Furong Daokai (1043–1118), and Lanxi Daolong (1213–1278).

As John R. McRae has noted:

> The tradition of exegesis on the *Heart Sutra* is absolutely exceptional in the history of Chinese Buddhism. The elegant brevity and multivalent profundity of the text have made it a favorite subject of commentators from the middle of the seventh century up until the present day, and there is no other single text — nor any single group of scriptures — that has been interpreted by such a long and virtually unbroken list of illustrious authorities.[8]

18

The Pan-Asian Experience

SINCE THE EXTRAORDINARY status of the *Heart Sutra* was established in China by the court of Emperor Gao in 672, as shown in the last chapter, the sutra has received much attention not only in China, but also in Korea, Vietnam, Central Asia, India, Nepal, Bhutan, Tibet, and Mongolia. This chapter briefly spots traces of the spread of the scripture in these regions. I will discuss some of the Japanese dharma practitioners' responses to the sutra in the next chapter.

In the late-seventh century, Wonch'uk (613–696), a monk from the kingdom of Silla, Korea, wrote a commentary titled *Praise to the Heart Sutra*.[1] Following his master Xuanzang's profound scholarship, Wonch'uk gave a well-balanced but highly theoretical interpretation of each line, extensively quoting a number of sutras, including the *Great Sutra* and the scripture *Unfolding the Secret*. Wonch'uk (whose Chinese name was Yuance) was an influential Yogachara thinker. Although he never returned to Korea, he did have a Korean disciple named Tojung.[2] Thus, it is conceivable that the *Heart Sutra* and Wonch'uk's *Praise to the Heart Sutra* were introduced to the Korean peninsula in the seventh century.

In 1445, Emperor Sejong of the Li Dynasty adopted a phonetic alphabet of twenty-eight letters (later called Hangul) to be used separately from ideography. In 1461 the emperor created a governmental agency to oversee publication of Buddhist texts, and the *Heart Sutra* became one of the first nine scriptures printed in this script.

When Xuanzang was working on the Chinese translation of the compilation of *Prajna Paramita* scriptures, one of his assistants was a Vietnamese monk by the name of Dai Thua Dang (whose Chinese name was Dacheng Deng).[3] Although there is no supporting evidence, it is thought that Dang may also have brought the *Heart Sutra* to his homeland, which was under the strict control of the Tang regime.[4]

In the twelfth century, the Vietnamese queen Y Lan of the Ly Dynasty composed a poem using phrases from the *Heart Sutra* when she appointed Thong Bien the national preceptor at the Khai Quoc Pagoda.[5] A number of commentaries on the sutra later emerged in Vietnam, including *Eloquent Commentary about the Prajna Paramita Heart Sutra* by Minh Chau Huong Hai (1628–1715)[6] and *Explanation of the Prajna Paramita Heart Sutra* by Thanh Dam, completed in 1843.[7]

Central Asia, the main route of pilgrimage and dharma transport between ancient India and China, produced a number of excellent translators of Buddhist texts, including Lokakshema from Bactria (second century C.E.) and, of course, Kumarajiva from Kucha.

Shikshananda (652–710) from Khotan translated the *Hridaya* into Chinese, though this version is no longer extant. In around 790, in Chang'an, Prajna of Kafiristan (who had studied in Kashmir and at Nalanda) translated the longer version of the *Hridaya* into Chinese with Liyan. Another translation was produced by Prajnachakra, who came to Chang'an from an unknown part of Central Asia, in the mid-ninth century.

As I described in chapter 11, a number of hand-copied manuscripts were unearthed by European archaeologists from a cave in Dunhuang, some of which were brought to Europe by Stein, Peliot, and others. These manuscripts include the shorter version of the *Hridaya* in Uighur (see fig. 11). The sutra had been translated into Central Asian languages either from Chinese or Sanskrit before the Dunhuang Caves were closed in the eleventh century.

In the late seventh century, India started to produce translations of the *Hridaya*. Divakara, a monk from central India, translated the *Hridaya* into Chinese in 683, only eleven years after the erection of Emperor Gao's imperial monument that marked the first public appearance of the sutra in Xuanzang's translation.

Bodhiruchi, from southern India, also translated the *Hridaya* into Chinese in 693. This version is extant. As mentioned earlier, the Vajrayana master Amoghavajra from Simha, who arrived in China in 720, recorded Xuanzang's shorter-version *Hridaya* in Chinese transliteration with the addition of his own translation. In 741, Dharmachandra from eastern India translated the longer version into Chinese.

While Buddhism — all forms from the earliest sects to the Mahayana — had been widely practiced in India, as Xuanzang and his biographers noted, there was also the growing popularity of Vajrayana — the most recent form of Buddhism, expressed in esoteric practices that emphasized secretly transmitted symbolism and complex magical rituals. Kings of the Pala Dynasty, who ruled over the northeastern region of India — Bengal (ca. 750–1150) and Magadha (ca. 750–1199) — gave Buddhism their powerful support. Buddhism at that time was primarily represented by a combination of Tantra and Prajna Paramita teachings. King Dharmapala (770–815) paid respect to all those who explained the *Prajna Paramita*, but he chiefly honored master Haribhada. This king founded a total of fifty religious schools, thirty-five of which were devoted to the exposition of the *Prajna Paramita*. Beginning with this king, the *Prajna Paramita* teaching spread more and more.[8] About twenty commentaries on the *Prajna Paramaita* scriptures from this period still exist.

The *Hridaya*, as a condensation of the enormous *Prajna Paramina* texts, must have enjoyed its prominence by the widespread study and recitation practice that took place during the Pala Dynasty. Seven Indian commentaries on the longer version *Hridaya* from this era still exist in the form of Tibetan translations.[9]

In the tenth century, as I mentioned earlier, Maitribhadra, a monk from Magadha, went to the northern Chinese kingdom of Khitan and transliterated the shorter text *Hridaya* with Chinese ideographs. In one of the *Hridaya* commentaries from the Pala Dynasty, Jnanamitra — a theorist whose dates and biography are unknown — emphasizes *shunyata* as that which is "without characteristic." Also, Prashastrasena, another figure obscured in history, explains that the mantra is unsurpassed because it clears away all signs of the internal and external.

In spite of its widespread practice, philosophical investigations, and provision of training in the *Prajna Paramita* and the *Hridaya,* as well as other esoteric and exoteric teachings in the Pala Dynasty, Buddhism gradually declined in India, losing its distinct identity and becoming assimilated with Hinduism. The Muslim invasions of India around 1200 and their thorough destruction of Buddhist holy sites and scriptures put an end to Buddhism in India.

By the sixth century, Buddhism had reached the Tibetan plateau. King Srong-btsan-sgam-po of the seventh century, founder of the first Tibetan dynasty, sent his minister with a delegation to India to learn Sanskrit script and create a Tibetan alphabet on their return. This made possible a gradual assimilation of the Mahayana scriptures into the kingdom. With the help of Indian masters, the vast work of translating Sanskrit Buddhist literature began in the following century and became a continuing priority for monasteries. Thus, literary centers began to flourish.

Vimalamitra — born in western India, probably in the eighth century — studied in Buddhagaya and is the earliest known tantric yogin to expound the *Hridaya* in Tibet. According to legend, Vimalamitra also studied yoga in China, then taught in Tibet for thirteen years before returning to China. He is regarded as the founder of the Dzogchen (Great Compassion) lineage. His long commentary on the sutra, the only known piece of his writing, includes sections written in the traditional question and answer format. He notes that true seeing is not to see things as their own independent entities; that seeing with ignorance is like viewing water in a mirage.[10]

Tibet vastly expanded its territory in western China in the mid-eighth century and in 781 occupied Dunhuang, where copying of the Tibetan canon flourished. Chosgrub (760?–860; named Facheng in Chinese), who created a unique synthesis of Tibetan and Chinese Buddhist studies came from this region and may have worked here on his translation of the longer-text *Hridaya* into Chinese.

The renowned scholar Atisha — born in Bengal, India, around 982 — was invited to Tibet in 1042. He engaged in an extensive translation of Sanskrit scriptures into Tibetan and remained in Tibet until his death in 1054. In his subcommentary on Vimalamitra's elucidation of the *Hridaya,* Atisha explains that the entire sutra up to the mantra is for bodhisattvas of dull faculties, while the mantra itself is for those of sharp faculties who understand everything in the sutra simply by hearing the mantra.[11]

Two commentaries on the *Hridaya* in Tibetan by anonymous authors are known. Both of them are titled *Mother of Bhagavan Prajna Paramita Hridaya.*[12]

Present-day Nepal, the birthplace of Shakyamuni Buddha, was one of the very first regions — along with northern India — where Buddhism spread. Until now, Nepal has preserved more Sanskrit scriptures than India, because of Nepal's active scribal tradition through centuries. The shorter and longer versions of the *Hridaya* texts introduced by Edward Conze are both from Nepal.

The fact that Vajrapani — from western India in the eleventh century — spent much of his time traveling in Nepal and Tibet shows that there was a strong Buddhist presence in this region. Vajrapani taught Vajrayana and bestowed a great number of initiations. Focusing on the practice of the teaching of the sutra, he writes in his commentary on the *Hridaya* — his only non-Tantric work — that when a meditation practitioner becomes accustomed to viewing persons and phenomena as selfless, with the goal of placing the mind in concentrated stillness for a prolonged period, one observes "the clear and joyous mind." He proclaims the mantra of realization of prajna as the heart of the meaning of all secret mantras.[13]

Nowadays, the highlands of Nepal bordering Tibet are inhabited by Tibetan-speaking Buddhists. Naturally, they chant the longer version of the *Hridaya* in Tibetan, as is the practice in the Buddhist kingdom of Bhutan. Versions of the *Hridaya* in Nepalese or Bhutanese are not known.[14]

Tantric Buddhism spread from Tibet to the nomads of the Mongolian steppes in the sixteenth century. A Mongolian monk who was active in Tibet, bsTan-dar-lha-ram-pa (1758–1839?), produced works on Buddhist philosophy, logic, grammar, and monastic discipline, as well as a Tibetan-Mongolian dictionary; he also wrote a commentary on the *Hridaya* entitled *Jewel Light Illuminating the Meaning*.[15] In it, he speaks of the Tibetan custom in great monasteries such as Drepung of reciting a verse of praise and obeisance before delivering the *Hridaya*.[16] He teaches that beyond the conventional is the ultimate, beyond samsara is nirvana, and beyond ignorance is knowledge. For him, nonduality of subject and object is a marvelous realization of one's own purpose. And he proclaims that the mantra that pacifies suffering is the path of no more learning.[17]

Tibetans and Mongolians alike used the *Heart Sutra* for prayers intended to repel demons as well as to offer protection, purification, and blessing for healing and longevity. A Tibetan ritualist, Sogdogpa (1552–1624), wrote a memoir entitled the *History of How the Mongols Were Turned Back*. After explaining the detailed exposition on thirty-two years of varied requirements and practices, Sogdogpa says, "From that year until the Hare Year (1601–1603), I myself accomplished a little over 100,000 recitations of the *Heart of Wisdom,* averter of demons, with the aim of turning back the Mongols." Several years later, he and other monks hurled their magical weapons, which, according to Sogdogpa, helped defeat the invading army.[18]

A Mongolian text called *Examination of Shoulder Blades* recommends recitation of the *Sutra of Golden Light,* the *8,000-Line Prajna Paramita,* or the *Heart Sutra,* in response to various physical symptoms.[19] Vesna Wallace, a U.S. scholar, suggests that only these sutras and the *Diamond Sutra* together with various *dharanis* (magical chants) have been put to use in Mongolian rituals of worshipping sutras. They function as "tutelary deities" and represent an integral part of daily religious life on the steppe.[20]

The Manchus, a tribal alliance in Mongolia, established their state in 1616 as the Later Jin Dynasty but changed the name in 1936 to Qing. Their forces took over the Chinese capital city of Beijing in 1644 and established the Qing Dynasty. The court of Qing had a strong connection with Mongolian and Tibetan Vajrayana and produced bilingual Manchu-Chinese or Tibetan-Manchu versions of the *Heart Sutra.* The Yenching Library of Harvard University owns some of these manuscripts, including a multilingual version of the longer *Heart Sutra* in Manchu, Chinese, Tibetan, Mongolian, and Sanskrit. The *Heart Sutra* was a favorite text of Emperor Qianlong (r. 1736–1796) who copied it countless times.[21]

Thus, we can see that the *Heart Sutra* spread fairly quickly in the ideographic world — China, Korea, Vietnam, and Japan — all countries represented by disciples of Xuanzang. The *Hridaya,* on the other hand, was carried west through Central Asia to India, against the normal eastbound flow of Buddhist scriptures to China, and then made its way to Nepal, Tibet, and Mongolia.

19

Japanese Interpretations

JAPANESE BUDDHISTS have put extraordinary effort into exploring the meaning of the *Heart Sutra*. The important reference work *Complete Catalog of Japanese Books* (Kokusho Somokuroku), which indexes all known books written in Japan before 1867 — more than half a million — lists 219 commentaries (or commentaries on commentaries) on the *Heart Sutra*. Not surprisingly, quite a few have similar titles.

The most revered of the Japanese commentaries is the *Secret Key to the Heart Sutra* (Hannya Shingyo Hiken) by Kukai (774–835), founder of the Shingon (Mantra) School. From his Vajrayana perspective, Kukai explains that the heart of *prajna*, wisdom, is not simply a summary of the sutra but the true word — the mantra. Kukai taught his disciples that the sound of each syllable of words in the *Heart Sutra* is greater than all discussions through the aeons, with its reality beyond the mastery even of countless awakened ones. Kukai states, on the other hand, that chanting and expounding this sutra relieves suffering and offers blessings, while studying and contemplating it leads to enlightenment and the realization of miracles.

Eihei Dogen (1200–1253), regarded as the founder of the Japanese Soto School of Zen, wrote an essay called "Manifestation of Great Prajna" and presented it as the second essay in the seventy-fascicle version of his lifework, *Treasury of the True Dharma Eye* (Shobo Genzo).[1]

His discussion begins: "At the moment when Avalokiteshvara Bodhisattva deeply practices prajna paramita, the total body clearly sees that all five skandhas are empty." He goes on to explain that prajna has various aspects, such as the six paramitas and the Four Noble Truths. They are, for Dogen, a single prajna paramita that is actualized right at this moment.

Dogen concludes: "To actualize the manifestation of boundless prajna is to actualize the Buddha, the World-Honored One. Look into this. Study this. To dedicate yourself to it and pay respect to the manifestation of boundless prajna is to see and accept the Buddha, the World-Honored One. It is to be the Buddha, the World-Honored One, seeing and accepting."

The *Illustrated Prajna Heart Sutra* (Hannya Shingyo Zue), attributed to the Zen monk Ikkyu (1394–1481), exists in two woodcut versions. One was published in 1844, while the other remains undated. Ikkyu, who called himself Crazy Cloud Person, was known for his eccentric life but profound poems. After his death, he became a popular figure. This book includes his anecdotes and poems as well as classical poems by earlier writers.

In the illustrated book, regarding the first part of the sutra's title, Ikkyu says:

> *Maka* (*maha*) means "big." If you want to know big mind, you must first become free from your small mind. The small mind makes deluded distinctions. With this mind, you separate yourself and others, buddhas and sentient beings. You divide existence from nonexistence, delusion from enlightenment, right from wrong, and wholesome from unwholesome. This is small mind.
>
> If you become free from small mind, there will be no distinction between buddhas and sentient beings, existence and nonexistence, delusion and enlightenment; they will all be equal, and there will be no more distinctions. This is called big mind. It is just like empty sky that is boundless. This is the original nature intrinsic to all of us sentient beings.[2]

The most iconoclastic commentary on the *Heart Sutra* may be *Poisonous Commentary on the Heart Sutra* (Hannya Shingyo Dokugo Chu), in which Hakuin (1685–1768), regarded as the restorer of the Rinzai School of Zen, wrote brief comments and verses. The book was edited by his successor, Torei.

Hakuin's comment on the statement "Form is no other than emptiness" reads as follows:

> In delicious soup you find two pellets of rat dung. You enjoy the soup and can never have enough of it. You brush off waves in search of water. But waves are water. Form does not shelter emptiness; the

essence of emptiness is form. Emptiness does not break form; the body of emptiness is form. Form and emptiness are within the dharma gate of nonduality. A lame turtle wipes off its eyebrows to call for the evening breeze.[3]

And he concludes his commentary:

If you become a greatly courageous person, you understand the meaning of this sutra and practice its teaching at each moment — while walking, coughing, spitting, or stretching your arms. In motion and stillness, you carry its entire power; you embody its entire awe. Then there will be no obstacle you cannot destroy; there will be no virtue you cannot realize. This is called the great *dharani*, the magical mantra.

20

Scriptwise

THE *HEART SUTRA* has been translated into a variety of Asian languages. Consequently, it has been written in different scripts. Let me present in this chapter some sample of these scripts. I will also explore visible and invisible connections among these scripts, many of which go back to the early Semitic script that marked the beginning of phonetic alphabets.

One of the earliest known styles of writing in India is Brahmi. According to one explanation, it is named Brahmi because this phonetic script was created by the god Brahma, the creator in ancient Indian mythology. Edicts of the Buddhist king Ashoka (circa 300–232 B.C.E.), the third monarch of Mauria, the first unified empire of India, were carved on rocks and stone pillars mainly in Brahmi script. Letters are written horizontally from left to right. A sample of one of the major Indic scripts deriving from Brahmi can be seen centuries later in the fragment of the early Prajna Paramita scripture found at Gilgit (see fig. 4, p. 58). The original Sanskrit scriptures translated by Kumarajiva were written in Brahmi. The Japanese Sanskritist Shoko Kanayama compares this script with Semitic and Phoenician scripts and points out that thirteen letters in Brahmi and in these scripts are nearly identical. Also, there are letters that have similar shapes although turned sideways or upside down. Thus, Kanayama asserts that some letters in the Brahmi script can be traced back to the Semitic and Phoenician scripts. He also explains that the ancient Indians created their own letters in addition to borrowed letters to fully represent their language.[1]

. . .

F IG . 9. *Roots of European and Indian scripts. A comparison
of Phoenician letters (left) and Brahmi letters (right).*

Gupta script is a variant of the Brahmi script that developed during India's
Gupta Dynasty (ca. 320–500 C.E.). Letters are written from left to right.
This script was commonly used in northern India until the eleventh century. The original Sanskrit texts translated by Xuanzang and Amoghavajra
were largely written in this script. The Horyu-ji version of the *Hridaya*, presented earlier (see p. 66) is also written in this script.

The Horyu-ji version of *Hridaya* has been regarded as one of the few
remaining examples of Gupta script. However, it is also explained as that of
Siddham-matrika (Original Siddham) script — one of the scripts developed
after the decline of the Gupta script in the sixth century. There is also a view
that the Horyu-ji version is of Siddham script.

Siddham script, meaning "completed" or "independent" script, is a variation
of the Gupta script. This script, which presents one Sanskrit syllable after
another, each in an independent form, emerged around the sixth century.[2]
It was widely used in the ideographic world by practitioners of Vajrayana

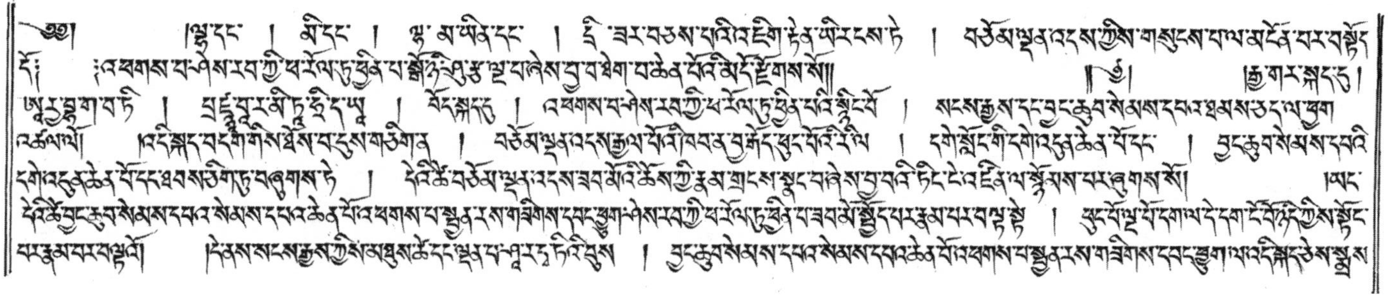

FIG. 10. Hridaya in Tibetan. Recovered from the rTog Palace near the city of Leh in present-day Ladakh. Copied during the reign of Jamyang Namgyal in the early seventeenth century. Portion.

Buddhism, in which individual syllables were often designated to symbolize particular deities. Chinese Buddhists would often write this script vertically with calligraphic strokes in ideography. The tantric Shingon monk Kukai introduced its use to Japan when he returned there from China in 806.

Devanagari (the name has been variously explained as "city of the gods" or "script of the city of the gods"), also a descendant of Brahmi, was established around the tenth century and replaced the Gupta script.[3] Texts in Classical Sanskrit, as well as contemporary Hindi, Marathi, and other Indian languages, are written in this script. Letters run from left to right on a horizontal headline, which is traditionally drawn throughout the sentence. The headline is met with vertical base lines of the same height, which are touched by shorter extension lines of various shapes.

Tibetan script is thought to have developed directly or indirectly from the Gupta script. Tibetan tradition explains that a monk named Thon-mi, under the command of King Srong-btsan-sgam-po (d. 649), studied in India and created this script when he returned. There is also a theory that it came from the ancient Khotanese script.[4] The Tibetan script can be written with or without a horizontal shoulder line, or headline; formal manuscripts and prints are written in the former way. Letters proceed from left to right. See a sample of the longer version of the *Hridaya* in this script in fig. 10.

Sogdian script, now extinct, was used by the Sogdians — speakers of a Central Iranian language — whose capital city was Samarkand, a key center of trading in western Central Asia. Their language was current throughout Central Asia. The script was adapted from the Aramaic-Syriac script (related to the Hebrew and Arabic alphabets).[5] A *Heart Sutra* manuscript written in Sogdian is extant.[6]

Khotanese script (also extinct), representing a Northeastern Iranian dialect, was used by the Khotanese living in the southwestern part of Central Asia. The style of this script is in the genealogy of the Gupta script[7] and thus goes back to Brahmi. Some of King Ashoka's edicts are written in Khotanese. The *Heart Sutra* manuscript written in this language is also extant.[8]

• • •

FIG. 11. Hridaya *in Uighur. Portion.*

Uighur script, also extinct, derived from the Sogdian script. It was used in the Uighur Empire, established in 745 by the nomadic Turks in western Mongolia. With the fall of the empire in 842, the Uighurs fled and settled around the Turfan region in eastern Central Asia. The Uighur script is written vertically, with a vertical line running on the right side of each word; columns run from left to right. Ancient manuscripts of the shorter-version *Hridaya* in this script are extant. An example is shown in fig. 11.[9]

Mongolian script is said to have developed from the Uighur script.[10] There is also a theory that it came from the Tibetan script and that a Tibetan monk named hPhags-pa created it in Mongolia. It became official in 1219.[11] It can be written horizontally, but it is primarily written vertically with a distinct center line in each word. Columns run from left to right. See fig. 13. At present the longer-text Mongolian *Hridaya* is printed in the Cyrillic alphabet, as shown in fig. 13. (I learned this from the Tibetan Mongolian Buddhist Cultural Center in Bloomington, Indiana.)

• • •

FIG. 12. Hridaya in Mongolian. In the Mongol Canon created under the auspices of the Manchu Emperor Kangxi during the period between 1717 and 1720. Portion.

ТӨГС БИЛГИЙН ЗҮРХЭН СУДАР
"ШЭРНИН"

Өгүүлшгүй төсөөлшгүй төгс чинадын билиг
Үүсэхгүй, эвдрэхгүй огторгуйн мөн чанарт
Өөрөө өөрийгөө таних суу билгийн л эзэмшихүүн
Өнгөрсөн, одоо, ирээдүйн гэгээрэгсдийн эх танаа мөргөе.

Би ийнхүү сонссон юм. Тэр үед Бурхан багш Ражагриха хотын Гридхакути уулнаа" дээд сахилтан, бодь сэтгэлтэн агуу шавь нартайгаа хамт заларч байлаа. Бурхан багш энэ үед юмс үзэгдлийн зүйл ангийг тольдох "Гүн гэгээ" хэмээх бясалгалд төвлөрсөн байв. Мөн тэр цагт агуу бодь сэтгэлтэн Арьяабал хутагт бээр төгс билгийн гүн замналаар таван цогцсын мөн чанар хоосон болохыг тольдох бөлгөө. Тэр цагт Бурхан багшийн адислалаар эрхэм хүндэт Шарибудра бээр агуу бодь сэтгэлтэн Арьяабал хутагтад ийм

FIG. 13. Hridaya *in Mongolian. Contemporary Cyrillic script. Portion.*

The Manchu script, used by the Manchu tribes of Mongolia, is an adapted form of the Mongolian script, written vertically or horizontally. At the beginning of the Qing Dynasty — established by the Manchus after they took the entire region of China in 1644 — the court ruled in the Mongolian language, then developed this script for official use. See a sample of the *Hridaya* in the Manchu script in fig. 14.

Sumerian cuneiform, the earliest known writing system, developed in Mesopotamia around 3300 B.C.E.[12] and may have influenced the formation of Egyptian hieroglyphs.[13] Then, as a base for their earliest alphabet, West Semites adopted Egyptian signs around 2000 to 1500 B.C.E.[14] Phoenicians used this Western Semitic or Canaan script.[15] (See fig. 15 for the evolution of the letter *A* as an example.) Around 1000 B.C.E. the Phoenician alphabet was created and it later became the source for Greek, Roman, and other European alphabets. From the Eastern Semitic or Aramaic script, the Arabic and modern Hebrew scripts descended.

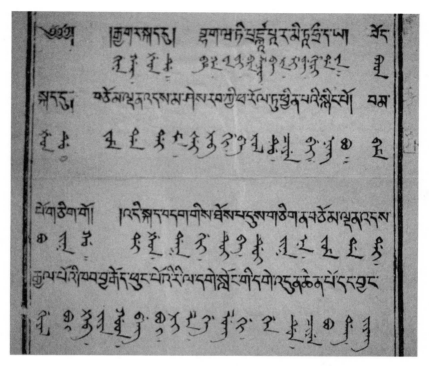

FIG. 14. Hridaya *in Tibetan and Manchu. Dated 1784.*

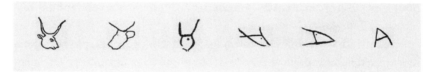

FIG. 15. *Evolution of the letter A. From Egyptian hieroglyph to Semitic alphabet. "Ox"—*alep, alp-, *to evolve into* alpha *in Greek.*

Thus, we could imagine an extensive group of alphabets that can be called the Semitic-Phoenician script family. All the scripts I have mentioned so far fall into this category. The Indo-European language family is a widely accepted category of a great number of languages including such large groups as the Indo-Iranian, Italic, Celtic, Germanic, and Balto-Slavic languages.[16] (Based on this understanding, I will later make a comparative study of Sanskrit and English terms in the "Terms and Concepts" part of this book.) Speakers of any member of this language family use scripts in the Semitic-Phoenician script family.

Meanwhile, speakers of any member of other language families, such as Semitic, Phoenician, Sogdian, Uighur, Tibetan, Mongolian, and Manchurian also use writings in the Semitic-Phoenician script family. So this is a huge, overarching family of letters. In fact, a great majority of alphabets in the world belong to this script family.

Compared with the Semitic-Phoenician script family, East Asian scripts — Chinese-derived ideography, Korean Hangul, and Japanese Kana — form a minority, although ideography alone is used by over 1.5 billion people today.

Ideography, or logography, is the only currently active writing system in the world in which a symbol represents a word. This writing system was created in China around 1400 to 1200 B.C.E.[17] It was later introduced to Korea, Japan, and Vietnam.

The languages of these four regions belong to different language families: Sino-Tibetan, Altaic, Ainu, and Austroasiatic.[18] Nevertheless, in these regions Chinese-derived ideographs are used with roughly common meanings, but pronounced differently according to the linguistic system of each region. For example, the title *Prajna Paramita Heart Sutra,* written with the same ideographs, is *Bore Boluomiduo Xinjing* in Chinese, *Banya Baramilda Simgyeong* in Korean, *Hannya Haramitta Shingyo* in Japanese, and *Batnha Balaatda Tamkinh* in Vietnamese.

For centuries the unabridged traditional form of ideography was commonly used in most parts of East Asia, but in 1946 the Japanese government instituted a simplified writing system and in 1956 the People's Republic of China established its own simplified system. So we now have three official systems of writing in ideography.

Japanese Kana, created at the beginning of the Heian Period (794–1185), is a phonetic script derived from ideography. Kana, usually written vertically, has three kinds — Man'yogana, Hiragana, and Katakana. In Man'yogana, which was used in *Anthology of Ten Thousand Leaves* (Man'yo-shu) compiled in the mid-eighth century, certain ideographs were designated, regardless of their meanings, to represent Japanese syllabic sounds. After this script became archaic, Hiragana and Katakana came to be commonly

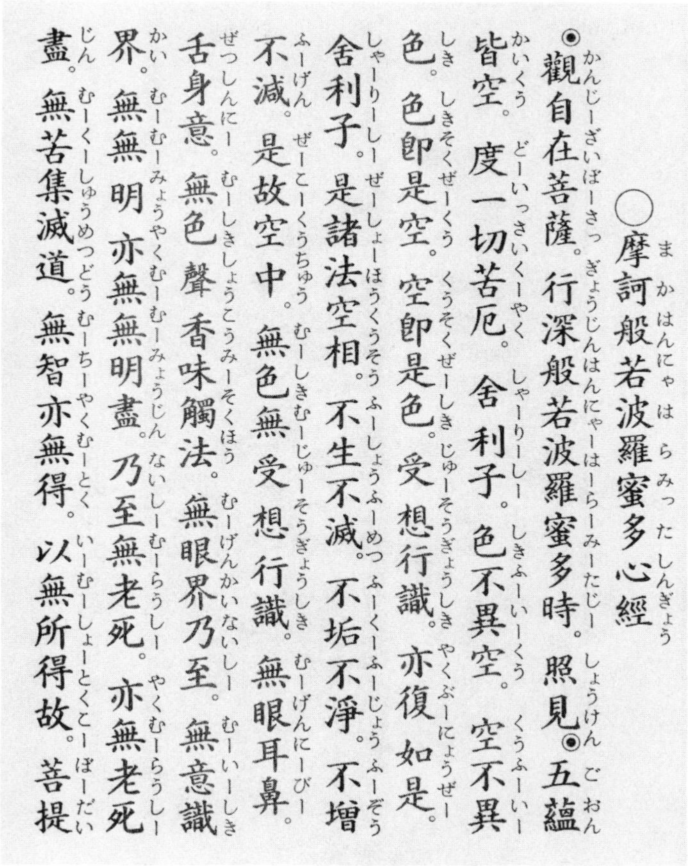

◎摩訶般若波羅蜜多心經（まかはんにゃはらみったしんぎょう）

○観自在菩薩。行深般若波羅蜜多時。照見◎五蘊（かんじーざいぼーさつ。ぎょうじんはんにゃーはーらーみーたじー。しょうけん ごおん）

皆空。度一切苦厄。舍利子。色不異空。空不異（かいくう。どーいっさいくーやく。しゃーりーしー。しきふーいーくう。くうふーい）

色。色即是空。空即是色。受想行識。亦復如是。（しき。しきそくぜーくう。くうそくぜーしき。じゅーそうぎょうしき。やくぶーにょうぜー）

舍利子。是諸法空相。不生不滅。不垢不淨。不增（しゃーりーしー。ぜーしょほうくうそう。ふーしょうふーめつ。ふーくーふーじょう。ふーぞう）

不減。是故空中。無色無受想行識。無眼耳鼻（ふーげん。ぜーこーくうちゅう。むーしきむーじゅーそうぎょうしき。むーげんにーび）

舌身意。無色聲香味觸法。無眼界乃至。無意識（ぜっしんにー。むーしきむーしょうこうみーそくほう。むーげんかいないしー。むーいーしき）

界。無無明。亦無無明盡。乃至無老死。亦無老死（かい。むーむーみょうやくむーむーみょうじん。ないしーむーらうしー。やくむーらうし）

盡。無苦集滅道。無智亦無得。以無所得故。菩提（じん。むーくーしゅうめつどう。むーちーやくむーとく。いーむーしょーとくこー。ぼーだい）

FIG. 16. *The* Heart Sutra *in ideography accompanied by Japanese phonetic letters. Portion.*

used. The former adapted the cursive script of ideographs and the latter the formal script of elements of ideographs. That is why Hiragana consists of curvy lines and Katakana of straighter lines.

While these two types of Kana were used interchangeably, Hiragana is often used in combination with ideographs in most Japanese writings now-adays. In this case, nouns and stems of verbs and adjectives are usually represented by ideographs, while conjunctions, inflected portions of words, and postpositions are represented by Hiragana. (One has a stylistic choice to substitute ideographs with Hiragana, or vice versa.) In early times in

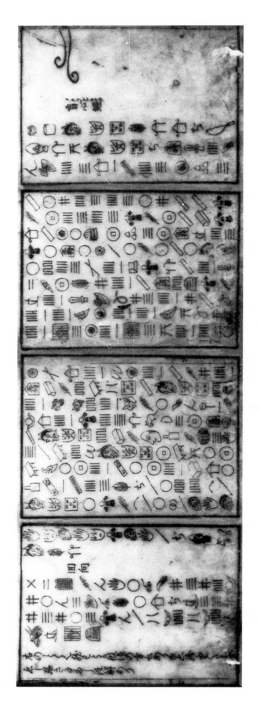

FIG. 17. *Illiterate version of the Heart Sutra.*

마하반야바라밀다심경
관자재보살 깊은 반야바라밀다 할 적, 오온 공함 비춰봐 일체 고액 건너라.
사리자여, 색이 공과 다르지 않고, 공이 색과 다르지 않아, 색 곧 공이요, 공 곧
색이니 수·상·행·식 역시 이럴러라.
사리자여, 이 모든 법 공한 상은 나지도 않고, 멸하지도 않고, 더럽지도 않고,
깨끗하지도 않고, 늘지도 않고, 줄지도 않나니, 이 까닭에 공 가운데 색 없어
수·상·행·식 없고 안·이·비·설·신·의 없어 색·성·향·미·촉·법 없되, 안계 없고
의식계까지 없다.
무명 없되 무명 다 됨 역시 없으며, 노사까지도 없되 노사 다 됨 역시 없고,
고·집·멸·도 없으며 슬기 없어 얻음 없나니, 얻을 바 없으므로 보리살타가
반야바라밀다 의지하는 까닭에 마음 걸림 없고, 걸림 없는 까닭에 두려움 없어,
휘둘린 생각 멀리 떠나 구경열반이며, 삼세제불도 반야바라밀다 의지한 까닭에
아뇩다라삼먁삼보리 얻었나니, 이 까닭에 반야바라밀다는 이 큰 신기로운 주며,
이 큰 밝은 주며, 이 위없는 주며, 이 등에 등 없는 주임을 알라.
능히 일체고액을 없애고 진실하여 헛되지 않기에 짐짓 반야바라밀다주를
설하노니 이르되,
아제 아제 바라아제 바라승아제 모지 사바하.
아제 아제 바라아제 바라승아제 모지 사바하.
아제 아제 바라아제 바라승아제 모지 사바하.

FIG. 18. *The* Heart Sutra *in Hangul.*

Buddhist texts, tiny renditions of Katakana were placed on the right-hand side of ideographs as a pronunciation aid. But today, Hiragana is often used for a pronunciation aid, while Katakana mainly serves to transliterate foreign words.

In addition, as before the development of modern-day Japan a great number of illiterate peasants lived in remote villages, pictorial versions of the sutra might have been created for them. In one instance, an eighteenth-century Japanese physician and writer wrote in his journal about the "illiterates' *Heart Sutra*" used in a remote village of Tayama, outside the northern city of Morioka. The title of the sutra, "Maka Hannya Haramitta Shingyo," is a rebus, represented by pictures of an upside-down iron pot, or *kama* (the two syllables of the word are to be read backward as *maka*); a *hannya* (wrathful demoness) mask for *hannya*; a belly (*hara*); a winnowing basket (*mi*); a rice field (*ta*); and a Shinto mirror (*shinkyo*).[19]

Hangul script, as mentioned earlier, is a phonetic script created in Korea in the mid-fifteenth century, although it received its name, meaning "great script," in the twentieth century. There are many theories about the origin of this script, including one that suggests an influence from Brahmi. Hangul is regarded as the most scientific system of writing in general use in any country or, simply, the world's best alphabet.[20] This is due to its having the highest correlation between its pronunciation and its spelling. This script is used independently or mixed with ideography. Figure 18 reproduces a modern Korean translation of a short-text *Heart Sutra* written in Hangul (not the traditional Sino-Korean transliteration).

21

Rituals in the Western World

BECAUSE THE *HEART SUTRA* is a Mahayana text, practitioners in the earlier Theravada tradition, which developed largely in South and Southeast Asia, don't recite it. Buddhists in Pure Land schools, whose main practice is the invocation of the name of Amitabha Buddha, don't recite this sutra, either.

Practitioners of some schools of Tibetan Buddhism, which are increasing their deep and wide presence in India as well as in the Western world, do recite the longer text of the sutra. The Fourteenth Dalai Lama's Heart of Wisdom Teachings, offered publicly in 2001 and later in book form as *Essence of the Heart Sutra,* are based on the Gelugpa transmissions he received as a lineage holder. When he teaches, he has the *Heart Sutra* recited first in one of the languages of the people attending, so that each day on a retreat they hear it in a different language. In many centers of the Gelugpa, Nyingma, and Kagyu schools worldwide the sutra is chanted daily.

In other schools of Tibetan Buddhism in the West, the sutra is recited weekly, monthly, or on certain occasions or retreats. There are also centers where sutras are not recited. Some teachers assign students the recitation of the sutra one hundred, one thousand, or even one hundred thousand times for a certain period of time as their personal practice. In 1973, the well-known teacher and meditation master Chögyam Trungpa wrote a commentary on *The Sutra on the Essence of Transcendent Knowledge.*[1]

In almost all Zen Buddhist monasteries, centers, and meeting groups worldwide, meditators make daily recitations of this scripture. The enthusiasm of Tibetan and Zen practitioners in North America and Europe seems to have contributed much to the popularization of the *Heart Sutra* around the globe.

The Japanese Buddhist scholar Daisetsu Teitaro Suzuki (1870–1966) played a catalytic role in introducing Zen to the West with the extensive essays he wrote in English before and after World War II. His eloquent descriptions of the intriguing paradoxes in the philosophy, art, and culture of Zen evoked a widespread curiosity and profoundly influenced the Beat generation. Consequently, the Japanese loanword *zen* became a household word in English. This type of Buddhism, initially developed in China, is called *chan* in Chinese, so "Chan" is actually the more precise name of the school. However, the first impact of the word "Zen" brought by Suzuki was so strong that the odd term "Chinese Zen" is commonly used. (I apologize to Chinese speakers that I am one of those who use the word "Zen" to include "Chan.")

From the early intellectual focus in the West, the actual practice of meditation evolved. In the 1950s, Zen teachers became increasingly prominent in North America and Europe. Among these were Shunryu Suzuki and Taisen Deshimaru from Japan; Seung Sahn from Korea; and Hsuan Hua and Sheng Yen from China and Taiwan. In 1966 Thich Nhat Hanh was exiled from Vietnam and eventually settled in France. Under the guidance of these teachers, Zen groups, centers, and monasteries developed their daily activities centering on meditation.

Recitation of the *Heart Sutra* is a regular part of Zen practice and is often conducted in a service after meditation. A chant leader announces the title in a melodic way, for example, "Maka Hannya Haramitta Shingyo" in Japanese or "Maha Prajna Paramita Hridaya Sutra" in a form familiar to speakers of English, borrowed from Sanskrit. Then all participants chant the text aloud, often accompanied by the chopping sound of a wooden catfish-shaped drum: "No eye, no ear, no nose . . ." My wife, Linda, says, "I like denying things. So when I chant the *Heart Sutra* and deny everything all the way, I get exuberant!" The high-volume synchronized recitation of the sutra by the gathering of meditators contrasts with the stillness and silence of meditation practice. It is a solemn but dynamic and joyous activity.

It makes sense that everyone present at a funeral or an ordination service cries out, "GATÉ GATÉ PARAGATÉ . . ." (Gone, gone, gone all the way . . .) Not only that — this sutra is chanted at all events, including weddings and the celebration of childbirth. Indeed, the *Heart Sutra* is the most commonly recited text on all Zen Buddhist occasions the world over.

In the West, the sutra is sometimes chanted in Chinese or Korean alone, in which case the text is incomprehensible for most of the participants. In a way, it serves as a long version of a dharani, or mantra,[2] which helps people to gather their minds away from the intellect. In some cases, for that reason, the meanings of words in the text are intentionally not explained. Nevertheless, people seem to enjoy chanting the incomprehensible foreign versions.

In Antwerp, Belgium, I noticed that all chanting was done in Japanese. When I asked Luc De Winter, the teacher of the Zen center, "Why don't you chant in Flemish or French?" he said, "Our sangha members speak six languages. It's not fair to use one of the languages. So we chant in Japanese." Thus, most participants are on equal footing.

In most cases, however, the sutra is chanted in English, French, German, or whatever language matches the region where it is chanted. Sometimes they chant in one of the East Asian languages and then in their own language.

All translations of the *Heart Sutra* used in Zen schools originate from Xuanzang's shorter version of the sutra. D. T. Suzuki's rendering is the basis for most English translations.[3] In some cases, people also seem to have checked with Edward Conze's translation.[4] (Suzuki's and Conze's translations of the sutra are included in the "Terms and Concepts" section of this book.)

One remarkable thing about the *Heart Sutra* in the Western world is that there are so many versions even within one language region. Zen centers and their sub-centers often have their own versions. It seems that not so many people have checked the original Chinese version; rather, they have made superficial changes to suit their need for chanting and explanation of the meanings.

Recitation of the *Heart Sutra* is often followed by a melodic prayer called "dedication of the merit." For example, in groups affiliated with San Francisco Zen Center, the prayer is: "We dedicate this merit to: Our great original teacher in India, Shakyamuni Buddha; our first ancestor in China, great teacher Bodhidharma; our first ancestor in Japan, great teacher Eihei Dogen; our compassionate founder, great teacher Shogaku Shunryu; the perfect wisdom Bodhisattva Manjushri. Gratefully we offer this virtue to all

HEART OF GREAT PERFECT WISDOM SUTRA

Avalokitesvara Bodhisattva, when deeply practicing prajna paramita, clearly saw that all five aggregates are empty and thus relieved all suffering. Shariputra, form does not differ from emptiness, emptiness does not differ from form. Form itself is emptiness, emptiness itself form. Sensations, perceptions, formations, and consciousness are also like this. Shariputra, all dharmas are marked by emptiness; they neither arise nor cease, are neither defiled nor pure, neither increase nor decrease. Therefore, given emptiness, there is no form, no sensation, no perception, no formation, no consciousness; no eyes, no ears, no nose, no tongue, no body, no mind; no sight, no sound, no smell, no taste, no touch, no object of mind; no realm of sight...no realm of mind consciousness. There is neither ignorance nor extinction of ignorance...neither old age and death, nor extinction of old age and death; no suffering, no cause, no cessation, no path; no knowledge and no attainment. With nothing to attain, a Bodhisattva relies on prajna paramita, and thus the mind is no hindrance. Without hindrance, there is no fear. Far beyond all inverted views, one realizes nirvana. All Buddhas of past, present, and future rely on prajna paramita and thereby attain unsurpassed, complete, perfect enlightenment. Therefore, know the prajna paramita as the great miraculous mantra, the great bright mantra, the supreme mantra, the incomparable mantra, which removes all suffering and is true, not false. Therefore we proclaim the prajna paramita mantra, the mantra that says:

GATE GATE PARAGATE PARASAMGATE BODHI SVAHA

FIG. 19. *The* Heart Sutra *in English. San Francisco Zen Center version.*

beings." In the Order of Interbeing founded by Thich Nhat Hanh, practitioners recite "Sharing the merit" after chanting the *Heart Sutra* or another sutra: "Reciting the sutras, practicing the way of awareness gives rise to benefits without limit. We vow to share the fruits with all beings. We vow to offer tribute to parents, teachers, friends, and numerous beings who give guidance and support the path." These kinds of prayers represent the aspiration, practice, and commitment of those who practice meditation.

Next, at San Francisco Zen Center, for example, practitioners put their palms together and chant: "All buddhas, three times, ten directions, bodhisattva mahasattvas, wisdom beyond wisdom, *maha prajna paramita*." This is like a simple listing of nouns. In English a sentence is not formed without a verb, so I would propose the following translation: "All awakened ones throughout space and time, honorable bodhisattvas, great beings — together may we realize wisdom beyond wisdom." Thus, this prayer becomes an acknowledgement of all buddhas and bodhisattvas in the past, present, and future, and the expression of everyone's intention to realize wisdom beyond wisdom together. With their chanting, practitioners confirm the experience of undividedness, which is the essential message of the *Heart Sutra*.

22

Scientific Thinking

THE NOTION OF SHUNYATA, or emptiness, which developed in ancient India and later became the central theme of the *Heart Sutra,* has fascinated a great many thinkers, including advanced scientists. Those with diverse backgrounds and interests may have their own unique ideas about emptiness. What one scientist means by emptiness may be completely different from what another scientist does, and the same is true of Buddhist teachers and theorists. Therefore, it is helpful to know the contexts of scientific discussions.

To review all the publications and remarks touching on the relationship between the message of the *Heart Sutra* and modern scientific thinking. would take up a second volume of the present book. Instead, allow me to introduce some notable examples:

1. Hideki Yukawa. In the 1930s, physicists knew that an infinitesimal atomic nucleus was closedly packed with protons (particles with a positive electrical charge) along with neutrons (particles with zero electrical charge). But they did not know why protons did not repel one another and cause an explosion, as nothing had been observed in the space between these protons to stabilize this interaction. In 1935, Hideki Yukawa, a twenty-eight-year-old Japanese theoretical physicist, theorized that this space was not completely void; there must be invisible fundamental particles within the space that held these protons together. He tentatively named these particles "mesons." In 1946, Cecil Frank Powell, a British theoretical physicist, along with others, discovered "pi-mesons" (or "pisons") as Yukawa had predicted. Yukawa received the Nobel Prize in Physics in 1949.

Yukawa acknowledged later that the thought behind his theory was that "void" or "vacuum" might not be completely empty. He said, "For establishing the meson theory, I relied on the spirit of Buddhism, which was part of my cultural education. The meson theory is related to the notion of 'Form is emptiness' in the *Heart Sutra*."[1]

2. The following excerpt is taken from statements by the Dutch astrophysicist and interdisciplinary scientist Piet Hut, a professor at the Institute for Advanced Study in Princeton, a position similar to those held earlier by Einstein and Yukawa:

> The Big Bang is an explosion. While all other explosions we know of take place inside space, the Big Bang is an explosion of space. You can talk about such an explosion in mathematics and physics, even if it is difficult to imagine it.
>
> We don't know if the Big Bang came out of a more true kind of emptiness. It could be that there was another space in which the Big Bang exploded so that our space is embedded in another space and maybe in another time. In physics they came up with the name "multiverse."
>
> Because the theory of the Big Bang is really a theory of space and time, it is possible that space and time both came out of the Big Bang. If that is true, you cannot say what was there before the Big Bang, because there was no "before." Our physics theory is not precise enough to know whether time started with the Big Bang or whether there was a time before it.
>
> The Big Bang took place 13.8 billion years ago. The degree of uncertainty is about 0.5 percent now. Fairly rapidly, modern observations have given us an understanding of the universe much more accurate than ten years ago, when we knew only within a factor of 2, which is 50 percent accuracy. I know the age of the universe, relatively speaking, better than my friends' ages.
>
> If you move at very high speeds, time slows down. But if you move together with the stars and galaxies around you, those galaxies will present you with a preferred frame of reference, and then you can really talk about time in that frame. Time is not absolute, but it is shared relative to the stars and the galaxies of our universe; so you can go back through that time and say how old the universe is.

At the beginning of the universe everything was moving much, much faster and the temperature was much higher. Initially, in each second a lot more happened than now. In the first millionth of a second everything was radiation. Then the radiation condensed into matter within the first second. Most of the matter we can see with our eyes now came out of the Big Bang in that first second, and that matter has been there since then, so it was a very important second.

The energy there was not visible light that you normally experience but light-like energy. While the universe expanded, it cooled, and by cooling the light condensed into droplets, so to speak, or particles of matter. Still very well mixed, the distribution of these droplets expanded. Then, after many millions of years, pieces of matter started to fall together to form the first galaxies and stars in the first hundred million or a few hundred million years.

The total energy of the universe may be zero. Our view depends on how we count or what theory we have. We don't know which theory is right. If you hold a ball in your hand, then it is at rest and doesn't move, but if you drop it, it goes faster and faster. That means the energy of movement becomes larger and larger, but we say that the potential energy in the gravitational field becomes smaller. So if you drop something and it starts to fall, it gains in kinetic energy — energy of motion — and it loses potential energy; so the energy remains zero. First it's zero energy at rest, and then it's zero energy in motion. In a very similar way, before the Big Bang the whole universe may have had zero energy, and it may still be so.

We don't know if this is the right theory yet. The hope is that with the Large Hadron Collider — the latest particle accelerator in Switzerland — we can discover new particles, which may give us a more precise understanding of the theory of elementary particles and a hint for better knowledge of the Big Bang.

What people thought a little more than one hundred years ago was that an electromagnetic field must be a vibration in some sort of substance. They called it *ether*. They tried to imagine the properties of the ether, but the more they measured, the more the measurements contradicted one another. Then they realized that it was actually a vibration in a vacuum.

A vacuum is empty space — as empty as we can get. A vacuum, however, contains an electromagnetic field, full of particles and anti-particles. It is normally quiet and you don't notice it, like a calm ocean when buoys and ships all sit still. But when a wave comes through the ocean, the buoys and ships start rocking. That shows us the presence of the wave. Likewise, we cannot see or measure the electromagnetic field, but it can produce forces that can move electrons and other particles. Thus, we can measure the waves in an electromagnetic field by the movement of charged particles.

In other words, to see electromagnetic effects, the vacuum needs to get excited. Without any perturbation, the electromagnetic field wants to be in the lowest state, like a bell that is hanging. If you hit the bell, it moves back and forth. The wave does not normally stay in one place, it just has to move, and doing so it typically gets weaker and weaker while spreading out over a larger and larger area.

The electromagnetic field itself is the same everywhere and has no substance. It is a kind of emptiness. We cannot empty the electromagnetic field out of the vacuum. In this field, there is duality between responding to a wave and a wave responding: a charged particle that is moving produces a wave and that wave can move other charged particles. In this process there is no underlying foundation called in the form of a substance like an ether.

The electromagnetic field is in a way not real, as it is empty. The waves are also in a way empty, as they are in something that is empty. But the waves cause real effects. They cause particles to respond. This is real. This is the mystery. The waves also contain energy, and because energy and mass are equivalent, you could also say that they contain a form of mass, while the electromagnetic field as such contains no energy or mass.

The universe was born, and then the universe cooled down. After a long time galaxies and stars were born, and for many stars, planets were born as well, circling their mother star. The Earth was one of them, circling our Sun. When the Earth was young, there were rocks, water, air, all containing many different chemical elements in the form of atoms, and molecules. There was a rich set of chemical reactions that took place between these atoms and molecules, but at first there was no life yet. At some point, some form of life must have started, signaling a transition from chemistry to biology. Following that event, biological evolution produced all different forms of life, from microbes to plants and animals and us.

In any type of life on Earth, whether it is a single cell, a plant, an animal, or any other form of life, some of the basic ingredients controlling the activities of the cells — the DNA molecules — all have the exact same structure. The information encoded in DNA is different for each organism, but the basic structure of DNA is universal, the same for any form of life that we have encountered on Earth.

We do not know in any detail how life originated on Earth. When atoms and molecules moved around in more and more complicated chemical reactions, somehow the molecules themselves became more and more complicated, and also the networks of interactions between them. These processes must have somehow given rise to form the cells from which all current life descended. We, too, came from this origin.[2]

3. Neil D. Theise, MD, a U.S. liver pathologist and adult stem cell researcher, discusses complexity theory in terms of the Buddhist concept of emptiness. According to him, human dependence on the scale of observation is parallel to the Buddhist idea that all things are devoid of inherent existence. What we take as the essence of an individual thing — be it an ant, person, or planet — is nothing more than the emergent self-organization of smaller things.[3] He further suggests:

Molecules are merely the emergent self-organization of atoms. In turn, atoms emerge from the self-organization of subatomic particles, which arise from smaller subatomic particles, and so on, down to the smallest possible units of existence; quixotically named units such as strings and branes, and others not yet posited by physicists.

However they are named or characterized, physicists describe these smallest things as coming and going in a quantum foam, popping in and out of a generative void, without qualities of space and time as we usually encounter them: no up, down, back, forth, before, after, dark, light; its features are beyond linguistic and, so far, mathematical description. It is at this point that physicists begin to sound like metaphysicists, and perhaps not by coincidence: this is the source from which everything arises.[4]

FIG. 20. *The* Heart Sutra *in German. An expressive rendering.*

4. I have been in correspondence with Alfred W. Kaszniak, professor in the departments of Psychology, Neurology, and Psychiatry and Director of Clinical Neuropsychology at the University of Arizona Medical Center. Kaszniak has shed interesting scientific light on the language and apparent claims of the *Heart Sutra*. He indicates that recent cognitive and neuroscientific research speaks "indirectly" to the core claim of the *Heart Sutra* — that our "self" and perceptions are "empty" or "boundless." As examples, he cites these findings:

- We cannot speak of a stimulus as something independent of the organism but must view and work with organism and environment as a single system.
- No such things as selves exist in the world. All that ever existed were conscious self-models that could not be recognized as models; the phenomenal self is not a thing but a process.
- Our sense of having a private nonmaterial soul "watching the world" is an illusion.
- Our experience of the visual world is not simply a "representation" of external stimuli impinging upon sense receptors, but is interactively constructed via "top-down" influences from "higher" brain regions involved in memory and future planning.[5]

Kaszniak concludes:

> In summary, I believe that much of current cognitive and neuroscientific research converges on the interpretation that what our conditioned experience takes to be the existence of external forms with inherent qualities, or an unchanging self, are illusory manifestations of interactive processes. In these interactive processes, it is impossible to identify one aspect (e.g., environment, brain, past experience) as cause and another as effect: each appears to be mutually and simultaneously causative and resultant, and conscious experience arises from this co-dependent interaction.[6]

5. Here is another quotation from Piet Hut:

> Natural science is based on experimentation and observation. Ultimately everything we know in science is tested by the fact that

scientists report experiential evidence, whether in a laboratory or in the field. However, every act of experience contains a subject pole, an object pole, and a form of interaction between the two. If I see a pen, I am the subject, the pen is the object, and seeing is the form of interaction between the two.

Natural science so far has focused on studying objects. For each form of experimentation, subjects and interactions are needed, but the results are typically described in objective ways, by listing changes in objects. By doing so, we have left out two-thirds of human experience. You could say that physics or biology, for example, is only one-third empirical, by focusing on objects, and leaving out an equally detailed study of subjects qua subjects, and interactions qua interactions.

I think that true emptiness as discussed in Buddhism, and to some extent in other religions as well, is something that goes beyond the subject/object duality that we normally rely on in daily life as well as in science. To compare science with spirituality or religious traditions in general, science has to expand beyond what it has covered so far. If science can eventually develop a new science of subject, of object, and of interaction, all together, then it would be much easier to compare it with spirituality.

When I read about dialogues between Buddhists and scientists, generally they are talking on completely different levels. Buddhists talk about all of reality, and physicists talk about the object part of reality. Physics can be very precise, because it leaves out a large part of reality.

It has taken about four hundred years from Galileo to the present to get this precise description of objects in physics. We may be able to develop an equally scientific description of the subject, not subject seen as object, but subject as subject. I think that can be done, but it will take a great deal of careful and dedicated work. When that is done, the next logical step would be to have a science of nonduality — a science that goes beyond both subjects and objects. On this level of nonduality, you could come closer to emptiness in which there is no self, and there is no subject/object split. But maybe that will take another four hundred years or a thousand years. So we have to be a little bit patient.[7]

The process of Buddhist understanding, including the understanding of the *Heart Sutra,* and the process of scientific research are completely different. In fact, the characteristics of their logic are completely opposite. The former is intuitive and self-experiential, calling for faith and spiritual practice. The latter is intellectual, calling for doubt and physical proof. And yet the teachings of the *Heart Sutra* can, at times, not only inspire scientists but help point them in the direction of new and visionary studies. The results of rigorous scientific research may also be in accordance with the new perspectives on its teachings. This has the potential to continue infinitely while science develops and study of the sutra deepens.

PART SIX

Terms and Concepts

I N T H I S P A R T I will examine all terms of the shorter text versions of *Hridaya* and *Heart Sutra*. I will explain the etymology of Sanskrit terms and, as much as possible, the concepts they carry.[1]

You may find some unexpected links between Sanskrit and English syllables and words. Such connections — more than thirty cases — will be shown here when I believe they are of common knowledge among linguists.[2]

The grammatical analysis of Sanskrit and Chinese presented in this section may at times appear to be cumbersome, but by knowing how particular words function in syntax, the reader may have a better and more appropriate understanding of the text as a whole.[3]

Three shorter versions of *Hridaya* are presented below. The three most important versions of the Chinese *Heart Sutra* will follow. I have arranged the texts in this order because, generally speaking, Sanskrit Buddhist terms are the basis of translated Chinese terms. This order does not reflect the presumed order of historical appearances of the text, as I suggested earlier. (The list in the "Comparative Texts" appendix is organized in the presumed chronological order, according to a new understanding about the formation of the sutra.)

Koreans, Japanese, and Vietnamese recite the sutra with their own sounds corresponding to the Chinese sounds of the Xuanzang version. Their transliterations are also included.

All texts of the sutra are divided into common segments, so that the terms in different languages are easily found and compared.

• • •

Before discussing terms, I would like to comment briefly on the Sanskrit and Chinese languages in general.

Sanskrit, which is no longer in daily use, is written in phonetics. Classical Sanskrit is a highly grammatical language, and many of its words are compounded with prefixes and suffixes. Nouns, pronouns, and adjectives inflect in three genders (masculine, feminine, and neuter) and three numbers (singular, dual, and plural). They have eight cases: nominative, accusative, instrumental, dative, ablative, genitive, locative, and vocative. A noun appears in dictionaries in its citation form without a prefix. Its uninflected part is called the stem, of which one function is to form the first word or one of the first words of a compound. Verbs, which conjugate in singular, dual, and plural cases, have present, future, aorist (indicative mood expressing past action), perfect, passive, and causative forms. No word spacing or capitalization is shown in ancient scripts, but when they are romanized, some of these features are usually added. The *e* and *o* are long vowels.

It should be noted that one cannot fully understand the *Heart Sutra,* like other North Indian Buddhist texts, by comprehending classical Sanskrit alone. The text reflects grammar in Buddhist Hybrid Sanskrit, which is primarily based on an old Middle Indic vernacular.[4]

Chinese, in turn, has more than fifty thousand ideographs. Each of them represents a syllable-word, pronounced in one of the four tones, and contains a range of meanings. In other words, a symbol constitutes a word in the ideographic system. Most words can function as different parts of speech. It is often up to the reader or listener to discern within context the part of speech of a certain word. The subject of a sentence and the tense of a verb are often implied. There are no inflections. No punctuation or paragraph changes are used in the olden-time ideographic system, although these features are often added in modern ideographic scripts.

In ideography, there are many homonyms — ideographs that have the same sounds. For example, *zi* for Guanzizai (Avalokiteshvara) may look similar to *zi* for Shelizi (Shariputra), but they are represented by different ideographs and have two dissimilar sets of meanings.

Although each ideograph originally represented a word, the ancient Sanskritists developed the system of transliteration — a way to make an ideograph, regardless of its meaning, represent a Sanskrit sound. You will see a number of samples of them below.

The translation of the *Heart Sutra* by Joan Halifax and me is based on Xuanzang's Chinese translation, as it is the most familiar, and, in fact, the only available version of the shorter text in the Western world. We have also referred to the *Hridaya*—the Sanskrit counterpart to the Xuanzang version—to clarify meanings of Buddhist technical terms, but our translation is not bound by the Sanskrit version. The ambiguity of the Chinese text helps us create an English version that suits the needs of dharma practitioners of our time.

Abbreviations

(See the "Comparative Texts" appendix for undivided texts, sources, and credits.)

> SH: Sanskrit, Horyu-ji version
> SA: Sanskrit, Amoghavajra version
> SN: Sanskrit, Nepalese version
> α: Chinese, α version (translation attributed to Kumarajiva)
> αtl: Chinese, transliteration of the α version
> CX: Chinese, Xuanzang version
> CXtl: Chinese, Xuanzang version, transliteration
> CA: Chinese, Amoghavajra version
> CAtl: Chinese, Amoghavajra version, transliteration
> Ktl: Korean transliteration of CX
> Jtl: Japanese transliteration of CX
> Vtl: Vietnamese, Northern transliteration of CX
> EM: English, F. Max Müller translation (note its early transliteration
>   system with single italic letters)
> ES: English, D. T. Suzuki translation
> EC: English, Edward Conze translation
> ETH: English, Tanahashi/Halifax translation

> [ ]: Terms in brackets were added in a later time but are frequently
>   used (for example, [*mo he*]).
> < >: Optionally added (i.e., *bosa<tsu>*).
> (x): Indicates a segment that has no correspondence in the Xuanzang
>   version

TITLE AND DEDICATION

(0) END TITLE/TITLE

SH, end title (44): *iti Prajñāpāramitā-hṛdayaṃ samāptaṃ*

SA: *prajñā-pāramitā-hṛdaya-sūtraṃ*

SN, end title (44): *iti prajñāpāramitā-hṛdayaṃ samāptam.*

α: 摩訶般若波羅蜜大明咒經

αtl: *mo he bo re bo luo mi da ming zhou jing*

CX: [摩訶] 般若波羅蜜多心經

CXtl: [*mo he*] *bo re bo luo mi duo xin jing*

CA: 般若波羅蜜多心經

CAtl: *bo re bo luo mi duo xin jing*

Ktl: [*Maha*] *Banya baramilda simgyeong*

Jtl: [*Maka*] *Hannya haramitta shingyō*

Vtl: *Bát Nhã Ba La Mật Đa Tâm Kinh*

EM: Pragñā-Pāramitā-Hṛidaya-Sūtra

ES: Prajñā-paramita-hridaya Sutra

EC: The Heart Sutra

ETH: The Sutra on the Heart of Realizing Wisdom Beyond
　　Wisdom

Originally, no versions of the *Hridaya* begin with a title, but they end with this line.

Iti is a conjunction, meaning "in this manner" or "thus."

Prajñāpāramitā is a combination of two stems—*prajñā* and *pāramitā*. These stems function as the first words of the compound *prajñāpāramitā-hṛdaya*. (The meanings of this compound will be explained below.)

Hṛdayaṃ, a word in the compound, is a phonetically changed form of *hṛdaya*. It is the nominative singular case of the neuter noun *hṛdaya,* meaning "heart."

Samāptaṃ is a phonetically changed form of *samāptam*. It is the nominative case of the neuter form of the adjective *samāpta,* meaning "completely obtained," "concluded," or "ended." It comes from the verb *āp,* which means "obtain" or "arrive at." The prefix *sam* means "all," "together," or "thorough."

There was perhaps no word *sūtra* in the Sanskrit versions. The Sanskrit title of the Amoghavajra version, which contains the word *sūtram* — the nominative singular case of the neuter noun *sūtra* — seems to be a back-translation of the Chinese title, as explained later on in the discussion of the sutra.

The end line of the Sanskrit versions (the Horyu-ji and Nepalese) can be translated as "Thus the *prajna paramita* heart is completed."

It is noteworthy that three out of the twelve Nepalese versions in Sanskrit, presented by Edward Conze, end with *nāma dhāraṇī* — for example, *Pañca-viṃśatikā prajñā-pāramitā nāma dhāraṇī*, meaning "The *dharani* named the five-part *prajna-paramita*." The word *hṛdaya* is replaced by *dhāraṇī*.[5]

It was customary to put the title of a sutra both at the beginning and the end of a text in China since ancient times. The oldest example I am aware of is the end title for fascicle 33 of the hand-copied manuscript of the Avatamsaka Sutra, dating from 513, a fragment of which is kept at Ku-kung Museum in Taiwan.[6]

This custom of having an end title is reflected in the East Asian and English versions of the texts for chanting. For example, those who practice in a center founded by a Japanese teacher must be familiar with the sutra's Japanese title *Maka hannya haramitta shingyō* chanted at the beginning as well as *Hannya haramitta shingyō* or *Hannya shingyō* at the end of each recitation. The English equivalents for these Japanese titles are *Maha Prajna Paramita Heart Sutra*, *Prajna Paramita Heart Sutra*, and *Prajna Heart Sutra*.

MAHĀ

The title of the α version begins with *mohe,* which is the Chinese translation of the Sanskrit word *mahā.* This word is not found in the Xuanzang version. The title with *maka* (the Japanese transliteration of *mahā*) is found in the scriptural commentary by Chiko, a Japanese monk of the Three Treatise School (Sanron-shu) in Nara, in the mid-eighth century.[7] The word was possibly taken from the α version.

The α version does not use the Chinese ideograph *dai* that means "great" here. Instead, the Chinese sound *mohe* is used. The romanized spellings *mohe* and *mahā* do not look so similar to each other. In olden times, however, the Chinese sound *mohe* was possibly closer to its Sanskrit counterpart than it appears in its spelling now.

The Sanskrit word *mahā,* if it were used here, would be the compound form of the adjective *mahat,* meaning "large," "great," "vast," "mighty," "splendid," or "glorious."

Mahā is a variant from the Indo-European root *meg-*, which developed into the English prefix "mega-" through the Greek word *megas,* meaning "great."[8]

Chinese translators had a principle of *bufan* (不翻), meaning "not to be translated." For example, Kumarajiva did not translate *"mahā," "prajñā,"* and *"pāramitā"* in his translation of the *Maha Prajna Paramita* scripture, and Xuanzang, along with many others, followed this tradition.

Xuanzang established five categories of terms not to be translated: secret terms, terms that have multiple meanings, names of things that did not exist in China, customarily used originals, and terms that have profound meanings.

The Chinese translators noticed that if they had translated *"mahā"* as *dai* in Chinese, that would merely have meant "great," but it would convey mystery if they kept the original Sanskrit sound. (Later in both the α and Xuanzang versions, the word *dai* is used to modify "mantra.")

PRAJÑĀ / WISDOM BEYOND WISDOM

Prajñā, a feminine noun, consists of two elements, *pra* and *jñā.*

Pra is a prefix, meaning "before," "forward," "in front," "on," "forth," "supreme," or "excellent."

This syllable is related to the English prefix "pro-" through the Greek word *pro,* meaning "before," "in front," and "forward."[9] Samples of the "pro-" words may include "proceed" and "prominent."

Jñā, as a verbal root, means "know," "perceive," "discover," "clarify," or "understand."

J and *g,* as well as *g* and *k,* are at times closely connected in the Indo-European language family. Thus, *jñā* is related to the English words "gnome" (in the sense of a maxim), "gnosis," and "know" through the Greek word *gnōsis,* meaning "knowledge."[10]

Prajñā may be understood as "supreme wisdom," "wisdom of enlightenment," "gnosis," "insight," "intuitive knowledge," or "salvific wisdom." It is regarded as the original pure mind or as the capacity of understanding that which goes beyond dualistic discerning—a transcendental and nondualistic wisdom. The grammatical gender of this word is feminine.

As mentioned earlier, Xuanzang cited *prajñā* as an example of a word whose meaning is so deep that it is essentially untranslatable. He used its Chinese transliteration, *bore* (般若). It is transliterated in Japanese as *hannya.*

In some cases, this word is translated as *zhihui* (智慧), meaning "wisdom," or *dazhi,* (大智), meaning "great wisdom" in Chinese.

Joan and I translate *prajñā* as "wisdom beyond wisdom." The word *prajñā* is comprehensively explained in the *Heart Sutra,* but for now we could call it a profound experience of freedom in meditation, where body, heart, and mind; self and other; life and death; transiency and timelessness, are not distinctly divided.

PĀRAMITĀ / REALIZING

There have been two major explanations of the etymology of the Pali and Sanskrit feminine noun *pāramitā,* according to the Japanese Buddhist scholar Hajime Nakamura.[11] Here are the two explanations, to which I have added some semantic and grammatical definitions:

1. A compound of *pāram* (to the other shore) and *ita* (having arrived). *Pāram* means "to the other shore" as the accusative case of the neuter noun *pāra* — "the opposite," "the other side," or "the opposite shore." The *i* is a verb meaning "go," "get to," or "arrive." And the *ta* makes it a state that has happened, which is turned into *tā* to make the word a feminine noun. Thus, *pāramitā* can be interpreted as "(the condition of) having arrived at the other shore," "complete attainment," or "perfection."

2. A compound of *pārami,* meaning "having arrived," plus *tā,* which makes a state of "having completely arrived."

In the common Buddhist analogy, "the other shore" means "awakening." "Arriving at awakening" is no other than enlightenment. This arriving makes a person a buddha. There is also another interpretation. Yuichi Kajiyama suggests:

3. A compound of *pārami,* which derived from *parami* meaning "the highest," plus *tā,* which shows a state or condition. It is an abstract noun meaning "extreme state" or "completion."[12]

As a compound, *prajñāpāramitā* is a feminine form. Its personified form, Prajnaparamita, is regarded as a goddess, Mother of All Buddhas, in the Mahayana pantheon.

The six *paramitas* are regarded as the means by which bodhisattvas lead beings to the shore of nirvana. They are: giving, keeping precepts, patience, vigorous effort, meditation, and *prajna*. And for Dogen, *prajna* is multifold.[13]

In English the six *paramitas* are often called the "six perfections." In a similar manner, *prajñāpāramitā* has often been translated as "perfection of wisdom." You might imagine that when wisdom is perfected, there is nothing more to do; when you have arrived at the shore of enlightenment, there is nowhere else to go.

I invite you to consider *paramita* as a dynamic state of arriving rather than a static state of having already arrived. The six *paramitas* may thus be interpreted as the six aspects of practice being actualized.

According to Dogen, as I suggested earlier, our practice should be a dynamic process of actualizing enlightenment and nirvana at each moment in a "circle of the way." This point of view suggests that at each moment in which we make an effort to practice, we are not necessarily perfecting something. Thus, *pāramitā* can be translated as "realizing," which can be seen as understanding and actualizing things that are not pre-fixed and not waiting to be perfected.

In the α version, *pāramitā* is transliterated as *boluomi* (波羅蜜).

In the Xuanzang version, it is *boluomiduo* (波羅蜜多). In Japanese these four ideographs are independently pronounced *ha ra mitsu ta,* but it is actually pronounced *ha-ra-mit-ta* as a compound by a phonetic change. A phonetic or euphonious change often means that two particular sounds pronounced one after the other create a single shorter sound, or the final sound of a word changes when followed by a certain sound. It happens in Sanskrit as well as in other languages.

Pāramitā is sometimes translated into Chinese as *daobian* (到彼岸), which means "arrival (or arriving) at the other shore." It is also translated as *du* (度), meaning "crossing over to" or "having crossed over to."

HEART

The neuter noun *hṛdaya* means "heart (as an organ)," "heart (as the seat of feelings and sensations)," "mind (as the seat of mental operations)," "center," "core," "condensation," "essence," "soul," or "most secret part."

This word is related to the Greek word *kardiā* and the Latin word *cordis,* both meaning "heart" and "center."[14] You could easily guess from here that *hṛdaya* is related to the English words "cardia," "cardiac," and "cardiology."

Hṛdaya can also be interpreted as *mantra* or *dhāraṇī,* meaning a "mystical verse." These Sanskrit words are often used interchangeably. In the α version, the counterpart for *hṛdaya* is *damingzhou* (大明咒), meaning "great bright mantra." *Mingzhou,* or bright mantra, usually indicates *dhāraṇī.*

Thus, the "heart" is seen as a mantra, the most secret of all teachings — the very heart of the Buddha. This notion of seeing the *Heart Sutra* as *dhāraṇī* is found in Kukai's assertion, quoted previously, that the "heart" of *prajñā* is the True Word — the mantra. Many practitioners of tantric Buddhism have accepted this view.

Xuanzang translated *hṛdaya* as *xin* (心). The Chinese word *xin* covers all the above semantics in *hṛdaya,* except *xin* usually does not mean *dhāraṇī.* His translation makes it possible to see the *Heart Sutra* beyond the context of *dhāraṇī.*

While the title of the α version emphasizes the tantric aspect of the sutra, that of the Xuanzang version keeps open to us whether we take it as a tantric text or as a condensation of the entire *Prajna Paramita* scripture group.

SUTRA

The primary meanings of the neuter noun *sūtra* are "thread," "string," "line," "cord," and "wire." It evolved to mean "the thread that runs through or holds everything." It also means a "manual of teaching," and "scripture."

Sūtra is related to the English word "suture" through the Latin word *suere,* meaning "to sew," whose past particle form is *sūtas.*[15]

The Chinese found its perfect counterpart, *jing* (經), in their language. The ideograph for *jing* has two elements: "thread" on the left side, and "stretching," "path," or "penetrating" on the right side. Thus, *jing* means "warp" and "path" as well as "unchangeable principle" and "scripture." This word indicated the presence of Daoist or Confucian scriptures even before Buddhism reached China. For example, Laozi's *Daodejing* (Tao Te Ching), the most sacred book of Daoism, has this ideograph at the end.

The Chinese translators used *jing* for the title of scriptures instead of using a transliteration of *sūtra.*

The Sanskrit text *Hridaya* does not have the word *sūtra,* which is not an unusual case. The Pali equivalent of this word is *sutta.* The titles of nearly all Pali scriptures are without the word *sutta.*[16]

The Sanskrit title for the *Lotus Sutra* is *Saddharma Puṇḍarīka.* All the Sanskrit titles of the *Maha Prajna Paramita Sutra,* the *Diamond Sutra,* the

Avatamsaka Sutra, and the *Maha Vairocana Sutra* are without the word *sūtra.* The Chinese had the tendency to add the word *jing* to titles of scriptures.

The oft-recited title in English, *Maha Prajna Paramita Hridaya Sutra,* consists entirely of Sanskrit words, so it may give you an impression that the Sanskrit title is written in this way. However, in fact, it is a back-translation from its Chinese or Japanese title. Note that Amoghavajra's Sanskrit version in the eighth century already has a similar title with the word *sutra* at its end. The actual Sanskrit title of this scripture, however, is, as previously explained, *Prajñāpāramitā-hṛdaya.*

(ox) DEDICATION

> SH: *namas sarvajñāya*
> SN: *Oṃ namo bhagavatyai Ārya-Prajñāpāramitāyai!*
> EM: Adoration to the Omniscient!
> EC: Homage to the Perfection of Wisdom, the lovely, the Holy!

Namas, at the beginning of the Horyu-ji version, is more commonly spelled *namaḥ,* which is the nominative singular case of the neuter noun *namas,* meaning "bow," "obedience," "adoration," or "homage." *Namo* in the Nepalese version takes this form as it is, followed by a voiced sound *bha.*

"Namaste," a word included in some English dictionaries, is a very common greeting word in India. It is originally Sanskrit, meaning "respect to you."

Sarva, meaning "all" or "every," is the stem of the pronoun that forms a compound with a following word.

Jñā means "know," as explained earlier. *Sarvajñā,* meaning "all-knower," is one of the honorific titles of Shakyamuni Buddha. *Sarvajñāya* is the dative form of this compound, meaning "to the all-knower."

Therefore, the dedication in the Horyu-ji version can be interpreted as "Homage to the all-knower." *Oṃ* at the beginning of the Nepalese version is an ancient Vedic word of invocation.

Bhagavatyai is the dative case of the feminine noun *bhagavatī,* meaning "(one who is) fortunate," "one who is happy," "one who is glorious," "one who is divine," or "one who is worthy of adoration." This word comes from the masculine noun *bhaga,* meaning "dispenser," "patron," or "glorious lord." *Bhagavatyai* modifies *prajñāpāramitāyai* in grammatical agreement.

Ārya, as an adjective, means "honorable" or "respectable." Its stem forms a compound with the next word. This word is related to the English word "Aryan."[17]

Prajñāpāramitāyai is the dative case of *prajñāpāramitā,* meaning "to the [goddess] Prajñāpāramitā."

The Amoghavajra versions, in Sanskrit and Chinese, do not have this dedication. Neither the α version nor the Xuanzang version has a corresponding line.

SETTING

The first line of the main part of the shorter text explains who experienced the *prajna paramita,* how it was experienced, and what benefit it has brought forth.

In the shorter text, as soon as the word *jing* (sutra) was added for its title, the opening line "Thus have I heard" was implied. The text became a discourse of Shakyamuni Buddha. He explains the teaching to his best listener disciple, Shariputra. In this case, the teaching is about a revelation of Avalokiteshvara. It is also possible to see Avalokiteshvara as the sutra's speaker.

In the later-developed longer text, the setting becomes much more interesting: At a great assembly on Vulture Peak, the Buddha goes into *samadhi.* Without uttering a word, he inspires Shariputra to ask Avalokiteshvara how to practice *prajna paramita.* Avalokiteshvara's explanation to Shariputra constitutes the main part of the *Heart Sutra.*

The longer text presents a conclusion: The Buddha, rising from his meditation, praises Avalokiteshvara and encourages everyone to practice *prajna paramita* as instructed. The multitudinous audience rejoices and hails the Buddha for his words.

(1) AVALOKITESHVARA

> SH: *Āryāvalokitevara-bodhisattvo*
> SA: *āryāvalokiteśvaro-bodhisattvo*
> SN: *ārya-Avalokiteśvaro bodhisattvo*
> α: 觀世音菩薩
> αtl: *Guan shi yin pu sa*
> CX: 觀自在菩薩

CXtl: *Guan zi zai pu sa*

CA: 聖觀自在菩薩

CAtl: *Sheng guan zi zai pu sa*

Ktl: *Gwanjajae bosal*

Jtl: *Kanjizai bosa<tsu>*

Vtl: *Quán Tự Tại Bồ Tát*

EM: The venerable Bodhisattva Avalokiteśvara,

ES: When the Bodhisattva Avalokitesvara

EC: Avalokita, the Holy Lord and Bodhisattva,

ETH: Avalokiteshvara, who helps all to awaken,

Ā for the *Āryāvalokiteśvara* and *ārya-Avalokiteśvaro* in the Sanskrit versions is written differently. The second *ā* in the first and the second samples, in the Horyu-ji and Amoghavajra versions, can be divided as *a-A*, as in the last sample in the Nepalese version.

Ārya is, again, an adjective meaning "honorable" or "respectable."

Avalokiteśvaro is a phonetically changed form of *Avalokiteśvaraḥ*, the nominative singular case of the masculine noun.

The Sanskrit spelling for Avalokiteshvara varies slightly: *Avalokitaśvara* and *Avalokiteśvara*. The etymological interpretations differ, according to Nakamura.[18]

Avalokitaśvara, the first variation, is a compound of *ava, lokita,* and *śvara.* Or it may be a compound of *ava, lokita,* and *aśvara,* in which case this name should be spelled *Avalokitāśvara.*

The prefix *ava* means "off," "away," or "down."

Lokita is a variation of the masculine noun *loka. Loka* means "open space," "place," "scope," "heaven," "earth," or "world."

In the meantime, the verb *lok* means "see," "perceive," "recognize," or "know." *Lokita* is its past participle form. The connection between *lok* and *loken,* the Old English word for "look," is not attested, although it seems rather obvious.

There is a pun between *loka* (world) and *lok* (look).

Śvara is an adjective meaning "delight in." It is contrary to *aśvara,* meaning "having a bad voice," "having a croaking voice," or "in a low voice."

Therefore, *Avalokitaśvara* means "one who perceives voices of delight in the world." On the other hand, *Avalokitāśvara* (with ā in the middle) means "one who perceives voices of suffering in the world."

When *ava* (down) is combined with *tāra* (protector), it becomes *avatāra* (descended deity on earth), of which the English form is "avatar."

Amoghavajra translated *ārya* as *sheng* (聖), meaning "sacred," "venerable," or "honorable."

Kumarajiva translated this bodhisattva's name as Guanshiyin (觀世音) in his acclaimed version of the *Lotus Sutra*. The α version of the *Heart Sutra* uses this translation — Guanshiyin.

Guan (觀) means "observe," "intuit," or "see with inner eyes."

Shi (世) means "the world."

Yin (音) means "sound" or "voice."

Thus, the translated name can mean "One who causes (sentient beings) to observe the voice" or "Perceiver of the cries of the world."

Kumarajiva obviously drew double meanings, *loka* and *lok,* from the word *lokita.* This is an example of Kumarajiva's spectacular translation.

This name is often simplified as Guanyin (觀音).

Avalokiteśvara, the second spelling of the bodhisattva's name, is a compound of *avalokita* and *īśvara. Avalokita* comes from the verb *avalok.* The prefix *ava* and the root of the verb *lok* are the same as above.

Īśvara is a masculine noun, meaning "master" or "supreme being." As a noun it also means "own," "possessing," "powerful," "able to do," or "capable of." Therefore, this Sanskrit name can be interpreted as "Lord who looks downward," "Perceiver with freedom," or "Perceiver who freely grants wishes."

In Buddhism, Īśvara (自在天) or Maheśvara (大自在天) is the name of Shiva, who was adapted into the Buddhist pantheon. In Hinduism "Īśvara" is one of the thousand titles of Shiva. In invisible ways, Avalokiteshvara and Shiva are related. Xuanzang, in his *Record of the Western Region Compiled during the Great Tang Dynasty,* reported: "In south of Mt. Malaya on southern end of India, there is a mountain called Potalaka, where Avalokiteshvara visits and stays. When people pray to him, he sometimes takes the form of Shiva or an ash-painted ascetic and responds to their prayers."[19]

In India, to this day, there are devotees of Shiva, ascetics with their naked bodies covered with ash. The magical chanting formula called "Great Compassionate Heart Dharani" for Avalokiteshvara, which is still recited daily in the Zen tradition, includes a distinct address to Shiva, "Blue-Necked One."[20]

Xuanzang translated the name as Guanzizai (觀自在).

Zi (自) means "self." *Zai* (在) means "be." The compound *zizai* is an idiom meaning "be oneself," "unrestricted," "free," or "freely."

It may be possible to say that Kumarajiva's translation of the name emphasizes the compassion of the bodhisattva, while Xuanzang's emphasizes the freedom and wisdom of the bodhisattva.

Regarding the gender of Avalokiteshvara, although the grammatical gender of the name is masculine in Sanskrit, the *Lotus Sutra* states that Avalokiteshvara manifests in thirty-three types of beings. Thus, this bodhisattva becomes androgynous. In China and Japan, the bodhisattva has been largely regarded as female since around the tenth century.[21]

BODHISATTVA / (ONE) WHO HELPS ALL TO AWAKEN

The Sanskrit term *bodhisattva* is a compound of *bodhi* and *sattva*. *Bodhi* is used as a masculine or feminine noun, meaning "awakening" or "enlightenment." The neuter noun *sattva* means "being," "person," or "essence." *Bodhisattva* is a masculine noun.

Sattva is related to the adjective *sat,* meaning "being existent" or "being present." *Sat* is related to *satya* (truth), which appears later in the text. It also has a remote connection to the English word "sooth" through the Old English word *sōth,* meaning "true."[22]

In early scriptures Shakyamuni was described as embodying various forms of bodhisattvas in *jatakas* — tales of the Buddha's former lives. In the Mahayana Buddhist tradition, those who endeavor for the awakening of other beings are called bodhisattvas.

Bodhisattva is sometimes translated as "seeker of awakening," while *buddha* means one who is already awakened. However, this does not mean that bodhisattvas are not awakened. Rather, instead of abiding in their own awakening, bodhisattvas make others' awakening a priority. Translating this word as "enlightening being," "one who enlightens (others)," "one who is dedicated to awakening," or "one who helps all to awaken" may represent this spirit more fully than "seeker of awakening."

Bodhisattvo is a phonetically changed form of *bodhisattvaḥ,* the masculine singular nominative form of the noun *bodhisattva,* owing to the following sound *ga.*

The word *bodhisattva* is transliterated in Chinese as *puti saduo* (菩提薩埵). Here at the beginning of the *Heart Sutra,* it is abbreviated as *pusa* (菩薩). In Japanese, it is pronounced *bosatsu,* or *bosa* in abbreviation.

Avalokiteshvara Bodhisattva is best described in the "Universal Gate" chapter of the *Lotus Sutra* as a bodhisattva of great compassion.

(2) MOVES DEEPLY

> SH: *gambhiraṃ prajñāpāramitāyāṃ caryāṃ caramāṇo*
>
> SA: *gambhīrāṃ prajñā-pāramitā-caryāṃ caramāṇo*
>
> SN: *gambhīrāṃ prajñāpāramitāyā-caryāṃ caramāṇo*
>
> α: 行深般若波羅蜜時
>
> αtl: *xing shen bo re bo luo mi shi*
>
> CX: 行深般若波羅蜜多時
>
> CXtl: *xing shen bo re bo luo mi duo shi*
>
> CA: 深般若波羅蜜多行行時
>
> CAtl: *shen bo re bo luo mi duo xing xing shi*
>
> Ktl: *haeng sim banya baramilda si*
>
> Jtl: *gyōjin hannya haramitta ji,*
>
> Vtl: *hành thâm Bát nhã Ba la mật đa thời,*
>
> EM: performing his study in the deep Pra*gñ*āpāramitā (perfection of wisdom),
>
> ES: was engaged in the practice of the deep Prajnaparamita,
>
> EC: was moving in the deep course of the wisdom which has gone beyond.
>
> ETH: moves in the deep course of realizing wisdom beyond wisdom,

Gambhīraṃ and *gambhīrāṃ* are forms of the adjective *gambhīra,* meaning "deep," "profound," "serious," "sacred," or "mysterious." (The last *m* turns into *ṃ* when followed by a consonant.)

Gambhīram (the Horyu-ji version) can be seen as the adverbial use of the accusative case of the masculine or neuter form of the adjective, meaning "deeply." *Gambhīrāṃ* (the Amoghavajra and the Nepalese versions), in its feminine accusative form, modifies *caryāṃ,* the accusative form of the feminine noun *caryā.*

Caryā means "motion," "course," "action," "conduct," "dealing," "performance," "observance," or "practice." Its accusative form makes this noun the objective of *caramāṇo.*

Caramāṇo is the present participle of the verb *car* in Buddhist Hybrid Sanskrit. *Car* means "go," "move," "walk through," or "perform." So *caramāṇo* makes it "(while) moving," "(while) performing," or "(when) conducting."

Prajñāpāramitāyām is a locative form, meaning "in (the midst of) *prajñāpāramitā*."

Thus, the Horyu-ji version can be translated as: "(Avalokiteshvara), while moving deeply in *prajna paramita* . . ." The Amoghavajra and Nepalese versions can be read: "(Avalokiteshvara), while conducting deep practice in *prajna paramita* . . ."

The Chinese word *xing* (行) has many meanings, including "go," "advance," "act," "action," or "practice." *Shen* (深) means "deep" or "deeply."

Prajñāpāramitā is transliterated differently in the Chinese versions: *boluomi* and *boluomiduo*.

The phrase *xing shen bore boluomi[duo]* (行深般若波羅蜜[多]) can be interpreted as "practicing deep *prajna paramita*," "practicing deeply *prajna paramita*," or "practicing the depth of *prajna paramita*." As you can see in this case, parts of speech are not strictly defined, and the relationship among words is flexible in the Chinese language.

If we read the Chinese translation apart from its Sanskrit counterpart, it would be natural to see *bore boluomi* or *bore boluomiduo* as the object of the verb *xing* (practicing), and *shen* as an adverb modifying *xing*. Thus, "deeply practicing *prajna paramita*" can be a fair translation of this Chinese line.

In the Chinese versions, the ideograph *shi* (時) comes next. *Shi* means "time" or "when." That makes the line read: "When Avalokiteshvara (is/was) deeply doing practice in *prajna paramita*." In Chinese, the tense can be either past or present.

Amoghavajra's version, which repeats the word *practice,* can be translated as: "Avalokiteshvara (is/was) deeply doing practice in *prajna paramita*. When (the bodhisattva) was practicing . . ."

Zen Master Bernie Glassman says:

> Some translations use the word *being* rather than *doing.* Being deep prajnaparamita, one does deep prajnaparamita. Since wisdom is the very state of what we are, being in that state without separation is nothing but wisdom. Bodhisattvas, being the state of enlightenment, do not remain or stop there, but in order to help all of us, they purposely function, they do deep prajnaparamita. This is compassion, which is the functioning of wisdom. Because they

are enlightened, they practice; because they're in the state of no-separation, which is wisdom, they practice compassion, the functioning of that state.[23]

(3) *SKANDHAS* / STREAMS

SH, SA: *vyavalokayati sma: pañca skandhās tāṃś*
SN: *vyavalokayati sma: pañca-skandās tāṃś*
α: 照見五陰
αtl: *zhao jian wu yin*
CX, CA: 照見五蘊
CXtl, CAtl: *zhao jian wu yun*
Ktl: *jogyeon o-on*
Jtl: *shōken go'on*
Vtl: *chiếu kiến ngũ uẩn*
EM: thought thus: 'There are the five Skandhas,
ES: he perceived: there are the five Skandhas; and these he saw
EC: He looked down from on high, he beheld but five heaps, and he saw that
ETH: sees that all five streams of body, heart, and mind

The Sanskrit word *vyavalokayati* is the third person singular case of *vyavalok,* which is a compound of *vytava* and *lok. Vytava* is a phonetic linkage of prefixes, *vi* and *ava. Vi* means "in two parts," "apart," or "in different directions." *Ava* means "off," "away," or "down."

Avalok, as in the name Avalokiteshvara, means "look down," "view," or "observe." *Sma* makes this verb a past tense.

Pañca is the stem of *pañcan,* meaning "five," at the beginning of the compound. *Pañca* is related to the English "penta-," "pentad," and "pentagon" through the Greek word *pente,* meaning "five."[24]

Skandhās is a phonetically changed form of *skandhaḥ,* which is the nominative plural case of the masculine noun *skandha.*[25] *Skandha* means "multitude," "quantity," "aggregate," "heap," "grasping," "part," "division," "constituents," "the stem or trunk of a tree," or "path."

Pañca-skandhās, or the five *skandhas,* are the five constituting elements of grasped or perceived phenomena. They are physical form, *rūpa,* plus the four mental and emotional activities: *vedanā, samjña, samskāra,* and *vijñana.* (These five terms will be examined later.) A Pali equivalent of this term already appears in *Suttanipata,* a sutra regarded as containing some of the earliest Buddhist teachings.

Tāṃś is a phonetically changed form of *tān* (meaning "them"), which is the accusative plural case of the third person pronoun *te,* meaning "they." *Te* seems to be related to the English word "they."

This line can be interpreted as: "(Avalokiteshvara) saw the five *skandhas* (and saw) them."

The Chinese word for "observe" is a compound of two verbs, *zhao* (照) and *jian* (見). *Zhao* means "shed light on," "illuminate," "know," "understand," or "shine." *Jian* simply means "see." This translation is often admired for its poetic beauty. This word is found in both the α version and Xuanzang versions. As with most other words in those versions, the unknown compiler of the α version should be credited.

While this verb is specified as the past form in Sanskrit, its Chinese counterpart does not indicate tense. In fact, tense is not specified in most cases in the Chinese language.

I prefer to use the dramatic present tense for our English translation. The present tense implies that Avalokiteshvara is still meditating in awakening and all those who meditate and chant this sutra can experience this illumination.

The translation of "the five *skandhas*" in the α version, as well as Kumarajiva's translation of the *Maha Prajna Paramita Sutra,* is *wuyin* (五陰). *Wu* is "five." *Yin,* the antonym of *yang* (陽), means "shade," "hidden," "covered," "subtle," or "quiet."

Xuanzang translated this term as *wuyun* (五蘊). *Wu,* again, means "five." *Yun* means "accumulate," layer," "stagnant," "assemble," "wrap," or "path."

If we compare these translations, Xuanzang's seems to be far clearer and closer to the Sanskrit term. The English word "aggregate" is still too static to describe the state of our body and mind that changes constantly. I personally prefer "path" among the above definitions. Our translated term "stream," which is even more dynamic than "path," comes from this understanding.

Thich Nhat Hanh says:

> These five elements flow like a river in every one of us. In fact, these are really five rivers flowing together in us: the river of form, which means our body, the river of feelings, the river of perceptions, the river

of mental formations, and the river of consciousness. They are always flowing in us.[26]

(4) EMPTY / BOUNDLESS

SH: *ca svabhāva-śūnyaṃ paśyasti sma.*
SA: *ca sva-bhāva-śūnyām paśyasti sma.*
SN: *ca svabhāvaśūnyān paśyast sma.*
α: 空
αtl: *kong*
CX: 皆空
CXtl: *jie kong*
CA: 彼自性空現
CAtl: *bi zi xing kong xian*
Ktl: *gaegong*
Jtl: *kaikū*
Vtl: *giai không,*
EM: and these he considered as by their nature empty (phenomenal)'
ES: in their self-nature to be empty.
EC: in their own-being they were empty.
ETH: are without boundary,

Ca means "and."

Svabhāva is a compound of *sva* and *bhāva.* It works as a masculine noun meaning "self," "ego," "own," "soul," or "inherent nature."

Here, in this case, *sva* functions as an adjective, meaning "own" and "one's own," at the beginning of the compound. *Sva* is related to the English word "suicide" through the Latin syllable *sui,* meaning "of oneself." It is also related to the Sanskrit-originated word "swami" (one's own master).[27]

Bhāva means "becoming," "being," "existing," "occurring," "appearance," "continuance," "state," "condition," "reality," "manner of being," or "nature." Thus, *svabhāva* is translated as "own-being," "self nature," "self-sufficient being," or "self-substantiated reality." *Bhāva* is rooted in the verb *bhū,* which means "arise," "come into being," "exist," "live," and "stay." It is related to the English word "be."[28]

Śūnyaṃ (in the Horyu-ji and the Amoghavajra versions) is a phonetically changed form of *śūnyam.* It is the accusative case of the adjective *śūnya,* making the compound *svabhāva-śūnya* the object of *paśyasti* ("perceive").

Śūnya as an adjective can be interpreted as "zero-like." This word also functions as a neuter noun meaning "swollen state," "increased state," "grown state," "emptiness," "lack," "void," "absence," "zero," "nonessential quality," or "ephemeral quality."

Śūnyatān (in the Nepalese version) is the accusative plural case of the same adjective. That makes the compound *svabhāvaśūnyān* agree with the five *skandhas.*

Śūnyatā is a feminine noun, and appears later in the sutra. *Śūnya* is made an abstract philosophical concept with the addition of the suffix *tā.* It means "hollowness," "loneliness," "emptiness," "nothingness," "nonexistence," "no self-existing entities," "nonsubstantiality," "illusory nature (of all things)," "nonreality," or "zeroness." Its Pali counterpart is *suññatā.*

The great early Mahayana philosopher Nagarjuna identifies *śūnyatā* with the interdependent origination of all existing phenomena.

Frederick J. Streng, a contemporary scholar of Buddhist studies, writes:

> "Empty," "open," "devoid," "nothing," and "nonexistent" are words used to translate the term *śūnyam.* "Emptiness," "openness," "nothingness," "nonsubstantiality," "relativity," and "the inexhaustible" have been used to translate *śūnyatā.* . . . The complexity of the concept expressed as "emptiness" derives from the recognition in Buddhism that teaching the truth about life is urgent for alleviating suffering, but that implicit in thinking and speaking resides a tendency to create an illusion (of self-sufficient realities) that is itself the cause of suffering. The teaching of "the emptiness of things" is a medicine for the spiritual illness seen wherever there is greed, hate, and self-delusion; it is a response to a universal, problematic condition that is found in particular specific forms and thus requires different kinds and levels of correction.[29]

Paśyasti is the third person singular of the verb *paś,* meaning "behold," "look at," "perceive," or "notice." *Sma* makes it a past form.

Thus, the Sanskrit line in the Horyu-ji and the Amoghavajra versions reads, "(Avalokiteshvara saw five *skandhas* and) perceived them as zero-like self-nature." The Nepalese version: "(Avalokiteshvara saw five *skandhas* and) perceived zero-like self-beings."

• • •

A symbol for zero was already being used by the Babylonians around 300 B.C.E.[30] In ancient India, the introduction of zero forever changed mathematical thinking. It was called *śūnya* in Sanskrit. Zero, as one minus one, is still called *shunya* in Hindi, an Indian language closely related to Sanskrit.

Mahayana's philosophical interpretation of "zeroness" (*śūnyatā*) led to a revolution in Buddhist thinking. Zeroness represented the lack of absolute value and substantiality of the phenomenal world. The notion of zeroness evolved from the earlier Buddhist teaching of *anātman*, or no-self — the denial of the substantial reality of the self and what belongs to the self — as a means to free one from attachment. The doctrine of zeroness, asserting the lack of self-identity and the lack of absolute separation in all things, became the central teaching of Mahayana Buddhism. In zeroness, all things are connected; nothing is absolute; nothing is separate; nobody is alone. Even Buddhist doctrines are seen as zeroness, not containing absolute fixed truths. Experience of this teaching is seen as awakening, as freedom, no other than *prajna paramita*.

In the α version this line is simply expressed by one ideograph, *kong* (空). The Xuanzang version reads *jie kong* (皆空).

Kong means "void," "space," "hollowness," "openness," "enormousness," "broadness," or "sky."

Jie means "all," "altogether," or "everything."

Thus, the α and Xuanzang versions read: "(Avalokiteshvara) illuminated that the five *skandhas* are (all) empty (or all open)."

Amoghavajra translated *svabhāva* as *bi zi xing* (彼自性). *Bi* means "he," "that," or "the." *Zi* means "self." And *xing* means "characteristic" or "nature."

Xian kong (空現) is *kong* (zeroness) plus *xian* (appear, emerge, or realize).

His line may be translated as "(Avalokiteshvara practiced and saw) the emerging zeroness of the self nature."

Just as zeroness is not only negative, *kong* is not only void but is broad and spacious. In fact, all things, including the earth, are in the sky. Joan and I translate this word as "without boundary," or "boundlessness."

(5) FREEDOM FROM ANGUISH

α, CX: 度一切苦厄

αtl, CXtl: *du yi qie ku e*

Ktl: *do ilche goaek.*
Jtl: *do issai kuyaku*
Vtl: *độ nhất thiết khổ ách.*
ETH: and frees all from anguish.

The two Chinese translations (the α and Xuanzang versions) mention freedom from suffering at this point. None of the existing Sanskrit texts has a corresponding line, nor do the English translations by Müller, Suzuki, or Conze.[31] Nor do the bilingual versions by Amoghavajra.

Du (度), as discussed before, means "crossing over to." To carry someone to the other shore of awakening is to "save," "relieve," or "free" the person.

Yiqie (一切) means "all," "entirely." It consists of two ideographs: *yi* (one) and *qie* (cut), thus meaning "sweeping in one large stroke." In Japanese, these two ideographs are individually pronounced *ichi* and *sai,* but, as a compound, they are pronounced *issai* by a phonetic change.

Ku (苦), the first part of the compound *kue,* means "bitter," "troublesome," "painful," "tormenting," "anguish," or "suffering." *E* (厄) is an ideograph meaning a "yoke" for a horse. It means "suffering," "calamity," "disaster," or "misfortune."

Thus, the line reads "(Avalokiteshvara) caused freedom from all suffering."

It is unclear from this line whether the bodhisattva became free from all suffering or freed others from all suffering. However, as Avalokiteshvara is revered as one who compassionately helps all beings, the latter interpretation seems to make better sense.

Form as Zeroness

(6) SHARIPUTRA

SH, SA, SN: *iha Śāriputra*
α: 舍利弗
αtl: *She li fu*
CX: 舍利子
CXtl: *She li zi*
CA: 此舍利子
CAtl: *ci She li zi*
Ktl: *Sarija,*

Jtl: *Sharishi,*

Vtl: *Xá Lợi Tử,*

EM: 'O Sāriputra,' he said,

ES: O, Sariputra,

EC: Here O Sariputra ,

ETH: O Shariputra [who listens to the teachings of the Buddha],

Iha is an adverb meaning "here," "in this case," or "now."

Śāriputra is the vocative case of the masculine name Śāriputra. A disciple of the Buddha known for his ability to listen, Shariputra represents in this sutra all those who listen to the Buddha's teaching.

Putra is related to the English syllables "pedo-" through the Greek word *paid,* meaning "child." [32]

In the α version, his entire name is transliterated as Shelifu (舍利弗).

In Chinese his name is sometimes translated as "Heron Child"—Quizi (鷲子), as *śāri* means "heron," and *putra* "son," "boy," or "child." Xuanzang transliterated *śāri* as *sheli* and translated *putra* as *zi* (子), meaning "child."

Amoghavajra's Chinese version has *ci* (此) before *Shelifu. Ci* means "this," or in this case, "here."

(6x) ADDITIONAL WORDS, NOT FOUND IN THE XUANZANG VERSION

SH: *rūpaṃ śūnyatā śūnyatā-iva rūpaṃ*

SN, SA: *rūpaṃ śūnyatā śūnyataiva rūpaṃ*

α: 色空故無惱壞相受空故無受相想空故無知相行空故無作相識空故無覺相何以故舍利弗

αtl: *se kong gu wu nao huai xiang shou kong gu wu shou xiang xiang kong gu wu zhi xiang xing kong gu wu zuo xiang shi kong gu wu jue xiang he yi gu She li fu*

CA: 色空空性是色

CAtl: *se kong kong xing shi se*

EM: form here is emptiness, and emptiness indeed is form.

ES: form is here emptiness, emptiness is form

EC: form is emptiness and the very emptiness is form

Rūpa—"that which is formed"—comes from the verb *rūp,* meaning "to form," "represent," "exhibit," or "appear." The neuter noun *rūpa* has a variety of meanings: "outward appearance," "outward phenomenon," "color," "case," "shape," "figure," "peculiarity," "character," "feature," "gracefulness," "beauty," "matter," or "material case."

Rūpaṃ is a phonetically changed form of *rūpam*. Its last sound *m* turns into *ṃ* as it precedes a consonant. *Rūpam* is the nominative singular case of the neuter noun.

Śūnyatā-iva or *śūnyataiva* is *śūnyatā* plus *eva*.

Eva is an adverb functioning as an emphatic postposition, meaning "just so" or "exactly."

This passage in section 6x in the α version has been adapted as it is from the Kumarajiva translation of the *Maha Prajna Paramita Sutra*. This, however, does not have a corresponding part in the Xuanzang version. It can be translated as follows:

> Form is *shunyata,* therefore (it has) no mark of angst and destruction. Perception is *shunyata,* therefore there is no mark of perception. Feeling is *shunyata,* therefore there is no mark of knowing. Inclination is *shunyata,* therefore there is no mark of doing. Discernment is *shunyata,* therefore there is no mark of awakening. Therefore, Shariputra...

There are some ideographs that are not used in other parts of the sutra. They are *nao* (惱), meaning "worry," "suffer"; and *huai* (壞), meaning "destroy," or "collapse." In addition, there is *jue* (覺), meaning "awake," "wake up," "realize," or "enlighten." Also, *zhi* (知), meaning "know"; *zuo* (作), meaning "do" or "make"; and *he* (何), meaning "what."

In my understanding, the significance of the fact that these lines do not have correspondence in the Xuanzang version is that they first existed in Kumarajiva's *Large Sutra* and were adapted by the α version, and their shorter forms included in the Sanskrit version. In translating the Sanskrit version into Chinese, Xuanzang did not include them. Amoghavajra made a brief translation of this passage: "Form (is) zeroness. Zeroness's characteristic is form."

(7) FORM AND ZERONESS

SH, SA, SN: *rūpan na pṛthak śūnyatā, śūnyatāyā na pṛthag rūpaṃ,*
α: 非色異空非空異色
αtl: *fei se yi kong fei kong yi se*
CX: 色不異空空不異色

CXtl: *se bu yi kong kong bu yi se.*

CA: 色不異空空亦不異色

CAtl: *se bu yi kong kong yi bu yi se*

Ktl: *saek bul i gong, gong bul i saek.*

Jtl: *Shiki fu i kū. Kū fu i shiki.*

Vtl: *sắc bất dị không, không bất dị sắc,*

EM: Emptiness is not different from form, form is not different from emptiness.

ES: form is no other than emptiness, emptiness is no other than form;

EC: emptiness does not differ from form, form does not differ from emptiness;

ETH: form is not separate from boundlessness; boundlessness is not separate from form.

Na means "no," or "not." *Na* is related to the English words "naught," "nil," "never," and "no" through the Old English *ne* and *nā,* "no."[33]

Pṛthak is an adverb meaning "different." *Pṛthag* is its phonetically changed form. It takes an ablative case here, as well as accusative or instrumental.

Rūpan is a phonetically changed form of *rūpat,* the ablative case of *rūpa,* meaning "from rupa." This word appears here again at the end of these paired sentences in its nominative form, *rūpaṃ.*

Śūnyatā is a nominative singular case of the feminine noun, which makes it the subject of the first sentence. *Śūnyatāyā* is the ablative case. This is another example of a Sanskrit sentence without a verb. The grammatical structure of the second sentence is identical to the first.

So these lines read: "From *rūpa, śūnyatā* (is) not different. From *śūnyatā, rūpa* (is) not different."

The Chinese translation for "form" is *se* (色). *Se* commonly means "color," "hue," "beauty," and "lust." For non-Buddhists who read Chinese, it may be hard to imagine that the word "color" can also mean "form," as there are other ideographs that mean "form." *Se,* however, is a technical term in Chinese Buddhism and is transliterated and used in other East Asian countries rather than translated. (Remember that the basic Korean, Japanese, and Vietnamese versions of the *Heart Sutra* are transliterations of Xuanzang's Chinese version. In addition, there are translated versions of it in these languages.)

Fei (非), in the α version, means "not." *Bu* (不) is "not," and *yi* (異) is "be different from" or "differ."

So these lines in the α version can be interpreted as: "It is not the case that *rūpa* (is) different from *śūnyatā*. It is not the case that *śūnyatā* (is) different from *rūpa*."

In the Xuanzang version, these lines read: "*Rūpa* is not different from *śūnyatā*; *Śūnyatā* is not different from *rūpa*."

Amoghavajra simply added the ideograph *yi* (亦), meaning "also."

(8) IS ITSELF

> SH, SN: *yad rūpaṃ sā śūnyatā yā śūnyatā tad rūpam.*
> SA: *yad rūpaṃ sā śūnyatā yā śūnyatā sā rūpam.*
> α, CX: 色即是空空即是色
> αtl, CXtl: *se ji shi kong kong ji shi se*
> CA: 是色彼空是空彼色
> CAtl: *shi se bi kong shi kong bi se*
> Ktl: *saek jeuk si gong, gong jeuk si saek.*
> Jtl: *Shiki soku ze kū. Kū soku ze shiki.*
> Vtl: *sắc tức thị không, không tức thị sắc,*
> EM: What is form that is emptiness, what is emptiness that is form.'
> ES: what is form that is emptiness, what is emptiness that is form.
> EC: whatever is form, that is emptiness; whatever is emptiness, that is form.
> ETH: Form is boundlessness; boundlessness is form.

Yad, a relative pronoun, means "who," "which," "what," or "that" in its nominative singular neuter case. *Yā* is the nominative feminine case of the same word.

Tad is an indicative pronoun meaning "it," "that," or "this." *Sā* is the nominative feminine case of the same word.

Tad is certainly related to the English words "that," "this," and "the."[34] These two pronouns — *yad* and *tad* — are in agreement with the nouns *rūpa* (neuter) and *śūnyatā* (feminine), both in nominative.

So these lines can be interpreted as: "Whatever is *rūpa,* that is *śūnyatā.* Whatever is *śūnyatā,* that is *rūpa.*"

Two Chinese versions (the α and the Xuanzang versions) agree with each other on these most-famous paired sentences.

Ji (即) means "immediately," "rightly," "then," "that is," or "in itself."

Shi (是) means "be," "this," "this is," "no other than," "correct," or "right on."

The combination of *ji* and *shi* makes these lines emphatic. So these lines may be interpreted as: "*Rūpa* is itself *śūnyatā. Śūnyatā* is itself *rūpa.*"

The Chinese lines in the Amoghavajra version have another ideograph, *bi* (彼), meaning "the" or "that very."

(9) FOUR OTHER *SKANDHAS*

SH: *evam eva vedanā-saṃjñā-saṃskāra-vijñāni.*

SA: *evam eva vedanā-saṃjñā-saṃskāra-vijñānam,*

SN: *evam eva vedanā-saṃjñā-saṃskāra-vijñānaṃ.*

α: 受想行識亦如是

αtl: *shou xiang xing shi yi ru shi*

CX: 受想行識亦復如是

CXtl: *shou xiang xing shi yi fu ru shi*

CA: 如是受想行識

CAtl: *ru shi shou xiang xing shi*

Ktl: *su sang haeng sik yeokbu yeosi.*

Jtl: *Ju sō gyō shiki yakubu nyoze.*

Vtl: *thu tưởng hành thức diệc phục như thị.*

EM: 'The same applies to perception, name, conception, and knowledge.'

ES: The same can be said of sensation, thought, confection, and consciousness.

EC: the same is true of feelings, perceptions, impulses, and consciousness.

ETH: Feelings, perceptions, inclinations, and discernment are also like this.

After discussing the *śūnya* nature of *rūpa,* which is the first *skandha,* the four other *skandhas* are listed.

Evam is an adverb meaning "as previously stated," or "as following." *Eva,* also an adverb, means "just," "exactly," "truly," or "indeed." After *rūpa,* the second to the fifth *skandhas* are joined, forming a compound. The first three nouns are in their stem forms. The last word shows its case as the nominative plural in the Horyu-ji version and as nominative singular in the Amogha-vajra and the Nepalese versions.

The second *skandha* is *vedanā*, a feminine noun, which means "feeling," or "sensation." *Vedanā* is in the same family as the masculine noun *veda*, which means "knowledge," "sacred knowledge," and "knowledge of rituals."

It is the root of the Sanskrit-originated English words "Veda" and "Vedic." The word *veda* is a root of several English words, including "view," "vision," "visit," "evident," and "survey," through the Latin word *videre*, meaning "see" or "look."[35] The Sanskrit word *veda* comes from the verb *vid*, which means "know," "perceive," "be conscious of," "understand," or "learn."

The third *skandha*, *saṃjñā*, a feminine noun, is a compound of *sam* and *jñā*. *Sam* is a prefix meaning "all," "together," or "thorough." *Jñā* is a verb, which appeared previously, meaning "know." Thus, *saṃjñā* means "concept" or "perception."

The prefix *sam*, or its varied form *saṃ*, appears several times in the *Heart Sutra*.

Sam and its changed form *san* are also found in Sanskrit-originated English words, such as "samsara," "sandhi," and "Sanskrit." *Sam* is also connected to *sama*, meaning "same," which leads to the English word "same."[36]

The fourth *skandha*, *saṃskāra*, a masculine noun, is *sam* ("all" or "together") and *skāra* combined. *Skāra* comes from the verb *kṛ* or *skṛ*, meaning "to form." *Kār* or *skār* means "that which is formed." Thus, *saṃskāra* (*saṃskāra*) is "putting together," "forming well," "conditioning force," "making ready," or "forming the mind." (*Kṛ* and *skṛ* are related to the word "Sanskrit," meaning "perfected.")

Edward Conze says, "The term includes all active dispositions, tendencies, impulses, volitions, striving, etc., whether 'conscious' or 'repressed.'"[37]

Thus, *saṃskāra* is interpreted as a mental function, voluntary and involuntary, that leads to action. It has been or can be translated as "impulse," "imprint," "preparation," "inclination," "conformation," "compositional factors," "mental formation," "mind-set," "will," "conditioning force," "confection," "conformation," "compounding," or "preparing."

The fifth *skandha*, *vijñāna*, is a compound of *vi* and *jñāna*. The prefix *vi* means "in two parts," "apart," or "in different directions." *Jñāna* means "knowing," "knowledge," or "higher knowledge." Thus, *vijñāna* means "discernment" or "discrimination." It is often translated as "consciousness."

Indeed, *vijñāna* can mean "consciousness" in general, as in Consciousness Only (*vijñānapti mātratā*) theory. But in the case of the *Heart Sutra*, it seems to indicate a part of general consciousness along with *vedanā*, *saṃjñā,* and *saṃskāra.* So Joan and I translated this term as "discernment" rather than "consciousness."

This word is related to the verb *vijñ,* which means "distinguish," "discern," "recognize," "know," or "understand."

Vijñāni (the Horyu-ji version) is the nominative plural, and *vijñānam* and *vijñānaṃ* (in the Amoghavajra and the Nepalese versions) are both nominative singular forms of the neuter noun *vijñāna.* In the former version the entire compound is treated as plural, and in the latter versions singular.

In Chinese the second *skandha* is translated as *shou* (受). It means "receive," "reception," or "acquire."

The third *skandha* is translated as *xiang* (想), meaning "thought," "consideration," "calling to mind," or "idea."

The fourth *skandha* is *xing* (行), which means "go," "advance," "act," "action," or "practice." It is the same word used in the first sentence of the sutra, but here it has a different meaning—"mental formation" or "inclination."

The last *skandha* is *shi* (識), which means "know," "recognize," "acquainted with," or "distinguish."

Yi (亦), in the α and Xuanzang versions, means "also," "in the same manner," or "greatly."

Ru (如) means "as," "like," "just like." And *shi* (是) means "this." *Rushi* means "like this."

So this line reads, "(*Vedanā, saṃjñā, saṃskāra,* and *vijñāna*) (are) again also like this."

The Xuanzang version uses *yi fu* (亦復) instead of *yi.* Xuanzang added the word *fu* (also) not for extra meaning but for emphasis and tonal beauty.

ASPECTS OF FREEDOM

This part of the *Heart Sutra* explains how zeroness relates to the activities of life. Shariputra is again addressed at the beginning.

(10) ALL THINGS

SH, SA, SN: *iha Śāriputra sarva-dharmāḥ śūnyatā-lakṣaṇā,*
α: 舍利弗是諸法空相
αtl: *She li fu shi zhu fa kong xiang*
CX: 舍利子是諸法空相
CXtl: *She li zi shi zhu fa kong xiang*

CA: 此舍利子諸法空相

CAtl: *ci She li zhu fa kong xiang*

Ktl: *Sarija, si jebeop gongsang,*

Jtl: *Sharishi, ze shohō kūsō*

Vtl: *Xá Lợi Tử, thị chư pháp không tướng,*

EM: "Here, O Sāriputra, all things have the character of emptiness,

ES: O Sariputra, all things are here characterized with emptiness:

EC: 'Here, O Sariputra, all dharmas are marked with emptiness;

ETH: O Sariputra, boundlessness is the nature of all things.

In the phrase *sarva-dharmāḥ, sarva* is the stem of the adjective, meaning "all." *Dharmāḥ* is the nominative plural case of the masculine noun *dharma.*

Dharma has a wide range of meanings: "that which is established," "that which is held firmly," "statute," "law," "doctrine," "teaching," "truth," "reality," "precept," "duty," "justice," "virtue," "religion," "nature," "mark," "character," "thing," "phenomenon," or "object of mind." This word derived from the verb *dhṛ,* which means "hold," "carry," "maintain," "preserve," "employ," or "practice."

In this section of the *Hridaya,* "all dharmas" can be interpreted as "all things" or "all phenomena."

Lakṣanā, a masculine noun, means "mark," "sign," "symbol," "nature," "attribute," "quality," or "characteristic." Here it is in its plural form *lakṣaṇāḥ,* describing *dharmāḥ,* but its last sound has been dropped because of a phonetic change.

The line *sarva-dharmāḥ śūnyatā-lakṣaṇā* literally means "all dharmas are characterized by *śūnyatā.*"

In our translation, Joan and I have reversed the subject and predicate and have translated this line as: "Boundlessness is the nature of all things."

The Chinese α and Xuanzang versions read: *shi zhufa* (是諸法). *Shi,* as mentioned previously, means "be," "this," "correct," or "right."

Zhu means "various" or "all," making the following noun plural.

Fa is a translation for "dharma" or "dharmas." This phrase can therefore be interpreted as "all dharmas" or "all things." Other meanings of *fa* are: "law," "regulation," and "method."

Shi, however, has another usage. That is a conjunctive use, subtly meaning "therefore." I am inclined to read it in that way, as "(these) all dharmas"

is rather redundant. Besides, "all dharmas" has not been mentioned before.

Shi zhufa is followed by *kongxiang* (空相). *Kong* is the translation of *śūnyatā*. *Xiang* means "form," "appearance," "state," "symbol," or "characteristic." (The Japanese sound for *xiang* is *sō*. The Zen circle, *ensō* [圓相] , means "circle symbol.")

The Chinese line means: "All dharmas (have/having) the zeroness characteristic."

(11) NOT ARISE, NOT PERISH

> SH: *anutpannā aniruddhā amalāvimalā nona na paripūrṇāḥ.*
> SA, SN: *anutpannā aniruddhā, amalā avimalā, anūnā aparipūrṇāḥ*
> α, CX, CA: 不生不滅不垢不淨不增不減
> αtl, CXtl, CAtl: *bu sheng bu mie, bu gou bu jing, bu zeng bu jian.*
> Ktl: *bul saeng, bul myeol, bul gu, bu jeong, bu jeung, bul gam.*
> Jtl: *fu shō, fu metsu, fu ku, fu jō, fu zō, fu gen.*
> Vtl: *bất sanh bất diệt, bất cấu bất tịnh, bất tăng bất giảm.*
> EM: they have no beginning, no end, they are faultless and not faultless, they are not imperfect and not perfect.
> ES: they are not born, they are not annihilated; they are not tainted, they are not immaculate; they do not increase, they do not decrease.
> EC: they are not produced or stopped, not defiled or immaculate, not deficient or complete.
> ETH: It neither arises nor perishes, neither stains nor purifies, neither increases nor decreases.

The Sanskrit line, in each version, forms "six negations"—a list of paired adjectives in plurals.

Anutpannā is a compound of *an* and *utpannā*. The *an* is a prefix meaning "not" or "no," as in the Sanskrit *anātman* (no self) and the English word "anaerobe." *Utpannā* means "born" or "produced."

The *a* for *aniruddhā* means "not" or "no," as in the English word "asymmetry." *Niruddhā* is a compound of *nir* (not or no) plus *uddhā*. *Uddhā* is *ud* (up or upward) plus *hā. Hā,* in this case, is the stem form of the verb *hā* (start or spring forward). Thus, *niruddhā* means "not risen," and *aniruddhā* means "not not risen" or "not stopped."

Amalā is *a* plus *malā. Malā* is "dirty," "dusty," "filthy," or "deluded."

This word is related to the English "melano-," "melena," and "melancholy" through the Greek word *melās,* meaning "black."[38]

Avimalā is *a* plus *vimalā. Vi* in *vimalā* is a prefix, meaning "apart," "away," or "without."

These four words — *anutpannā, aniruddhā, amalā,* and *avimalā* — are all adjectives in masculine nominative plural case.

Nona (in the Horyu-ji version) should be *nonā,* which is *na* plus *ūnā.*[39] *Na* means "no." *Ūnā* means "wanting," "becoming fewer," "becoming less," or "becoming smaller." *Anūnā* (in the Amoghavajra and the Nepalese versions) is *an* plus *ūnā.* The *an* is, again, a prefix meaning "not" or "no."

Na paripūrṇāḥ (the Horyu-ji version) and *aparipūrṇāḥ* (the Amoghavajra and the Nepalese versions) are the masculine plural forms with an addition of *ḥ* at the end. Its citation form is *paripūṇa,* meaning "fill." The entire compound, in either case, is masculine plural in agreement with "all dharmas."

Bu (不), meaning "not," modifies both verbs and nouns. In this case, the three sets of phrases are presented as symmetric parallels. All the words that follow *bu* can be taken as verbs.

Sheng (生) means "be born," "appear," emerge," or "live." *Mie* (滅) means "destroy," "be destroyed," "disappear," or "die."

Gou (垢) is usually a noun, meaning "dirt" or "filth," but in this case it functions as a verb meaning "get dirty," or "to stain." *Jing* (淨) is usually an adjective or a noun meaning "pure" or "purity," but it can be a verb meaning "purify," "become pure," or "cleanse."

Zeng (增) means "increase," and *jian* (減) means "decrease."

(11X) BEYOND TIME

α: 是空法非過去非未來非現在

αtl: *shi kong fa fei guo qu fei wei lai fei xian zai*

The α version is the only text in the *Heart Sutra* that has this passage: "Thus, zeroness of dharmas (is) not the past, not the future, and not the present."

Guoqu (過去) means "past." *Weilai* (未來) means "future." And *xianzai* (現在) means "present," or "now."

The Sanskrit versions, the Chinese Xuanzang versions, and the Amoghavajra versions do not have these lines. It is interesting that these time elements were omitted from the *Heart Sutra* at one point.

(12) THEREFORE IN ZERONESS

SH, SA, SN: *tasmāc Chāriputra śūnyatāyāṃ*
α: 是故空法
αtl: *shi gu kong fa*
CX: 是故空中
CXtl: *shi gu kong zhong*
CA: 是故舍利子空中
CAtl: *shi gu She li zi kong zhong*
Ktl: *sigo gongjung,*
Jtl: *Zeko kūchū*
Vtl: *Thị cố không trung*
EM: Therefore, O Sāriputra, in this emptiness
ES: Therefore, O Sariputra, in emptiness
EC: Therefore, O Sariputra, in emptiness
ETH: Boundlessness is

The Sanskrit word *tasmāc* is a phonetically changed form of *tasmāt* as it precedes the sound *ś*. It is the ablative case of the pronoun *tad*—a counterpart of "that" in English. Thus, *tasmāc* and *tasmāt* mean "because of that" or "therefore."

In the Sanskrit versions Shariputra is addressed again. In this line, the first consonant of his name is spelled *ch* as a result of the phonetic change brought about by its following *tasmāt*.

Śūnyatāyāṃ is the locative singular case of *śūnyatā*. It means "in *śūnyatā*" or "in regard to *śūnyatā*."

The Chinese *shi* (是) means "this," and *gu* (故) means "reason" or "because."

Kong (空), again, is the translation of *śūnyatā*. *Fa* means "dharmas" or "things." *Zhong* (中) means "in," "inside," or "within."

So this phrase reads: "Therefore in zeroness..."

(13) NO..., NO...

SH: *na rūpaṃ na vedanā na saṃjñā na saṃskāra na vijñāni.*
SA: *na rūpaṃ na vedanā na saṃjñā na saṃskāra na vijñānam,*
SN: *na rūpaṃ na vedanā na saṃjñā na saṃskārāḥ na vijñānam.*
α, CX: 無色無受想行識
αtl, CXtl: *wu se, wu shou xiang xing shi.*

CA: 無色無受無想無行無識

CAtl: *wu se wu shou wu xiang wu xing wu shi*

Ktl: *mu saek, mu su sang haeng sik,*

Jtl: *mu shiki, mu ju sō gyō shiki,*

Vtl: *vô sắc, vô thụ tưởng hành thức.*

EM: there is no form, no perception, no name, no concept,
no knowledge.

ES: there is no form, no sensation, no thought, no confection,
no consciousness;

EC: there is no form, nor feeling, nor perception, nor impulse,
nor consciousness;

ETH: not limited by form, nor by feelings, perceptions, inclinations,
or discernment.

These Sanskrit lines indicate a negation of all five *skandhas* "within *śūnyatā.*"

In regard to the second through the fifth *skandhas,* the Nepalese version previously stated: *vedanā-saṃjñā-saṃskāra-vijñānam.* Now the fourth *skandha* is spelled *saṃskārāḥ.*[40]

It may sound odd, but negations are not always negative: there are positive negations. When you say, "There is no doubt about it" or "Nothing is better than that," you use a negative form to say something positive.

Negation can also be transcendental. When it is said in Buddhism, "Not one, not two," it is not a negation of both monistic and dualistic views but an expression of the dynamic interaction of the two perspectives. Negation can also represent freedom, just as if you say, "We don't need to do it."

Thus, this set of negations in the *Heart Sutra* can be seen as transcending and liberating negations. That is why Joan and I have translated this line as: "Boundlessness is not limited by form, nor by feelings, perceptions, inclinations, or discernment."

The Chinese w*u* (無) means "no," "there is no," or "have no." It often precedes a noun and negates the existence or possession of it.

So this line can be interpreted as: "(In zeroness) there is no *rūpa,* (and) there is no *vedanā,* no *saṃjñā,* no *saṃskārā,* and no *vijñāna.*"

(14) SIX SENSE ORGANS

SH, SA, SN: *na cakṣuḥ-śrotra-ghrāṇa-jihvā-kāya-manāṃsi,*

α, CX, CA: 無眼耳鼻舌身意

αtl, CXtl, CAtl: *wu yan er bi she shen yi.*

Ktl: *mu an i bi seol sin ui,*

Jtl: *mu gen ni bi zes shin [n]i,*

Vtl: *Vô nhãn nhĩ tỷ thiệt thân ý,*

EM: No eye, ear, nose, tongue, body, mind.

ES: no eye, ear, nose, tongue, body, mind;

EC: No eye, ear, nose, tongue, body, mind:

ETH: It is free of the eyes, ears, nose, tongue, body, and mind;

The Sanskrit *na,* meaning "not" or "there is (are) not," is followed by the long compound, representing six sense organs.

Cakṣuḥ is a phonetically changed form of *cakṣus,* which is the stem of the neuter noun *cakṣus,* meaning "eye." *Śrotra* is a neuter noun meaning "ear." *Ghrāṇa* is a neuter or masculine noun meaning "nose." *Jihvā* is a feminine noun meaning "tongue."

Kāya is a masculine noun meaning "body." In this case, it indicates "touching organs" such as skin and hair, corresponding to "touch" or "touchables" in the next line.

The stems of these five nouns are linked together.

Manāṃsi, the nominative plural form of the neuter noun *manas,* defines the grammatical function of this compound. *Manas* means "mind," "intellect," or "perception." *Manas* is related to the English word "mind" through the Latin word *mens,* meaning "mind."[41]

Yan (眼) means "eye." *Er* (耳) means "ear." *Bi* (鼻) is "nose." *She* (舌) is "tongue." And *shen* (身) is "body."

Yi (意), meaning "thought," "idea," "wish," and "will," can be compared with *xin* (心). While *xin* often refers to the fundamental mind or heart, *yi* may be seen as a functional aspect of the mind.

Thus, the Chinese line can be interpreted as: "(In zeroness) there are no eyes, ears, nose, tongue, body, (and) mind."

Translating this phrase as a set of singular nouns reading "No eye, no ear . . ." is also acceptable, as nouns are not restricted to either singular or plural in Chinese.

Chögyam Trungpa says:

> As your bodhisattva practice begins to evolve, you realize that ego-pain can be overcome and destroyed. The source of the destruction is compassion, a bodhisattva approach to yourself. When you practice the *Heart Sutra,* you chant that there is "no eye, no ear, no nose, no tongue, no body, and no mind." But that actually means "I love my eyes, I love my ears, I love my nose, I love my tongue, I love my body, and I love my mind. I feel sympathetic to all of that." When you develop that kind of sympathetic attitude, all that ego-pain actually begins to dissolve.[42]

(15) SIX SENSE OBJECTS

SH, SA: *na rūpa-śabda-gandha-rasa-spraṣṭavya dharmāḥ,*
SN: *na rūpa-śabda-gandha-rasa-spṛṣṭavya-dharmāḥ.*
α, CX, CA: 無色聲香味觸法
αtl, CXtl, CAtl: *wu se sheng xiang wei chu fa*
Ktl: *mu saek seong hyang mi chok beop,*
Jtl: *mu shiki shō kō mi soku hō,*
Vtl: *vô sắc thanh hương vị xúc pháp,*
EM: No form, sound, smell, taste, touch, objects.'
ES: no form, sound, odour, taste, touch, objects;
EC: No forms, sounds, smells, tastes, touchables or objects of mind;
ETH: free of sight, sound, smell, taste, touch, and any object
      of mind;

The grammatical structure of the Sanskrit line is identical to its previous sentence.

Rūpa, meaning "form" or "color," is the object of the function of eyes. *Śabda* is a masculine noun meaning "sound" "or "voice," which is the object of the function of ears. *Gandha* is a masculine noun meaning "smell" or "odor." *Rasa* is a masculine noun meaning "taste."

Spraṣṭavya is a neuter noun meaning "touch," "touchable," or "feeling," which is the object of the function of skin contact. It is related to the adjective *spṛṣta,* meaning "touched" or "felt with a hand." It is the gerundive of the verb *spṛś,* meaning "touch," "feel with the hand," or "lay the hand on." (In the Horyu-ji and the Amoghavajra versions, it is transliterated as *sparśtavya.*)

These five nouns are in the form of stems.

Dharmāḥ, meaning "dharmas" or "all phenomena," in this case, is the object of the function of mind. It is the nominative plural case of the masculine noun *dharma.*

Se (色) is, again, "color" or "form." *Sheng* (聲) means "voice" or "sound"; *xiang* (香), "smell" or "fragrance." *Wei* (味), "taste," and *chu* (觸), "touch." *Fa* (法) is, again, "dharma" or "thing."

This Chinese line can be interpreted as: "(In zeroness) there is no sight, sound, smell, taste, touchables, (or) dharmas."

(16) REALMS OF PERCEPTION

> SH, SA: *na cakṣur-dhātur yāvan na mano-vijñāna-dhātuḥ.*
>
> SN: *na cakṣur-dhātur yāvan na manovijñāna-dhātuḥ.*
>
> α, CX, CA: 無眼界乃至無意識界
>
> αtl, CXtl, CAtl: *wu yan jie nai zhi wu yi shi jie*
>
> Ktl: *mu angye, naeji mu uisikgye,*
>
> Jtl: *mu genkai, naishi mu ishikikai,*
>
> Vtl: *vô nhān giới nãi chí vô ý thức giới.*
>
> EM: 'There is no eye,' &c., till we come to 'there is no mind.' [What is left out here are the eighteen Dhatu or aggregates, viz. eye, form, vision; ear, sound, hearing; nose, odour, smelling; tongue, flavour, tasting; body, touch, feeling; mind, objects, thought.]
>
> ES: no Dhatu of vision, till we come to no Dhatsu of consciousness
>
> EC: No sight-organ element, and so forth, until we come to: No mind-consciousness element;
>
> ETH: free of sensory realms, including the realm of the mind.

The Sanskrit *dhātur* is a phonetically changed form of *dhātuḥ,* which is the nominative singular case of the masculine noun *dhātu. Dhātu,* here, means each of the eighteen realms of perception. These realms include the six sense organs; the six sense objects, mentioned above in the sutra; plus six corresponding consciousnesses — seeing, hearing, smelling, tasting, touching, and knowing.

Dhātu in general means "layer," "stratum," "constituent part," "ingredient," or "element." In Buddhism this word is also used to mean "principle," "category," "realm," or "world."

Yāvan is a phonetically changed form of the adverb *yāvat,* meaning "until," "through," or "up to (a certain point)."

The Chinese *jie* (界), a translation of *dhātu,* means "realm," "range," "bounds," or "world."

Naizhi (乃至) is a compound of *nai,* meaning "then," and *zhi,* meaning "through" or "arrive." This compound indicates the skipping of the contents in between. What is being skipped after the eye realm are the ear realm, the nose realm, the tongue realm, the body realm, and the mind realm; the form realm, the sound realm, the odor realm, the flavor realm, the touchable realm, and the object-of-mind realm; the seeing realm, the hearing realm, the smelling realm, the tasting realm, and the touching realm.

Yishijie (意識界) is the "consciousness realm," which is the last of the eighteen sensory realms. *Yi,* as discussed earlier, means "mind." *Shi* means "know." As a compound, *yishi* means "consciousness."

The six sense organs, the six sense objects, and the six corresponding consciousnesses are called the eighteen dusts or elements. In early Buddhist teachings, this classification of perception was presented to prove the nonsubstantiality of *atman,* or self. This list already appears at an early time of Buddhist teaching in the Pali text *Suttanipata.*

(17) TWELVEFOLD CAUSATION, PART I

SH: *na vidyā nāvidyā na vidyākṣayo nāvidyākṣayo.*
SA: *nāvidyā na vidyā nāvidyā-kṣayo nāvidyā-kṣayo*
SN: *na-avidyā na-avidyā kṣayo.*
α, CX: 無無明亦無無明盡
αtl, CXtl: *wu wu ming, yi wu wu ming jin,*
CA: 無明無明無明盡無明盡
CAtl: *wu ming wu ming wu ming jin wu ming jin*
Ktl: *mu mumyeong yeok mu mu myeong jin,*
Jtl: *mu mumyō yaku mu mu mumyō jin.*
Vtl: *Vô vô minh, diệc vô vô minh tận,*
EM: 'There is no knowledge, no ignorance, no destruction of
   knowledge, no destruction of ignorance,' &c., till we come to
ES: there is no knowledge, no ignorance, no extinction of
   knowledge, no extinction of ignorance
EC: There is no ignorance, no extinction of ignorance, and so forth
ETH: It is free of ignorance and the end of ignorance.

The Sanskrit *na* means "not."

Avidyā is *a* and *vidyā* combined. The *a* is a prefix, meaning "not," "contrary to," or "lack of." *Vidyā,* a feminine noun, means "knowledge," "science," "learning," or "philosophy." That makes *avidyā* mean "lack of knowledge," "ignorance," "delusion," or "afflicted mind." It is in the nominative singular case.

Avidyā is regarded as fundamental stupidity, the cause of all delusions. It is the first link of the twelvefold causation of dependent origination, one of the basic Buddhist doctrines.

Kṣayo is a phonetically changed form of *kṣayaḥ,* which is the nominative singular form of the masculine noun *kṣaya.* It means "exhaustion" or "destruction."

The Sanskrit line here in the Horyu-ji version consists of four negations: "(there is) no knowledge, no ignorance, no extinction of knowledge, (and) no extinction of ignorance." The first and the third of these negations, which are not part of the twelvefold causation, are not found in the Nepalese or Chinese versions.

The Chinese *wu* (無) is "no." *Ming* (明) means "brightness," "clarity," or "knowledge." *Wuming* is a technical Buddhist term meaning "ignorance," or "delusion."

Yi (亦) means "also." *Jin* (盡) is "exhaustion," "finishing," "ending," or "extinction."

If we compare Amoghavajra's line here in Sanskrit with his Chinese translation, the Chinese should be *wu wuming wu ming* (無無明無明), meaning "no ignorance and no knowledge." The next line may be translated as: "No end of ignorance. (Because of having) no end of ignorance . . ."

(18) TWELVEFOLD CAUSATION, PART 2

SH, SA: *yāvan na jarā-maraṇaṃ na jarā-maraṇa-kṣayo.*

SN: *yāvan na jarāmaraṇaṃ na jarāmaraṇakṣayo.*

α, CX: 乃至無老死亦無老死盡

αtl, CXtl: *nai zhi wu lao si, yi wu lao si jin*

CA: 乃至無老死無老死盡

CAtl: *nai zhi wu lao si wu lao si jin*

Ktl: *naeji mu nosa yeok mu nosajin,*

Jtl: *naishi mu rōshi yaku mu rōshi jin*

Vtl: *nāi chí vô lão tử, diệc vô lão tử tận.*

EM: 'there is no decay and death, no destruction of decay and death;

ES: till we come to there is no old age and death, no extinction of old age and death;

EC: until we come to: there is no decay and death, no extinction of decay and death

ETH: Boundlessness is free of old age and death, and free of the end of old age and death.

Yāvan is a phonetically changed form of the adjective *yāvat,* which means "just so much" or "that is to say."

Jarā, the nominative singular case of the feminine noun, is "decay," "old age," or "aging." This word is related to the English "geronto-," meaning "old age" or "aged one."[43]

Maraṇa, a neuter noun, means "dying" or "death." *Maraṇam* is in its nominative singular form. *Maraṇa* comes from the verb *mṛ* (die), which is related to the English words "mort," "mortal," and "immortal" through the Latin word *mors,* meaning "death."[44] The Sanskrit loan word "amrita," meaning "ambrosia," also comes from *mṛ.*

The first and the second Sanskrit lines combined here can be interpreted as: "(In zeroness) there is [no knowledge], no ignorance, [no extinction of knowledge] (and) no extinction of ignorance; there is no decay and death, and also no end of decay and death."

Naizhi (乃至), in this case, means "and then."

Lao (老) is "old age," and *si* (死) is "death."

Yi (亦) means "also." *Jin* (盡) is "exhaustion," "finishing," "ending," "extinction."

Thus, the Chinese line reads: "(In zeroness) (there is) no delusion, also (there is) no end of delusion." And then, "(there are) no old age and death; (there is) no end of old age and death."

Here the Chinese versions consist of two pairs of negations, keeping the symmetric integrity.

The twelve-link chain of causality, or the twelvefold dependent co-origination, is represented here by its first and last links. What is implied here is freedom from knowledge as well as from all the twelve links: "(In zeroness) there is no knowledge, no ignorance, no formative forces, no consciousness, no name-and-form, no sense-fields, no contact, no feeling, no craving, no grasping, no becoming, no birth, and no decay and death."

The twelvefold dependent co-origination is regarded as one of the earliest Buddhist teachings. It appears in many places in Pali scriptures.

(19) FOUR NOBLE TRUTHS

> SH, SA, SN: *na duḥkha-samudaya-nirodha-mārgā.*
> α, CX, CA: 無苦集滅道
> αtl, CXtl, CAtl: *wu ku ji mie dao*
> Ktl: *mu go jip myeol do,*
> Jtl: *mu ku shū metsu dō.*
> Vtl: *Vô khổ, tập, diệt, đạo.*
> EM: there are not [the four truths, viz. that there] is pain, origin of
>   pain, stoppage of pain, and the path to it.
> ES: there is no suffering, no accumulation, no annihilation, no path;
> EC: There is no suffering, no origination, no stopping, no path.
> ETH: It is free of suffering, arising, cessation, and path,

Duḥkha is the stem of a neuter noun. *Duḥkha* means "pain," "suffering," "unsatisfactoriness," "dis-ease," "difficulty," "sorrow," or "anguish." It is probably a form of the adjective *duḥ-stha.*[45] The prefix *duḥ* means "malicious" or "wicked." *Stha* means "standing."

This represents the first Noble Truth: Reality is permeated with suffering.

Samudaya is the stem of a masculine noun. It is a compound of *sam* and *udaya. Sam* means "together." *Udaya* means "going up," "rising," or "swelling up." Thus, *samudaya* means "coming together," "union," "junction," "combination," "collection," "assemblage," "multitude," "aggregation," "producing cause," or "clinging."

This represents the second Noble Truth: Clinging is the cause of suffering.

Nirodha is the stem of a masculine noun. This word comes from the verb *nirudh,* which is a compound of *ni* (down, back, into, or within) and *rudh* (obstruct, withhold, stop, or restrain). Thus, *nirudh* means "hold back," "stop," "hinder," "confine," "destroy," or "cessation."

This represents the third Noble Truth: The cessation of suffering is possible.

Mārgā is a phonetically changed form of *mārgāḥ,* the nominative plural case of the masculine noun *mārga.* It means "search," "tracing out," "hunting," "way," "passage," "channel," "means," "method," "direction," or "proper course." This nominative plural case defines the grammatical function of the four-word compound.

Mārga represents the last Noble Truth: There is a path that leads to the cessation of suffering.

This is the Eightfold Path, which consists of wholesome view, wholesome thought, wholesome speech, wholesome conduct, wholesome livelihood, wholesome effort, wholesome mindfulness, and wholesome meditation.

The Chinese *ku* (苦), as mentioned previously, means "bitter," "troublesome," "painful," "tormenting," or "suffering."

Ji (集) is read as "assembling," "collecting," "gathering," or "coming together," meaning one's assembling of actions and their effects by craving and ignorance. This "assembling" is regarded as the origin or cause of suffering.

Mie (滅), mentioned earlier, means "destruction," "removal," "elimination," or "abandonment," indicating cessation of suffering.

Dao (道) is "way" or "path."

The Four Noble Truths are explained in the Pali canon as the first teaching of Shakyamuni Buddha after he attained enlightenment. The *Heart Sutra* states here that in *śūnyatā* there are none of these aspects that are self-existing.

Red Pine says:

> The Buddha's sermon on the Four Truths has been called the First Turning of the Wheel, and the teaching of Prajnaparamita has been called the Second Turning of the Wheel. In the traditional formula of the First Truth, suffering is equated with the Five Skandhas, with which it is necessarily co-extensive. But since the Five Skandhas are empty of self-existence, suffering must also be empty of self-existence. But if suffering is empty of self-existence, then there is no self that suffers. Thus, in emptiness there is no suffering, no source of suffering, no relief from suffering, and no path leading to relief from suffering. This is the basis of Avalokiteshvara's interpretation of the Four Truths.[46]

From the Mahayana viewpoint of *shunyata,* or nondualistic interconnectedness, the *Heart Sutra* presents a condensed map of the entire Buddhist teaching that leads toward nirvana. An experience of enlightenment, nirvana is taught as an ultimate state of peace and freedom from attachment, suffering, and reincarnation.

(20) WISDOM AND ATTAINMENT

SH: *na jñānam, na prāptitvaṃ*

SA: [*jñā*] *na jñānaṃ, na prāptiś*

SN: *na jñānam, na prāptir na aprāptiḥ*

α, CX: 無智亦無得

αtl, CXtl: *wu zhi, yi wu de*

CA: 無智無得無證

CAtl: *wu zhi wu de wu zheng*

Ktl: *mu ji yeok mu deuk.*

Jtl: *Mu chi yaku mu toku*

Vtl: *Vô trí diệc vô đắc.*

EM: There is no knowledge, no obtaining of [Nirvāna].'

ES: there is no knowledge, no attainment, [and] no realization

EC: There is no cognition, no attainment and no non-attainment.

ETH: and free of wisdom and attainment.

This Sanskrit line represents a combination of negated nouns.

Jñānam is the nominative singular case of the neuter noun *jñāna*. *Jñāna* is derived from the verb *jñā*, meaning "know, "have knowledge," "perceive," or "understand." *Jñāna* means "cognition," "gnosis," or "wisdom," indicating higher wisdom that is cultivated through meditation.

Prāptitvaṃ is a phonetically changed form of *prāptitvam*, which is *prāpti* plus *tvam*. *Prāpti*, which is the feminine noun form of the verb *prāp*, consists of *pra* and *āp*. *Pra* is a prefix meaning "before," "forward," or "forth." The verbal root *āp* means "obtain" or "take possession." Thus, *prāp* means "reaching," "arrival," "attaining," "obtaining," or "acquisition." *Āp* is related to the English words "apt" and "aptitude" through the Latin *apere*, meaning "join" and "tie to."[47] *Tvam* is the nominative singular case of the suffix *tva*, which means "-ness" or "state of." So *prāptitvam* means "attainment." *Prāptir* is a phonetically changed form of *prāptiḥ*, which is the nominative singular case of *prāpti*. Its base noun is the feminine *prāpti*. *Aprāptiḥ* is *a* (no) plus *prāptiḥ*. *Prāptiś* is a phonetically changed form of *prāptir* due to following the consonant *ch*.

This Sanskrit line in the Horyu-ji and Amoghavajra versions can be interpreted: "(In zeroness there is) no wisdom, also no attainment."

The Nepalese version reads: "(In zeroness there is) no wisdom, also no non-attainment."

The Chinese *wu* (無) means "no."

Zhi (智), meaning "wisdom" or "wisdom of awakening," is sometimes used as a translation of *prajñā,* but in this case it corresponds to another Sanskrit word, *jñāna* (knowledge or understanding).

De (得) can be a verb, meaning "obtain," "acquire," or "attain." It can also function as a noun, meaning "obtaining" or "attaining."

This line in the α and Xuanzang versions reads: "(There is) no wisdom; (there is) no attainment."

Amoghavajra added another phrase, *wu zheng* (無證). *Zheng* means "realization," "witness," or "authentication."

SERENITY AND AWAKENING

Next, the *Heart Sutra* discusses the illusion of attainment in meditation practice.

(21) FREE OF ATTAINMENT

> SH: *tasmāc*
> SA: *ca tasmān nāprāpti-tvā*
> SN: *tasmāc Chāriputra aprāptitvād*
> α, CX, CA: 以無所得故
> αtl, CXtl, CAtl: *yi wu suo de gu*
> Ktl: *i mu sodeuk go,*
> Jtl: *i mu shotok ko,*
> Vtl: *Dī vô sở đắc cố,*
> ES: because there is no attainment.
> EC: Therefore, O Sariputra, it is because of his non-attainmentness
> ETH: Being free of attainment

Tasmāc and *tasmān* are phonetically changed forms of *tasmāt,* meaning "therefore."

Ca means "and." *Na* means "no."

Prāpti-tvā, or *prāptitvā,* is a phonetically changed form of *prāptitvād.*

Aprāptitvād is a compound of *aprāpti* and *tvād. Aprāpti* is a compound of *a* (no) and the feminine noun *prāpti* (attainment or gain). *Prāpti* comes from the verb *prāp,* which consists of *pra* (before or forward) and *āp* (reach or obtain).

Tvād is a phonetically changed form of *tvāt,* which is the ablative case of the suffix *tva.* It inflects as an "*a*-ending" neuter noun. *Tva* means "-ness" or "state of." The ablative case changes it to "because of" or "relying on."

In Sanskrit, this is just the start of a longer sentence ending with *cittā-varaṇaḥ* (segment 24).

The Nepalese version addresses Shariputra again.

The Chinese *yi* (以) means "with," "by," "because," or "because of." *Gu* (故), which has appeared previously, means "reason" or "because." The combination of these similar words is in a way redundant, but it creates a strong sound.

Suo (所) means "place" but also makes the following verb passive. *De* (得) means "attain" or "acquire." So *suode* means "what is attained."

This line in Chinese can be interpreted as: "Because nothing is attained" or "Because there is nothing to be attained."

The Japanese *shotokko* is a phonetic form of *shotoku* (所得) followed by *ko* (故).

(22) BODHISATTVAS

> SH, SN: *bodhisattvasya*
> SA: *bodhisattvasyām*
> α: 菩薩
> αtl: *pu sa*
> CX, CA: 菩提薩埵
> CXtl, CAtl: *pu ti sa duo*
> Ktl: *borisalta*
> Jtl: *bodaisatta*
> Vtl: *bồ đê tát đõa,*
> EM: the Bodhisattva dwells
> ES: In the mind of the Bodhisattva
> EC: that a Bodhisattva,
> ETH: those who help all to awaken

Bodhisattvasya is a genitive singular form of the masculine noun *bodhi-sattva,* which means "of a bodhisattva" or "for a bodhisattva." The grammatical form of *bodhisattvasyām* is questionable.

The phrase up to this point can be translated as: "Relying on the attainment of a bodhisattva . . ."

(23) ABIDING IN *PRAJNA PARAMITA*

SH, SN: *prajñāpāramitām āśritya*

SA: *prajñā-pāramitām āśritya*

α: 依般若波羅蜜故

αtl: *yi bo re bo luo mi gu*

CX: 依般若波羅蜜多故

CXtl: *yi bo re bo luo mi duo gu*

CA: 般若波羅蜜多依於住

CAtl: *bo re bo luo mi duo yi yu zhu*

Ktl: *ui banya baramilda go,*

Jtl: *e hannya haramitta ko.*

Vtl: *y Bát nhã Ba la mật da cố,*

EM: A man who has approached the Pra*gñ*āpāramitā of

ES: who dwells depending on the Prajnaparamita

EC: through having relied on the perfection of wisdom,

ETH: abide in the realization of wisdom beyond wisdom

Prajñāpāramitām is the accusative case of *prajñāpāramitā,* making it the object of *āśritya.*

Āśritya is the indeclinable form, or gerund, of the verb *āśri.* A compound of *ā* (near to, or toward) and *śri* (depend on or abide in), *āśri* means "join," "adhere," "rest on," or "depend on."

The Chinese *yi* (依) here is different from the several versions of *yi* that appeared before. Chinese has a number of ideographs represented by one romanized spelling. For example, *A Chinese-English Dictionary* by Herbert A. Giles contains fifty-five ideographs that are spelled *yi.* Some of them are homonyms and others are not, as they can have different tones. *Yi* in this case is a verb meaning "depend on," "trust to," "be near to," or "obey." *Gu* (故) means "because" or "therefore."

Bore boluomiduo (般若波羅蜜多) is a transliteration of *prajñā-pāramitā.*

So this Chinese line in the α and Xuanzang versions reads: "(Because bodhisattvas) depend on *prajñāpāramitā . . .*"

Amoghavajra has *yi yu zhu* (依於住). *Yi* means "depend on." *Yu* means "in," "at," or "by." *Zhu* means "live" or "abide," corresponding with the Sanskrit *āśritya.*

(24) MIND HAS NO HINDRANCE

SH: *viharaty a-cittāvaraṇaḥ. cittāvaraṇa*
SA, SN: *viharaty acittāvaraṇaḥ. cittāvaraṇa-*
α, CX: 心無罣礙無罣礙故
αtl, CXtl: *xin wu gua ai. wu gua ai gu*
CA: 心無罣礙心無罣礙
CAtl: *xin wu gua ai xin wu gua ai*
Ktl: *sim mu gaae. Mu gaae go,*
Jtl: *shin mu keige. Mu kei ge ko,*
Vtl: *tâm vô quái ngại, vô quái ngại cố,*
EM: enveloped in consciousness. But when the envelopment of
   consciousness has been annihilated,
ES: there are no obstacles; and because there are no obstacles in
   his mind
EC: dwells without thought-coverings. In the absence of
   thought-coverings
ETH: and live with an unhindered mind. Without hindrance,

Viharaty is a phonetically changed form of *viharati*. *Viharati* is the third person singular active present tense of the verb *vihṛ*, which means "take away," "remove," "separate," "be absent," "spend time," or "retreat." *Vihṛ* is *vi* (apart) plus *hṛ* (carry, remove, or turn away).

Vihṛ is related to the loan word in English "vihara," derived from the Sanskrit noun *vihāra*, meaning "monastery" or "temple."

Acittāvaraṇaḥ can be broken up as *a, citta,* and *āvaraṇaḥ*. The *a* means "no" or "without." *Citta,* a neuter noun, means "thinking," "reflecting," "imagining," "intention," "wish," "heart," or "mind." It comes from the verb *cit,* meaning "perceive," "observe," "take notice of," "know," or "understand." *Acitta,* in this case, functions as the first member of the compound.

Āvaraṇaḥ is the nominative singular case of the neuter noun *āvaraṇa*. It takes a masculine ending, modifying the *bodhisattva*. The second occurrence of *āvaraṇa* is joined to *-nāstitvād* (segment 25), forming a compound. *Āvaraṇa* means "covering," "hiding," and "concealing." It comes from the verb *āvṛ,* meaning "hide," "conceal," or "enclose." This verb can be traced down to the verb *vṛ,* which means "stop," "restrain," "hinder," or "withhold." *Acittāvaraṇa* can be translated as "no thought-covering."

This Sanskrit line (segments 21 to 24) can be literally translated as: "Therefore, relying on the *prajñāpāramitā* of a bodhisattva, (the bodhisattva) abides in seclusion with no thought enclosure. (This) no-thought-enclosure..."

Xin (心) is "mind" or "heart." *Gua'ai* (罣礙) is a compound of similar verbs, *gua* and *ai*. *Gua* means "hinder," "be hindered," "be anxious," or "fall into a snare." *Ai* means "obstruct," "hinder," "stop progress," or "be blocked."

Thus, this line in Chinese reads: "(A bodhisattva depends upon *prajñā-pāramitā*, therefore the bodhisattva's mind) is not hindered. Because the mind is not hindered..."

Amoghavajra simply repeats, "(the bodhisattva's) mind is not hindered. (As) the mind is not hindered..."

(25) NO FEAR

> SH, SA, SN: *nāstitvād atrasto*
> α, CX, CA: 無有恐怖
> αtl, CXtl, CAtl: *wu you kong bu*
> Ktl: *mu yu gongpo,*
> Jtl: *mu u kufu*
> Vtl: *vô hữu khủng bố,*
> EM: then he becomes free of all fear,
> ES: he has no fear
> EC: he has not been made to tremble
> ETH: the mind has no fear.

Nāstitvād is *na* (no), plus *asti,* plus *tvād,* which is a phonetically changed form of *tvāt*. *Asti* is the third person present indicative active form of the verb *as,* which means "be," "exist," take place," or "become." *Tvāt,* as discussed previously, is the ablative form of the suffix *tva* (-ness, or state of). *Nāstitvād,* therefore, means "because of the nonexistence."

Cittāvaraṇa-nāstitvād (in segments 24 and 25) can be seen as a four-word compound—*citta-āvaraṇa-na-astitvād* (meaning, "because of non-existence of mind covering").

Atrasto is *a* plus *trasto,* which is a phonetically changed form of *trastaḥ,* as a result of being followed by the sound *vi. Trastaḥ* is the nominative singular masculine case of the past passive participle of the verb *tras. Tras* means "tremble," "frighten," or "scare." Its masculine noun form is *trāsa.*

Trastaḥ means "frightened." *Atrastaḥ* means "not frightened" or "fearless." *Trāsa* is related to the English words "terror" and "terrible" through the Latin word *terrere,* meaning "frighten."[48]

This line can be interpreted thus: "(a bodhisattva is) fearless because of the nonexistence of thought enclosure."

The Chinese *you* (有), as the antonym of *wu* (無) or "no," means "have," "exist," "existence," or "there be."

Kongbu (恐怖) is a compound of similar nouns. *Kong* means "fear," "fearfulness," or "apprehension." *Bu* means "fear," "fright," "surprise," or "dread."

(26) FREEDOM FROM CONFUSION

> SH, SA: *viparyāsātikrāntaḥ*
> SN: *viparyāsa-atikrānto*
> α: 離一切顛倒夢想苦惱
> αtl: *li yi qie dian dao meng xiang ku nao*
> CX: 遠離 [一切] 顛倒夢想
> CXtl: *yuan li [yi qie] dian dao meng xiang*
> CA: 顛倒遠離
> CAtl: *dian dao yuan li*
> Ktl: *wonri jeondo mongsang,*
> Jtl: *onri [issai] tendō musō*
> Vtl: *viễn ly diên đảo mộng tưởng,*
> EM: beyond the reach of change,
> ES: and, going beyond the perverted views
> EC: he has overcome what can upset
> ETH: Free from confusion, those who lead all to liberation

Viparyāsa, a masculine noun, is derived from a compound of *vi* (apart, or to and fro), *pary* (a form of *pari,* meaning "around"), and *ās.* This verb *ās* means "throw," "cast," "shoot at," or "frighten away." Thus, *viparyāsa,* which appears here in its stem form, means "overturning," "overthrow," "upsetting," "confusion," "perverted views," or simply "change" or "delusion."

Atikrāntaḥ is the masculine nominative singular case of the adjective *atikrānta. Atikrānto* in the Nepalese version is a phonetically changed form of *atikrāntaḥ. Atikrānta* is related to the verb *atikram.* A compound of *ati* (over or beyond) and *kram* (go over, go across, or advance), *atikram* means "walk over," "pass," "cross," "surpass," or "transgress." *Atikrānta* means "having passed," "having transgressed," "having passed beyond." Its nominative case determines the grammatical form of the compound *viparyāsa-atikrānta*.

Thus, this line means "(a bodhisattva) is confusion-free . . ."

The Chinese *yuan* (遠) and *li* (離) can be interpreted as a compound. *Yuan* means "far," which was added by Xuanzang. *Li* means "be apart," "be distant." So *yuanli* is "far apart." These two words, however, can also be interpreted as an adverb and a verb.

Yiqie (一切, *issai* in Japanese), as discussed previously, means "all." This word is not in the original Xuanzang version but was added later in Japan, perhaps having been retrieved from the α version.[49] It is always found in the currently chanted Japanese version.

Diandao (顛倒) is a compound of *dian* and *dao*. *Dian* means "upset," "turn over," or "fall." *Dao* means "fall over," "lie down," or "knock down." In this way, *diandao* can be interpreted as a noun meaning "confusion" or as a verb participle meaning "confused." (*Dao* here is not the *dao* as in Daoism; they are different words represented by distinct ideographs.)

Amoghavajra simply swapped *yuanli diandao* into *diandao yuanli*.

The Japanese sound *tendō* is a euphonic form of *ten* (顛) and *tō* (倒).

Mengxiang (夢想) is, again, a compound. *Meng* is "dream." *Xiang,* the same word as in the third *skandha,* means "thought." Thus, *mengxiang* can be translated as "illusion" or "delusion."

After this word, the α version lists *kunao* (苦惱), meaning "pain and distress" or "suffering and anguish." However, neither the Xuanzang version nor the Amoghavajra version includes this word.

(27) NIRVANA

SH: *niṣṭhā nirvāṇaḥ.*

SA: *niṣṭhānirvāṇam.*

SN: *niṣṭhā-nirvāṇa-prāptaḥ.*

α, CX, CA: 究竟涅槃

αtl, CXtl, CAtl: *jiu jing nie pan*

Ktl: *gugyeong yeolban*

Jtl: *kukyō nehan*

Vtl: *cứu cánh Niết bàn*

EM: enjoying final Nirvāna.

ES: he reaches final Nirvana
EC: and in the end he attains to Nirvana
ETH: those who lead all to liberation embody profound serenity

The feminine noun *niṣṭhā* is the same word in a different part of speech as the verb *niṣṭhā*. It is a compound of *ni* (down, in, into, or within) and *sthā* (stand).

Sthā is related to the English verb "stand" through the Old English word *standan,* meaning "stand." *Sthā* is also related to "stage," "stay," "stanza," "constant," "instant," and "rest" through the Latin word *stāre,* meaning "to stand."[50]

Niṣṭhā means "being situated on," "grounded on," or "devoted to." *Niṣṭhā,* in this case, is the beginning word of the compound.

Nirvāṇaḥ in the Horyu-ji version is the nominative singular case of the neuter noun *nirvāṇat. Nirvāṇam* in the Amoghavajra version is also the nominative case. *Nirvāṇa* in the Nepalese version is a part of the compound, followed by *bodhisattva.*

Nir is an alternative for the prefix *nis,* meaning "out" or "away." Coming from the verb *vā* (blow), *vāṇa* means "blowing." *Nirvāṇa* is a state where the fire of craving is blown out. *Vā* is related to the English words "vent" and "ventilate" through Latin *ventus,* meaning "wind," and to the English word "weather" through Germanic *vedram,* meaning "wind" or "weather."[51]

Prāptaḥ is the nominative singular masculine case of the adjective *prāpta,* which is *pra* plus *āpta. Pra* is a prefix, meaning "before" or "forward," and *āpta* is a past participle, meaning "reached" or "obtained." *Āpta* is derived from the verbal root *āp,* meaning "reach" or "obtain."

Thus, the Sanskrit line reads: "(a bodhisattvas is) nirvana abiding."

Jiujing (究竟) is another compound. You can see how the Chinese translators liked to use two-ideograph compounds. This was a common way to create Buddhist technical terms. *Jiu* means "examine," "investigate," or "reach an extreme." *Jing* means "exhaust," "end," or "realm." Thus, *jiujing* can be interpreted as "fully experience" or "reach all the way."

Niepan (涅槃) is the transliteration of the Sanskrit word *nirvāṇa.*

This Chinese line can be read thus: "(Bodhisattvas) get all the way to nirvana."

. . .

In the early Buddhist tradition, *nirvana* was taught to be the extinction of craving, as in the third of the Four Noble Truths. As the highest state achieved by practitioners, *nirvana* is seen as a release from *samsara* — the chain of birth, death, and rebirth. It is a state of peace, bliss, and liberation — freedom from attachment or clinging. To experience this state was the main objective of the Buddha's disciples, and those who had attained it were called *arhats*.

On the other hand, the Mahayana tradition views *nirvana* as not separate from *samsara*. Dogen may be the most radical of these Mahayana thinkers on this topic: as I suggested earlier, he says one can experience *nirvana* and enlightenment in each moment of practice.

(28) AWAKENED ONES

> SH: *tryadhvavyavasthitāḥ sarva-buddhāḥ*
> SA: *tryadhva-vyavasthitāḥ sarva-buddhāḥ*
> SN: *tryadhva vyavasthitāḥ sarva-buddhāḥ*
> α, CX: 三世諸佛
> αtl, CXtl: *san shi zhu fo*
> CA: 三世所住諸佛
> CAtl: san shi suo zhu zhu fo
> Ktl: *samse jebul*
> Jtl: *Sanze shobutsu*
> Vtl: *tam thế chư Phật,*
> EM: All Buddhas of the past, present, and future,
> ES: All the Buddhas of the past, present, and future
> EC: All those who appear as Buddhas in the three periods of time
> ETH: All those in the past, present, and future,

The numeral *try* is a phonetically changed form of *tri,* meaning "three." *Tri* is related to the English "three," "tri-," "trio," and "triple" through the Latin *tres* or *tri-,* both meaning "three."[52]

Adhva is the stem of the masculine noun *adhvan,* used in a compound. *Adhvan* means "road," "way," "course," "time," or "period." The three periods are past, present, and future.

Vyavasthitāḥ is the masculine plural form of the adjective *vyavasthita.*

Vyavasthita means "placed in," "being in," "taking part with," or "staying." This word is the past passive participle of the verb *vyavasthā. Vy,* a phonetically changed form of *vi,* in this case means "to and fro." *Ava* means "off," "away," or "down." *Sthā,* as mentioned before, means "stand." *Avasthā* means "stand" or "remain."

Sarva, again, means "all."

Buddhāḥ is the nominative plural case of the masculine noun *buddha.* It is the past passive participle of the verb *budh. Budh* means "wake," "be awake," "become aware," or "understand." *Buddha,* as an adjective, thus means "awakened," "woken up," or "enlightened." *Buddha* as a noun means "awakened one" or "enlightened one."

This phrase may be translated word by word: "All buddhas abiding in the three periods..."

The Chinese *sanshi* (三世) is a compound: *san,* meaning "three," and *si,* meaning "world(s)" — that is, past, present, and future.

Amoghavajra added the compound *suo zhu* (所住). *Suo* in this case means "that which" or "one(s) who." *Zhu,* as discussed previously, means "abide."

Zhu (諸) is "all," or "various," as in "all dharmas," previously mentioned. *Fo* (佛) means "Buddha," as in a particular Buddhist deity or Shakyamuni Buddha, as well as "a buddha," meaning "an awakened person" or "buddhas."

(29) DEPENDING ON

> SH, SN: *prajñāpāramitām-āśritya-*
> SA: *prajñā-pāramitām āśritya-*
> α: 依般若波羅蜜故
> αtl: *yi bo re bo luo mi gu*
> CX, CA: 依般若波羅蜜多故
> CXtl, CAtl: *yi bo re bo luo mi duo gu*
> Ktl: *ui banya baramilda go*
> Jtl: *e hannya haramitta ko,*
> Vtl: *y Bát nhā Ba la mật đa cố,*
> EM: after approaching the Pragñāpāramitā,
> ES: depending on the Prajnaparamita,
> EC: because they have relied on the perfection of wisdom
> ETH: who realize wisdom beyond wisdom,

Prajñāpāramitām is the accusative singular case of the feminine noun *prajñāpāramitā*.

Āśritya is the gerund form of the verb *āśri* (join, rest on, or depend on). This word is the prefix *ā* (near or toward) plus the verb *śri* (lean on, rest on, depending on, or abide in). The gerund makes it "abiding in" or "relying upon."

The Sanskrit line continues: "(All buddhas abiding in the three periods) depending on *prajñāpāramitā . . .*"

Yi (依) means "depending on." *Bore boluomiduo* is, again, the Chinese transliteration of *prajñāpāramitā*. *Gu* (故) means "therefore."

(30) ENLIGHTENMENT

SH: *anuttarāṃ samyaksambodhiṃ abhisaṃbuddhāḥ.*
SA: *anuttarāṃ samyak-[sam]bodhim abhisambuddhāḥ.*
SN: *anuttarāṃ samyaksambodhim abhisambuddhāḥ.*
α, CX: 得阿耨多羅三藐三菩提
αtl, CXtl: *de a nou duo luo san miao san pu ti.*
CA: 得無上等正覺
CAtl: *de wu shang deng zheng jue*
Ktl: *deuk anyok dara sammyak sambori.*
Jtl: *toku anoku tara sammyaku sambodai.*
Vtl: *đắc A nậu da la Tam miệu Tam bồ đê.*
EM: have awoke to the highest perfect knowledge.'
ES: attain to the highest perfect enlightenment.
EC: fully awake to the utmost, right and perfect enlightenment
ETH: manifest unsurpassable and thorough awakening.

Anuttarāṃ is a phonetically changed form of *anuttarām*. It is the feminine accusative singular case of the adjective *anuttara,* which is a compound of *an* and the adjective *uttara.* The *an* is a prefix, meaning "not," as in the above-mentioned word *anutpannā* (not born).

Uttara means "higher," "better." Thus, *anuttarā* means "not excelled (by others)" or "supreme." *Uttara* is related to the English words "utter" and "utmost" through the Old English word *ūtera,* meaning "complete."[53]

Samyak is a form used in a compound of the adjective *samyañc,* which means "true," "correct," "accurate," or "right." *Sambodhim* is the accusative case of *sambodhi,* in this case a feminine noun modified by *anuttarām.*

Sam, as mentioned previously, is a prefix meaning "all," "together," or "thorough." Coming from the verb *budh,* meaning "wake," "be awake," "become aware," or "understand," the noun *bodhi,* used either in feminine or masculine form, means "awakening," "perfect wisdom," "illuminated intellect," or "enlightenment."

Abhisambuddhāḥ is the masculine nominative plural form of the adjective *abhisambuddha,* which can also be divided as *abhi-sam-buddha.* *Abhi* is a prefix meaning "to," "toward," "into," "over," or "upon." *Sam,* again, is a prefix meaning "all," "together," or "thorough." *Abhisambuddha* means "thoroughly awaken."

Thus, the Sanskrit line reads: "(All buddhas abiding in the three worlds depending on *prajñāpāramitā*) are fully awakened (to) unequaled, true enlightenment."

De (得) means "attain."

Anouduoluo (阿耨多羅) *sanmao* (三藐) *sanputi* (三菩提) is the Chinese transliteration of its Sanskrit counterpart, *anuttarāṃ samyaksambodhi.*

For this compound, Amoghavajra uses a standard Chinese translation, *wu shang deng zheng jue* (無上等正覺). *Wu* means "no," *shang* means "high" or "higher," *deng* means "equal," *zheng* means "correct" or "right," and *jue* means "awakening" or "enlightenment."

This Chinese sentence reads: "(All buddhas in the three worlds depend on *prajñāpāramitā,* therefore they) attain *anuttarāṃ samyak sambodhi.*"

MANTRA AS REALIZATION OF
WISDOM BEYOND WISDOM

In this section, the *Heart Sutra* challenges us with a puzzling equation: *prajñāpāramitā* is itself the mantra. What does it mean? The Fourteenth Dalai Lama says:

> The perfection of wisdom itself, *prajnaparamita,* is here referred to as a "mantra." The etymological meaning of *mantra* is "to protect the mind." Thus, through attaining the perfection of wisdom, one's mind will be completely protected against erroneous beliefs, against the mental afflictions that arise from such beliefs, and against the suffering produced by the mental afflictions.[54]

(31) THEREFORE KNOW

SH: *tasmāj jñātavyam prajñāpāramitā*
SA: *tasmāj jñā-tavyaṃ prajñāpāramitā*
SN: *tasmāj jñātavyam: prajñāpāramitā*
α: 故知般若波羅蜜
αtl: *gu zhi bo re bo luo mi*
CX: 故知般若波羅蜜多
CXtl: *gu zhi bo re bo luo mi duo*
CA: 是故應知般若波羅蜜多
CAtl: *shi gu ying zhi bo re bo luo mi duo*
Ktl: *go ji banya baramilda*
Jtl: *ko chi hannya haramitta*
Vtl: *Cố tri Bát nhā Ba la mật đa,*
EM: 'Therefore one ought to know the great verse of
     Prag*ñ*āpāramitā,
ES: Therefore, one ought to know that the Prajnaparamita is
EC: Therefore one should know the prajñāpāramitā as
ETH: Know that realizing wisdom beyond wisdom

Tasmāj is a phonetically changed form of *tasmāt*. This is the second occurrence of the word *tasmāt,* which means "therefore."

Jñātavyam is the gerundive of the verb *jñā. Jñā,* as discussed previously, means "know," "perceive," "discover," "clarify" or "understand."

So *jñātavyam* may be interpreted as: "(This is) to be known" or "(This) should be known."

Gu (故), as discussed previously, means "therefore."

Zhi (知) means "know," "knowledge." The traditional interpretation in this case is to treat it as a verb in its imperative form. *Bore boluomiduo* is, again, a transliteration of *prajñāpāramitā*.

Shi gu (是故) in the Amoghavajra version means "thus," "therefore," or "because of this."

Ying in *ying zhi* (應知) makes the verb following the term imperative.

(32) MANTRA

SH, SA, SN: *mahā-mantro*
CX: 是大神咒
CXtl: *shi da shen zhou*

CA: 大呪
CAtl: *da zhou*
Ktl: *si daesin ju,*
Jtl: *ze daijin shu,*
Vtl: *thị đại thần chú,*
ES: is the great Mantram
EC: the great spell,
ETH: is no other than this wondrous mantra,

Mahā, as in the title of the sutra, means "great."

Mantro is a phonetically changed form of *mantraḥ.* It is a nominative singular case of the masculine noun *mantra,* meaning "instrument of thought," "sacred speech," "prayer," "incantation," "magical formula," "charm," or "spell."

The Sanskrit line reads: "(This should be known: *prajñāpāramitā* is) a great mantra..."

Shi (是) means "be," "this," "this is," "be no other than," "correct," or "right."

Da (大) means "large," "big," "great."

Shen (神) has a wide range of meanings: "spirit," "god," "spiritual," "inscrutable," "divine," "supernatural," "mind," "energy," "mysterious," or "mystical."

Zhou (咒 or 呪) means "swear an oath," "spell," "curse," or "incantation." This is a translation of the Sanskrit word *mantra.*

This line is not found in the α version.

Mantra comes from the verb *man,* which means "think," "imagine," "honor," or "set one's mind on." *Man* is in the same family as the noun *manas,* which, as shown before, means "mind," "intellect," or "perception."

Mantra is also related to the verb *mantṛ,* meaning "consider," "consult," "recite," "consecrate," and "mutter." As a noun of the same form, it means "thinker" or "advisor."

Mantṛ is a source of the English word "mentor" through the Latin words *mens* (mind) and *mentiō* (remembrance).[55]

In the ancient Vedic tradition, which preceded Hinduism, *mantra* meant "sacred utterance," "encompassing speech, text, prayer, or song of praise." In Hinduism, mystical verses are believed to be a sonic form of divinity. Over time, the practice of reciting magical sonic formulas for gaining power over objects or problems became central.

An early sutra says that the Buddha first prohibited the incantation of such verses but later permitted their use as a remedy for pain or disease. Prayer for healing is a common human need, found in all religions. Thus, the prototantric elements of magical chanting were practiced for many centuries before the *Heart Sutra* was formed.

There is a word similar in meaning to *mantra*, used in Buddhism. That is *dhāraṇī*, a feminine noun. It is related to the verb *dhṛ*, meaning "carry," "maintain," "spell," or "practice." It is sometimes translated in Chinese as *zongchi* (總持), meaning "holding all."

In the 25,000-line version of the *Prajna Paramita* text, there are some descriptions of chanting *dharani* before it was developed as a practice of magic. For example, the Buddha says:

> And this perfection of wisdom is the entrance to all the syllables and the door to the dharanis in which the Bodhisattva, the great being, should be trained. The Bodhisattvas, the great beings, who bear in mind these dharanis will come face to face with all the flashes of insight and all analytical knowledges. I have taught this deep perfection of wisdom as the inexhaustible storehouse of the true Dharma of the past, future, and present Buddhas and Lords. Therefore, then, Ananda, I solemnly declare to you, I make known to you, that one who will take up this deep perfection of wisdom, bear it in mind, recite and study it, he will bear in mind the enlightenment of the past, future, and present Buddhas and Lords. I have taught this perfection of wisdom as a dharani. When you bear in mind those dharanis of the perfection of wisdom, you bear all dharmas in mind.[56]

On the other hand, *dharani* has been associated with magic and exorcism, in particular, since the development of Esoteric Buddhism. *Dharani* often indicates longer mystical verses than *mantra*. *Mantra* is sometimes seen as the essence of *dharani*. These two words, however, can be used interchangeably. Chanting *mantra* or *dharani* goes beyond ordinary language and thus keeps one from dualistic thinking. In this way, it is regarded as a method of concentration and remembrance and is often used for gaining mystical power in meditation.

This line of the *Heart Sutra* suggests that *prajna paramita* is no other than *dharani,* or "the holder of all." It means that *prajna paramita,* as the totality of Buddhist practice, is concentrated in its short mantra. In fact, the *Heart Sutra* is radical enough to proclaim that the totality of Buddhist practice *is* this mantra.

Here is D. T. Suzuki's explanation from his Zen point of view:

> Utterly exhausted intellectually and emotionally, he (Avalokiteshvara) made a final leap. The last tie which held him to the world of relativity and "self-power" completely snapped. He found himself on the other shore. Overwhelmed with his feelings, he could only keep uttering the "*Gate!*" The "*Gate!*" then became his Mantram, the "*Gate!*" became the Mantram of the Prajnaparamita. With this ejaculation everything was cleared up, and Avalokitesvara's discipline in the Prajna was brought to a finish.[57]

The recitation of the *Heart Sutra* is done in two ways: the entire sutra and the mantra by itself. The latter is less intellectual and perhaps more intense, as a practice of wholehearted recitation. In fact, the chanting of the *Heart Sutra* mantra has been done as a "single practice."

A "single practice" means to select and focus on one type of practice — chanting a buddha's name, chanting the title of a sutra, or engaging in Zen meditation as the entire experience of Buddhism. The chanting of the mantra, in this regard, has been one of the oldest continuous single practices in Buddhism. The accumulated chanting completed in the past provides practitioners with a tool that inspires, guards, and heals with utmost intensity.

(33) VIDYA

SH, SA: *mahā-vidyā-mantraḥ*
SN: *mahā-vidyā-mantro*
α, CX: 是大明咒
αtl, CXtl: *shi da ming zhou*
CA: 大明咒
CAtl: *da ming zhou*
Ktl: *si daemyeong ju,*
Jtl: *ze dai myō shu,*
Vtl: *thị đại minh chú,*
EM: the verse of great wisdom,

ES: the Mantram of great wisdom,

EC: the spell of great knowledge,

ETH: luminous,

Vidyā, a part of this compound, is the stem of the feminine noun *vidyā.* As shown earlier, it means "knowledge," "science," "learning," or "philosophy." But in this case its likely meaning is "*dhāraṇī.*"

Mantraḥ (in the Horyu-ji and the Amoghavajra versions) is in its nominative singular case. *Mantro* (in the Nepalese version) is a phonetically changed form of *mantraḥ.*

Shi (是) means "is."

Da (大) means "large," "big," "great."

Ming (明) means "bright," "clear," "intelligent," "light," "brilliant," "know," "understand," "cleanse," or "knowledge." This ideograph is used for translation of *vidyā,* which is the antonym of *avidyā* (ignorance), mentioned previously.

Mingzhou (明咒) is a Chinese translation of *dhāraṇī. Dhāraṇī* is sometimes called *mantra* or *dhāraṇī vidyā.* In the tantric teaching, it is explained that the incantation of *dhāraṇī* removes obstacles that derive from *avidyā,* or ignorance.

(34) HIGHEST MANTRA

SH, SA: *anuttara-mantraḥ*

SN: *'nuttara-mantro*

α: 無上明咒

αtl: *wu shang ming zhou*

CX: 是 無上咒

CXtl: *shi wu shang zhou*

CA: 無上彼呪

CAtl: *wu shang bi zhou*

Ktl: *si musang ju,*

Jtl: *ze mujō shu,*

Vtl: *thị vô thượng chú,*

EM: the unsurpassed verse,

ES: the highest Mantram,

EC: the utmost spell,

ETH: unequalled,

Anuttara means, which appeared earlier in segment 30, "supreme." *'Nut-tara* is a phonetically changed form of *anuttara,* meaning "unsurpassable," as explained earlier.

Wushang (無上) means "not higher," "unequaled," or "unsurpassable."

In the α version, *shi* (是) is not repeated.

In the Amoghavajra version, *bi* (彼), meaning "that" or "the very," is added.

(35) INCOMPARABLE MANTRA

> SH, SA: *asamasama-mantraḥ*
> SN: *'samasama-mantraḥ*
> α: 無等等明咒
> αtl: *wu deng deng ming zhou*
> CX: α: 是無等等咒
> CXtl: *shi wu deng deng zhou.*
> CA: 無等呪
> CAtl: *wu deng zhou*
> Ktl: *si mudeungdeung ju,*
> Jtl: *ze mutōdō shu,*
> Vtl: *thị vô đẳng đẳng chú,*
> EM: the peerless verse,
> ES: the peerless Mantram,
> EC: the unequalled spell,
> ETH: and supreme.

Asamasama, an adjective, is also a form of the compound *a* plus *sama* plus *sama.* The apostrophe at the beginning of the Nepalese version represents the letter *a.* The *a,* which appeared previously a number of times, means "not."

Sama is an adjective meaning "same," "equal," "similar," "parallel," or "together," which is related to the English word "same," as suggested earlier. *Samasama* means "quite equal" or "exactly alike."

Asamasama then means "not equal to anything that is equal." It is a unique expression in Buddhist literature.[58] It can be seen as a postclassical Sanskrit idiom.

Then this entire line (segments 31–35) is interpreted as: "Therefore, be it known. *Prajñāpāramitā* is a great *mantra,* a great *vidyā mantra,* an unsurpassable *mantra,* and an incomparable *mantra.*"

Deng (等) means "class," "grade," or "equal." Repeating the word as *dengdeng* means "equal, equal" or "comparable in any means." That makes *wudengdeng* "incomparable."

This line in the Xuanzang version reads: "(*Prajna paramita* is) a great *mantra*, a great bright *mantra*, an utmost *mantra*, an incomparable *mantra*."

(36) RELIEVES SUFFERING

> SH, SA, SN: *sarva-duḥkha-praśamanaḥ,*
> α, CX: 能除一切苦
> αtl, CXtl: *neng chu yi qie ku*
> CA: 一切苦正息
> CAtl: *yi qie ku zheng xi*
> Ktl: *neungje ilche go.*
> Jtl: *nōjo issai ku.*
> Vtl: *năng trừ nhất thiết khổ,*
> EM: which appeases all pain
> ES: which is capable of allaying all pain;
> EC: allayer of all suffering,
> ETH: It relieves all suffering.

Sarva-duḥkha means "all suffering."

Praśamanaḥ is the nominative singular masculine case of the adjective *praśamana*. This word comes from the verb *praśam*. *Pra* is a prefix meaning "before" or "forward." *Śam* means "finish," "rest," or "calm." Thus, *praśamana* means "tranquilizing," "pacifying," "curing," or "healing."

This line can be translated as: "(This mantra is) all pain pacifying."

The Chinese *neng* (能) means "can," "able to," "do well," "power," or "ability."

Chu (除) means "remove" or "do away with."

Yiqie ku (一切苦) means "all pain," or "all the sufferings."

Zheng for *zheng xi* (正息) means "truly" in this case. *Xi* means "rest" or "end."

(37) GENUINE

> SH, SA, SN: *satyam amithyatvāt.*
> α, CX, CA: 眞實不虛
> αtl, CXtl, CAtl: *zhen shi bu xu*
> Ktl: *jinsil bul heo.*

Jtl: *Shinjitsu fu ko.*
Vtl: *chân thực bất hư.*
EM: — it is truth, because it is not false —
ES: it is truth because it is not falsehood;
EC: in truth — for what could go wrong?
ETH: It is genuine and not illusory.

Satyam, meaning "truly," is an indeclinable (adverb) form of the adjective *satya. Satya* means "true," "real," "actual," "genuine," "honest," or "pure." *Satya* comes from the same root as the adjective *sat* (happening or being present) and, as mentioned previously, is related to the English word "sooth."

Satya became the basis of "satyagraha" (truth resistance, literally meaning "taking hold of the truth"), which Gandhi coined to express the principle of his nonviolent political action.

Amithyatvāt is *amithya* plus *tvāt.* The *a,* again, is a prefix meaning "not." *Mythya* comes from a feminine adjective *mithyā* that means "incorrect," "wrong," or "improper." *Tvāt* is the ablative case of the suffix *tva,* meaning "-ness" or "state of," as mentioned previously. The ablative case changes it to "because of" or "on account of."

This Sanskrit phrase can be interpreted as: "(This mantra is all pain removing) truly on account of (its) nonincorrectness."

Zhenshi (眞實) is a compound of *zhen* and *shi. Zhen* means "true," "real," or "genuine." *Shi* means "fruit," "substantial," or "true."

Bu (不) means "not." *Xu* (虛) means "false," "untrue," "unreal," "vacant," "empty," "hollow," or "insubstantial."

(38) THEREFORE THIS MANTRA

SH, SN: *prajñāpāramitāyām ukto mantraḥ*
SA: *prajñāpāramitām ukto mantraḥ,*
α: 故説般若波羅蜜咒
αtl: *gu shuo bo re bo luo mi zhou*
CX: 故説般若波羅蜜多咒
CXtl: *gu shuo bo re bo luo mi duo zhou*
CA: 般若波羅蜜多
CAtl: *bo re bo luo mi duo*
Ktl: *go seol banya baramilda ju,*
Jtl: *Ko setsu hannya haramitta shu,*

Vtl: *Cố thuyết Bát nhã Ba la mật đa chú,*
EM: the verse proclaimed in the Prag*ñ*āpāramitā:
ES: this is the Mantram proclaimed in the Prajnaparamita.
EC: By the prajñāpāramitā has this spell been delivered.
ETH: So set forth this mantra of realizing wisdom beyond wisdom.

Prajñāpāramitāyām, the locative case of the feminine noun *prajñā-pāramitā,* means "in *prajñāpāramitā*" or "in regard to the *prajñāpāramitā.*" *Prajñāpāramitām* is in its accusative case, whose grammatical function in this case is questionable.

Ukto is a phonetically changed form of *uktaḥ.* It is the masculine nominative singular case of *ukta,* meaning "uttered," "said," or "spoken." *Ukta* is the past participle of the verb *vac. Vac* means "speak," "utter," "declare, "proclaim" or "recite."

Vac is related to the English words "vocal," "voice," and "vowel" through the Latin *vocāre,* meaning "call."[59]

Mantraḥ is the nominative singular case of the masculine noun *mantra.*

The Sanskrit line means: "With respect to the *prajñāpāramitā,* (this) *mantra* has been uttered."

Gu (故) means "therefore." *Shuo* (説) means "speak," "say," "tell," "explain," or "expound." In this case, it can be seen as an imperative.

The Chinese phrase can be interpreted as: "Therefore, expound the *prajñāpāramitā mantra . . .*"

(39) PROCLAIM

SH, SA: *tad yathā:*
SN: *tadyathā*
α, CX: 即説咒曰
αtl, CXtl: *ji shuo zhou yue*
CA: 説呪曰
CAtl: *shuo zhou yue*
Ktl: *jeuk seol ju wal:*
Jtl: *soku setsu shu watsu:*
Vtl: *túc thuyết chú viết:*
ES: It runs:
EC: It runs like this:
ETH: Set forth this mantra that says:

Tad, again, is the pronoun that means "this" or "that."

Yathā is an adverb meaning "as" or "like." *Tadyathā* means "as following."

Thus, the Sanskrit line reads: "(It is) as following:"

Ji (即) means "immediately," "rightly," "then," "that is," "in itself," or "now."

Shuo (説), again, means "speak," "say," "tell," "explain," or "expound." In this case, it can be seen as an imperative.

Shuo zhou (説咒) means "say the mantra." *Yue* (曰) means "say" or "say in the following way."

Thus, the Chinese line reads: "Now say the mantra in this way:"

(40) *GATÉ, GATÉ*

> SH: *gate, gate,*
> SA: *(Oṃ) gate, gate,*
> SN: *oṃ gate gate*
> α: 竭帝竭帝
> αtl: *jie di jie di*
> CX: 揭帝揭帝
> CXtl: *jie di jie di*
> CA: 誐諦誐諦
> CAtl: *e'e di e'e di*
> Ktl: *aje aje*
> Jtl: *Gyatei gyatei,*
> Vtl: *Yĕt đế yĕt đế,*
> EM: gone, gone,
> ES: Gate, gate, (gone, gone,)
> EC: Gone, gone,
> ETH: Gaté, gaté,

Mantra is among the first words in Xuanzang's list of *bufan* — words that are not to be translated — by virtue of its esoteric and mystical nature. Traditionally, the *Heart Sutra* mantra is not translated. Besides, it is not written in standard Sanskrit but, rather, in a special incantation form. Therefore, any interpretation or translation of the mantra remains in the realm of conjecture.

The Sanskrit *gate* (pronounced *gaté* — with *e* as in "get," but stretched) is a form of the verb *gam*, which means "go," "move," "set out," or "come."

This verb is remotely related to the English word "come."[60]

It is tempting to compare *gam* with *gā,* another Sanskrit word similar in sound and meaning to it. *Gā* is remotely related to the English word "go" through the Old German word *gām,* meaning "go."[61]

In a common interpretation, *gate* is a feminine form of the past participle *gatā,* which means "gone," "gone away," "departed," or "deceased." (This is a different word from the familiar Buddhist word *gatha,* meaning "verse.") In addition, it is seen as a feminine vocative case or masculine or feminine locative case.

It is possible to see *gate* as a form of the feminine noun *gati. Gati* means "going," "moving," "passage," "path," "progress," "movement," or "arriving." *Gate* can be seen as the vocative case of *gati.*

In Chinese, this mantra is transliterated in different ways but perhaps pronounced in the same way or with slight variations.

(41) *PARAGATÉ*

SH, SA, SN: *pāragate,*
α: 波羅竭帝
αtl: *bo luo jie di*
CX: 般羅揭帝
CXtl: *bo luo jie di*
CA: 播囉誐諦
CAtl: *bo luo e'e di*
Ktl: *bara aje*
Jtl: *hara gyatei*
Vtl: *ba la yêt đě,*
EM: gone to the other shore,
ES: paragate, (gone to the other shore,)
EC: gone beyond
ETH: paragaté

Pāra, as in *pāramitā,* is a noun meaning "the opposite," "the other side," or "the opposite shore." There seems to be a connection between *pāra* and the Sanskrit prefix *para,* which means "far," "distant," "remote," "opposite," or "beyond." It may be related to the English prefix "para," as in "paradox" (beyond opinion) or "parapsychology."

Gate is the same as above.

(42) *PARASAMGATÉ*

SH, SN: *pārasaṃgate*
SA: *pāra-saṃgate*
α: 波羅僧竭帝
αtl: *bo luo seng jie di*
CX: 般羅僧揭帝
CXtl: *bo luo seng jie di*
CA: 播囉僧誐諦
CAtl: *bo luo seng e'e di*
Ktl: *bara seung aje*
Jtl: *hara sō gyatei,*
Vtl: *ba la tăng yết đế,*
EM: landed at the other shore.
ES: parasamgate, (landed at the other shore),
EC: gone altogether beyond,
ETH: *parasamgaté*

Pāra and *gate* are the same as above.

Sam, as discussed previously, is a prefix meaning "all," "together," or "thorough." Thus, *saṃgate* can be interpreted as "gone altogether," "arrived altogether," or "fully arriving together."

(43) *SVAHA*

SH, SA, SN: *bodhi svāhā.*
α, CX: 菩提僧莎訶
αtl, CXtl: *pu ti seng suo he*
CA: 冒地娑嚩賀
CAtl: *pu ti suo fu he*
Ktl: *moji sabaha*
Jtl: *bōji sowaka.*
Vtl: *bồ đề tát bà ha.*
EM: 'O wisdom, . . . Svāhā!'
ES: bodhi, svaha!
EC: O what an awakening, all-hail!
ETH: *bodhi! Svaha!*

Bodhi is a noun, used in both masculine and feminine forms, meaning "awakening" or "enlightenment." Here it is possibly used as a nominative case.

Svāhā is a Vedic word used for prayer or offering. It is regarded as a compound of *su* and *ah*. *Su* is a prefix meaning "accord." *Ah* is a verb meaning "say," "express," or "call." Thus, *svāhā* is a word of exclamation: "hail," "hail to," or "blessing to."[62] I would add " joy" and "ecstasy."

So this mantra can be interpreted as: "Arriving, arriving, arriving all the way, arriving all the way together: awakening. Joy!"

(44) END TITLE

SH: *iti Prajñāpāramitā-hṛdayaṃ samāptaṃ*
SN: *iti prajñāpāramitā-hṛdayaṃ samāptam.*
α: 摩訶般若波羅蜜大明咒經
αtl: *mo he bo re bo luo mi da ming zhou jing*
CX: [摩訶]般若波羅蜜多心經
CXtl: [*mo he*] *bo re bo luo mi duo xin jing*
CA: 梵本般若心經
CAtl: *fan ben bo re xin jing*
Ktl: [*Maha*] *Banya baramilda simgyeong*
Jtl: [*Maka*] *Hannya haramitta shingyō*
EM: Thus ends the heart of the Pra*gñ*āpāramitā.
EC: This completes the Heart of perfect wisdom.

The Sanskrit versions conclude the sutra with this line. It can be read: "Thus, (I have chanted) a complete *prajñāpāramitā* heart." It can also be understood as: "Thus, (I have chanted) a completed *prajñāpāramitā dhāraṇī*," as in the title of the α version. As I mentioned earlier, "heart" is seen as the most secret of all teachings.

The Chinese versions repeat their titles at the ends.

Amoghavajra has its end title as *fan ben bo re xin jing* (梵本般若心經). *Fan* means "Sanskrit" and *ben* means "book" or "text." *Bore xin jing* means "*Prajna* Heart Sutra."

In Japanese, the end title is sometimes read in an abbreviated form, *Hannya shingyō* (般若心經).

Appendix 1: Texts for Comparison

SOME KEY TEXTS of the *Heart Sutra* and the *Hridaya* in seven Asian languages are presented below, together with several English versions. These seven Eastern-language texts represent the principal world languages in which the sutra has been recited in the past. First, however, I offer some earlier texts as materials for examining the formation of the sutra. The Asian texts are presented in chronological order, roughly following the sequence of emergence suggested by Jan Nattier, as I introduced in chapter 13.

I use Xuanzang's Chinese version as the primary text. To make a quick reference and comparison possible, I have divided the Xuanzang version into forty-four segments. Each segment consists of terms, a phrase, or a sentence. Lines in other texts that do not have corresponding parts in Xuanzang's Chinese text are marked with the preceding line number followed by "x." The bracketed words have been added later. For the shorter-version *Heart Sutra* and *Hridaya* texts, I have added in parentheses the abbreviations explained on page 139.

EARLIER TEXTS

25,000-LINE *PRAJÑĀ PĀRAMITĀ* (also known as *Mahā Prajñā Pāramitā Sūtra* or *Large Sūtra*), Sanskrit manuscript (circa sixth century). See fig. 4.

The core section of the *Hridaya* corresponds to this section of this version of the *Prajñā Pāramitā*. The first and last sections of the *Hridaya* did not come from this sutra. That is why Segments 0–5 and 21–44 are not found in this text.

Initial transcription by Gregory Schopen, revised by Paul Harrison for this book on the basis of a re-reading of the Gilgit manuscript. According to Paul Harrison, the manuscript consistently reads *śunyatā* for *śūnyatā* (a common variant spelling), and is full of minor mistakes from the point of view of classical Sanskrit (mostly in matters of *sandhi*), including some obvious scribal blunders (e.g. *kāye* is clearly a misread *kāyaṃ,* which would look very similar; this sort of mistake suggests the scribe wasn't thinking about what he was writing, or didn't understand it). Parentheses (. . .) indicate unclear or damaged *akṣaras;* square brackets [. . .] indicate omissions in the manuscript which Schopen or Harrison have supplied.

(6) na hi Śāradvatīputrānyad (7) rūpam anyā śunyatā nānya {*should be* nānyā*}* śunyatānyad rūpam | (8) rūpam eva śunyatā śunyataiva rūpam | (9) evaṃ nā(ny)ā vedanānyā śunyatā | nā(ny)ā saṃjñ(ā) nānyā {*should be* saṃjñānyā*}* śunyatā | nānye saṃskārā anye {*should be* anyā*}* śunyatā | 3 nānya[d] vijñānam anyā śunyatā | (9x) nānyaḥ {*should be* nānyā*}* śunyatānyad vijñānaṃ | vijñānam eva śunyatā śunyataiva vijñānaṃ | (10) (yā) Śāradvatīputra śunyatā (11) na sā utpadyate na nirudhyate | na saṃkliśyate na vyavadāyate | na hīyate na vardhate | (11x) nātītā nānāgatā na pratyutpannā yā notpadyate na nirudhyate na saṃkliśyate na vyavadāyate | na hīyate na vardhate | nātītā nānāgatā na pratyutpannā | (13) na tatra rūpaṃ na vedanā na saṃjñān na saṃskārān {*should be* na saṃjñā na saṃskārā*}* na vijñānaṃ (14) na cakṣur na śrotraṃ na ghrāṇaṃ na jīhvā na kāye {*should be* kāyaṃ*}* na manaḥ (15) na rūpaṃ na śabdo na gandho na rasa {*should be* raso*}* na sparśo na dharmāḥ (16) na tatra skandhā na dhātavo nāyatanāni na tatra cakṣurdhātu[r] na rūpadhātur na cakṣurvijñānadhātu[r] (16x) na (śro)tradhātu[r] na śabdadhātur na śrotravijñānadhātuḥ na ghrāṇadhātur na gandhadhātur na ghrāṇavijñānadhātu[r] na jīhvādhātur na rasadhātur na jīhvāvijñā-nadhātuḥ na kāyadhātur na spraṣṭavyadhātur na kāyavijñānadhātur na manodhātur na dharmadhātur na manovijñāna[dhā]tuḥr (sic) (17) na tatrāvidyā nāvidyānirodhaḥ (17x) na saṃskārān {*should be* saṃskārā*}* na saṃskāranirodhaḥ na vijñānaṃ na vijñānanirodhaḥ na nāmarūpaṃ na nāmarūpanirodhaḥ na ṣaḍāyatanaṃ na ṣaḍāyatananirodhaḥ na sparśo na sparśananirodhaḥ na vedanā na vedanānirodhaḥ na tṛṣṇā na tṛṣṇānirodhaḥ nopādānaṃ nopādānanirodhaḥ na bhavo na bhavanirodhaḥ na jātir na jātinirodhaḥ (18) na jarāmaraṇaṃ na jarāmaraṇanirodhaḥ (19) na duḥkhaṃ na samudayo na nirodho na mārgaḥ (20) na prāptir nābhisamayaḥ

25,000-LINE *PRAJÑĀ PĀRAMITĀ* (*Maha Prajñā Pāramitā Sūtra,* or *Large Sūtra*), Fascicle 1, translated by Kumarajiva in 404
   (From *Taisho,* no. 223, vol. 8, p. 223a.)

(6)舍利弗(6x)色空故無惱壞相受空故無受相想空故無知相行空故
無作相識空故無覺相何以故舍利弗(7)色不異空空不異色(8)色即
是空空即是色(9)受想行識亦如是(10)舍利弗是諸法空相(11)不生
不滅不垢不淨不增不減(11x)是空法非過去非未來非現在(12)是故
空中(13)無色無受想行識(14)無眼耳鼻舌身意(15)無色聲香味觸法
(16)無眼界乃至無意識界(17)亦無無明亦無無明盡(18)乃至亦無老
死亦無老死盡(19)無苦集滅道(20)亦無智亦無得

25,000-LINE *PRAJÑĀ PĀRAMITĀ*, transliteration of the above

(6) she li fu (6x) se kong gu wu nao huai xiang shou kong gu wu shou xiang
xiang kong gu wu zhi xiang xing kong gu wu zuo xiang shi kong gu wu jue
xiang he yi gu she li fu (7) se bu yi kong kong bu yi se (8) se ji shi kong kong ji
shi se (9) shou xiang xing shi yi ru shi (10) she li fu shi zhu fa kong xiang (11)
bu sheng bu mie bu gou bu jing, bu zeng bu jian (11x) shi kong fa fei guo qu
fei wei lai fei xian zai (12) shi gu kong zhong (13) wu se wu shou xiang xing
shi (14) wu yan er bi she shen yi (15) wu se sheng xiang wei chu fa (16) wu
yan jie nai zhi wu yi shi jie (17) yi wu wu ming yi wu wu ming jin (18) nai zhi
yi wu lao si yi wu lao si jin. (19) wu ku ji mie dao (20) yi wu zhi yi wu de

DAZHIDU LUN (Treatise on Realization of Great Wisdom), attributed to Nagarjuna. Fascicle 36, 406 C.E., a quotation of the *25,000-line
Prajñā Pāramitā (Mahā Prajñā Pāramitā Sūtra,* or *Large Sūtra*) as translated by Kumarajıva
   (From *Taisho,* no. 1509, vol. 25, p. 327c.)

(6) 舍利弗 (6x) 色空 故 無 惱壞相 受空 故 無 受相 想空 故 無 知相
行空 故 無 作相 識空 故 無 覺相 何以故 舍利弗 (7) 非色 異空 非空
異色 (8) 色 即是 空 空即是 色 (9) 受想行識 亦如是 (10) 舍利弗 是
諸法 空相 (11) 不 生 不 滅 不 垢 不 淨 不 增 不 減 (11x) 是 空法 非 過
去 非 未來 非 現在 (12) 是故 空中 (13) 無 色 無 受想行識 (14) 無 眼
耳鼻舌身意 (15) 無 色聲香味觸法 (16) 無 眼界 乃至 無 意識界 (17)
無 無明 亦 無 無明盡 (18) 乃至 無 老死 亦 無 老死盡 (19) 無 苦集滅
道 (20) 亦 無 智 亦 無 得

DAZHIDU LUN, transliteration of the above text

(6) she li fu (6x) se kong gu wu nao huai xiang shou kong gu wu shou xiang
xiang kong gu wu zhi xiang xing kong gu wu zuo xiang shi kong gu wu jue
xiang he yi gu she li fu (7) fei se yi kong. fei kong yi se (8) se ji shi kong kong
ji shi se (9) shou xiang xing shi yi ru shi (10) she li fu shi zhu fa kong xiang
(11) bu sheng bu mie bu gou bu jing, bu zeng bu jian (11x) shi kong fa fei
guo qu fei wei lai fei xian zai (12) shi gu kong zhong (13) wu se wu shou
xiang xing shi (14) wu yan er bi she shen yi (15) wu se sheng xiang wei chu fa
(16) wu yan jie nai zhi wu yi shi jie (17) wu wu ming yi wu wu ming jin (18)
nai zhi wu lao si yi wu lao si jin (19) wu ku ji mie dao (20) yi wu zhi yi wu de

SHORTER TEXTS

***α* VERSION**, Chinese translation attributed to Kumarajiva (α)
(From *Taisho,* no. 250.)

(0)摩訶般若波羅蜜大明咒經(1)觀世音菩薩(2)行深般若波羅蜜時
(3)照見五陰(4)空(5)度一切苦厄(6)舍利弗(6x)色空故無惱壞相受
空故無受相想空故無知相行空故無作相識空故無覺相何以故舍
利弗(7)非色異空非空異色(8)色即是空空即是色(9)受想行識亦如
是(10)舍利弗是諸法空相(11)不生不滅不垢不淨不增不減(11x)是空
法非過去非未來非現在(12)是故空法(13)無色無受想行識(14)無眼
耳鼻舌身意(15)無色聲香味觸法(16)無眼界乃至無意識界(17)無無
明亦無無明盡(18)乃至無老死亦無老死盡(19)無苦集滅道(20)無智
亦無得(21)以無所得故(22)菩薩(23)依般若波羅蜜故(24)心無罣礙
無罣礙故(25)無有恐怖(26)離一切顛倒夢想苦惱(27)究竟涅槃(28)
三世諸佛(29)依般若波羅蜜故(30)得阿耨多羅三藐三菩提(31)故知
般若波羅蜜(33)是大明咒(34)無上明咒(35)無等等明咒(36)能除一
切苦(37)眞實不虛(38)故説般若波羅蜜咒(39)即説咒曰(40)竭帝竭
帝(41)波羅竭帝(42)波羅僧竭帝(43)菩提僧莎訶(44)摩訶般若波羅
蜜大明咒經

***α* VERSION**, transliteration of the above (αtl)

(0) mo he bo re bo luo mi da ming zhou jing (1) Guan shi yin pu sa (2) xing
shen bo re bo luo mi shi (3) zhao jian wu yin (4) kong (5) du yi qie ku e (6)
She li fu (6x) se kong gu wu nao huai xiang shou kong gu wu shou xiang

xiang kong gu wu zhi xiang xing kong gu wu zuo xiang shi kong gu wu jue xiang he yi gu She li fu (7) fei se yi kong. fei kong yi se (8) se ji shi kong kong ji shi se (9) shou xiang xing shi yi ru shi (10) She li fu shi zhu fa kong xiang (11) bu sheng bu mie bu gou bu jing, bu zeng bu jian (11x) shi kong fa fei guo qu fei wei lai fei xian zai (12) shi gu kong fa (13) wu se, wu shou xiang xing shi (14) wu yan er bi she shen yi (15) wu se sheng xiang wei chu fa (16) wu yan jie nai zhi wu yi shi jie (17) wu wu ming yi wu wu ming jin (18) nai zhi wu lao si yi wu lao si jin. (19) wu ku ji mie dao (20) wu zhi yi wu de (21) yi wu suo de gu (22) pu sa (23) yi bo re bo luo mi gu (24) xin wu gua ai. wu gua ai gu (25) wu you kong bu (26) li yi qie dian dao meng xiang ku nao (27) jiu jing nie pan (28) san shi zhu fo (29) yi bo re bo luo mi gu (30) de a nou duo luo san miao san pu ti (31) gu zhi bo re bo luo mi (33) shi da ming zhou (34) wu shang ming zhou (35) wu deng deng ming zhou (36) neng chu yi qie ku (37) zhen shi bu xu (38) gu shuo bo re bo luo mi zhou (39) ji shuo zhou yue (40) jie di jie di (41) bo luo jie di (42) bo luo seng jie di (43) pu ti seng suo he (44) mo he bo re bo luo mi da ming zhou jing

SANSKRIT, HORYU-JI VERSION (SH)

Transcribed by Ryosaburo Sakaki, Unrai Ogiwara, Shindo Shiraishi, and Shuyu Kanaoka. Fig. 8.

(ox) namas sarvajñāya (1) Āryāvalokiteśvara-bodhisattvo (2) gambhīram prajñāpāramitāyām caryām caramāno (3) vyavalokayati sma: pañca skandhās tāmś (4) ca svabhāva-śūnyam paśyasti sma. (6) iha Śāriputra, (6x) rūpam śūnyatā śūnyatā-iva rūpam. (7) rūpan na pṛthak śūnyatā, śūnyatāyā na pṛthag rūpam, (8) yad rūpam sā śūnyatā yā śūnyatā tad rūpam. (9) evam eva vedanā-samjñā-samskāra-vijñāni. (10) iha Śāriputra, sarva-dharmāḥ śūnyatā-lakṣaṇā, (11) anutpannā aniruddhā amalāvimalā nona na paripūrṇāḥ. (12) tasmāc Chāriputra śūnyatāyām (13) na rūpam na vedanā na samjñā na samskāra na vijñāni. (14) na cakṣuḥ-śrotra-ghrāṇa-jihvā-kāya-manāmsi. (15) na rūpa-śabda-gandha-rasa-spraśtavya dharmāḥ, (16) na cakṣur-dhātur yāvan na mano-vijñāna-dhātuḥ. (17) na vidyā nāvidyā na vidyākṣayo nāvidyākṣayo. (18) yāvan na jarā-maranam na jarā-marana-kṣayo. (19) na duḥkha-samudaya-nirodha-mārgā. (20) na jñānam, na prāptitvam (21) tasmāc (22) bodhisattvasya (23) prajñāpāramitām āśritya (24) viharaty a-cittāvaranaḥ. cittāvarana (25) nāstitvād atrasto (26) viparyāsātikrāntaḥ (27) niṣṭhā-nirvāṇaḥ (28) tryadhvavyavasthitāḥ sarva-buddhāḥ (29) prajñāpāramitām-āśritya- (30) anuttarāṃ samyak-sambodhiṃ abhisambuddhāḥ. (31) tasmāj jñātavyam: prajñāpāramitā (32) mahā-mantro (33) mahā-vidyā-mantraḥ (34) anuttara-mantraḥ (35) asamasama-mantraḥ, (36) sarva-duḥkha-praśamanaḥ (37) satyam amithyatvāt, (38) prajñāpāramitāyām ukto mantraḥ, (39) tadyathā: (40) gate, gate, (41) pāragate, (42) pārasaṃgate (43) bodhi svāhā. (44) iti Prajñāpāramitā-hṛdayaṃ samāptam.

CHINESE, XUANZANG VERSION, 694 C.E. (CX)
(From *Taisho,* No. 251.)

(0)[摩訶]般若波羅蜜多心經(1)觀自在菩薩(2)行深般若波羅蜜多時(3)照見五蘊(4)皆空(5)度一切苦厄(6)舍利子(7)色不異空空不異色(8)色即是空空即是色(9)受想行識亦復如是(10)舍利子是諸法空相(11)不生不滅不垢不淨不增不減(12)是故空中(13)無色無受想行識(14)無眼耳鼻舌身意(15)無色聲香味觸法(16)無眼界乃至無意識界(17)無無明亦無無明盡(18)乃至無老死亦無老死盡(19)無苦集滅道(20)無智亦無得(21)以無所得故(22)菩提薩埵(23)依般若波羅蜜多故(24)心無罣礙無罣礙故(25)無有恐怖(26)遠離[一切]顛倒夢想(27)究竟涅槃(28)三世諸佛(29)依般若波羅蜜多故(30)得阿耨多羅三藐三菩提(31)故知般若波羅蜜多(32)是大神咒(33)是大明咒(34)是無上咒(35)是無等等咒(36)能除一切苦(37)眞實不虛(38)故説般若波羅蜜多咒(39)即説咒曰(40)揭帝揭帝(41)般羅揭帝(42)般羅僧揭帝(43)菩提僧莎訶(44)[摩訶]般若波羅蜜多心經

CHINESE, XUANZANG VERSION, transliteration of the above (CXtl)

(0) [mo he] bo re bo luo mi duo xin jing (1) Guan zi zai pu sa (2) xing shen bo re bo luo mi duo shi (3) zhao jian wu yun (4) jie kong (5)du yi qie ku e (6) She li zi (7) se bu yi kong kong bu yi se (8) se ji shi kong kong ji shi se (9) shou xiang xing shi yi fu ru shi (10) She li zi shi zhu fa kong xiang (11) bu sheng bu mie bu gou bu jing, bu zeng bu jian (12) shi gu kong zhong (13) wu se, wu shou xiang xing shi (14) wu yan er bi she shen yi (15) wu se sheng xiang wei chu fa (16) wu yan jie nai zhi wu yi shi jie (17) wu wu ming yi wu wu ming jin (18) nai zhi wu lao si yi wu lao si jin (19) wu ku ji mie dao (20) wu zhi yi wu de (21) yi wu suo de gu (22) pu ti sa duo (23) yi bo re bo luo

mi duo gu (24) xin wu gua ai. wu gua ai gu (25) wu you kong bu (26) yuan
li [yi qie] dian dao meng xiang (27) jiu jing nie pan (28) san shi zhu fo (29)
yi bo re bo luo mi duo gu (30) de a nou duo luo san miao san pu ti (31) gu
zhi bo re bo luo mi duo (32) shi da shen zhou (33) shi da ming zhou (34)
shi wu shang zhou (35) shi wu deng deng zhou. (36) neng chu yi qie ku (37)
zhen shi bu xu (38) gu shuo bo re bo luo mi duo zhou (39) ji shuo zhou yue
(40) jie di jie di (41) bo luo jie di (42) bo luo seng jie di (43) pu ti seng suo
he (44) [mo he] bo re bo luo mi duo xin jing

KOREAN, transliteration of the Chinese Xuanzang version (Ktl)
Transcription by Dongho for this book.

(0) [Maha]Banya baramilda simgyeong (1) Gwanjajae bosal (2) haeng sim
banya baramilda si (3) jogyeon o-on (4) gaegong (5) do ilche goaek. (6)
Sarija, (7) saek bul i gong, gong bul i saek. (8) saek jeuk si gong, gong jeuk
si saek. (9) su sang haeng sik yeokbu yeosi. (10) Sarija, si jebeop gongsang,
(11) bul saeng, bul myeol, bul gu, bu jeong, bu jeung, bul gam. (12) sigo
gongjung, (13) mu saek, mu su sang haeng sik, (14) mu an i bi seol sin ui,
(15) mu saek seong hyang mi chok beop, (16) mu angye, naeji mu uisik-
gye, (17) mu mumyeong yeok mu mu myeongjin, (18) naeji mu nosa yeok
mu nosajin, (19) mu go jip myeol do, (20) mu ji yeok mu deuk. (21) i mu
sodeuk go, (22) borisalta (23) ui banya baramilda go, (24) sim mu gaae. Mu
gaae go, (25) mu yu gongpo, (26) wonri jeondo mongsang, (27) gugyeong
yeolban (28) samse jebul (29) ui banya baramilda go (30) deuk anyok
dara sammyak sambori. (31) go ji banya baramilda (32) si daesin ju, (33) si
daemyeong ju, (34) si musang ju, (35) si mudeungdeung ju, (36) neungje
ilche go. (37) jinsil bul heo. (38) go seol banya baramilda ju, (39) jeuk seol
ju wal: (40) aje aje (41) bara aje (42) bara seung aje (43) moji sabaha. (44)
[Maha]Banya baramilda simgyeong

JAPANESE, transliteration of the Chinese Xuanzang version (Jtl)

(0) [Maka] Hannya haramitta shingyō. (1) Kanjizai bosa<tsu> (2) gyōjin
hannya haramitta ji (3) shōken go'on (4) kaikū (5) do issai kuyaku. (6)
Sharishi, (7) shiki fu i kū. Kū fu i shiki. (8) Shiki soku ze kū. Kū soku ze
shiki. (9) Ju sō gyō shiki yakubu nyoze. (10) Sharishi, ze shohō kūsō, (11)
fu shō, fu metsu, fu ku, fu jō, fu zō, fu gen. (12) Zeko kūchū, (13) mu shiki,

mu ju sō gyō shiki, (14) mu gen ni bi zes shin (n)i, (15) mu shiki shō kō mi
soku hō, (16) mu genkai, naishi mu ishikikai, (17) mu mumyō yaku mu mu
mumyō jin, (18) naishi mu rōshi yaku mu rōshi jin, (19) mu ku shū metsu
dō. (20) Mu chi yaku mu toku. (21) I mu shotok ko, (22) bodaisatta (23)
e hannya haramitta ko, (24) shin mu keige. Mu kei ge ko, (25) mu u kufu,
(26) onri [issai] tendō musō, (27) kukyō nehan. (28) Sanze shobutsu (29)
e hannya haramitta ko, (30) toku anoku tara sammyaku sambodai. (31) ko
chi hannya haramitta (32) ze daijin shu, (33) ze daimyō shu, (34) ze mujō
shu, (35) ze mutōdō shu, (36) nōjo issai ku. (37) Shinjitsu fu ko. (38) Ko
setsu hannya haramitta shu, (39) soku setsu shu watsu: (40) Gyatei gyatei,
(41) hara gyatei, (42) hara sō gyatei, (43) bōji sowaka. (44) [Maka] Hannya haramitta shingyō

VIETNAMESE, SOUTHERN, transliteration of the Chinese Xuan-zang version
Transcribed by Quang Huyen for this book.

(0) Bát Nhã Ba La Mật Đa Tâm Kinh (1) Quán Tự Tại Bồ Tát (2) hành
thâm Bát nhã Ba la mật đa thời, (3) chiếu kiến ngũ uẩn (4) giai không, (5)
độ nhứt thiết khổ ách. (6) Xá Lợi Tử, (7) sắc bất dị không, không bất dị
sắc, (8) sắc tức thị không, không tức thị sắc, (9) thọ tưởng hành thức diệc
phục như thị. (10) Xá Lợi Tử, thị chư pháp không tướng, (11) bất sanh bất
diệt, bất cấu bất tịnh, bất tăng bất giảm. (12) Thị cố không trung (13) vô
sắc, vô thọ tưởng hành thức. (14) Vô nhãn nhĩ tỷ thiệt thân ý, (15) vô sắc
thanh hương vị xúc pháp, (16) vô nhãn giới nãi chí vô ý thức giới. (17) Vô
vô minh, diệc vô vô minh tận, (18) nãi chí vô lão tử, diệc vô lão tử tận. (19)
Vô khổ, tập, diệt, đạo. (20) Vô trí diệc vô đắc. (21) Dĩ vô sở đắc cố, (22) bồ
đề tát đõa, (23) y Bát nhã Ba la mật đa cố, (24) tâm vô quái ngại, vô quái
ngại cố, (25) vô hữu khủng bố, (26) viễn ly điên đảo mộng tưởng, (27) cứu
cánh Niết bàn (28) tam thế chư Phật, (29) y Bát nhã Ba la mật đa cố, (30)
đắc A nậu đa la Tam miệu Tam bồ đề. (31) Cố tri Bát nhã Ba la mật đa, (32)
thị đại thần chú, (33) thị đại minh chú, (34) thị vô thượng chú, (35) thị vô
đẳng đẳng chú, (36) năng trừ nhứt thiết khổ, (37) chân thiệt bất hư. (38)
Cố thuyết Bát nhã Ba la mật đa chú, (39) tức thuyết chú viết: (40) Yết đế
yết đế, (41) ba la yết đế, (42) ba la tăng yết đế, (43) bồ đề tát bà ha.

VIETNAMESE, NORTHERN, transliteration of the Chinese Xuan-zang version (Vtl)
 Transcribed by Quang Huyen for this book.

(0) Bát Nhã Ba La Mật Đa Tâm Kinh (1) Quán Tự Tại Bồ Tát (2) hành thâm Bát nhã Ba la mật đa thời, (3) chiếu kiến ngũ uẩn (4) giai không, (5) độ nhất thiết khổ ách. (6) Xá Lợi Tử, (7) sắc bất dị không, không bất dị sắc, (8) sắc tức thị không, không tức thị sắc, (9) thụ tưởng hành thức diệc phục như thị. (10) Xá Lợi Tử, thị chư pháp không tướng, (11) bất sinh bất diệt, bất cấu bất tịnh, bất tăng bất giảm. (12) Thị cố không trung (13) vô sắc, vô thụ tưởng hành thức. (14) Vô nhãn nhĩ tỷ thiệt thân ý, (15) vô sắc thanh hương vị xúc pháp, (16) vô nhãn giới nãi chí vô ý thức giới. (17) Vô vô minh, diệc vô vô minh tận, (18) nãi chí vô lão tử, diệc vô lão tử tận. (19) Vô khổ, tập, diệt, đạo. (20) Vô trí diệc vô đắc. (21) Dĩ vô sở đắc cố, (22) bồ đề tát đỏa, (23) y Bát nhã Ba la mật đa cố, (24) tâm vô quái ngại, vô quái ngại cố, (25) vô hữu khủng bố, (26) viễn ly điên đảo mộng tưởng, (27) cứu cánh Niết bàn (28) tam thế chư Phật, (29) y Bát nhã Ba la mật đa cố, (30) đắc A nậu đa la Tam miệu Tam bồ đề. (31) Cố tri Bát nhã Ba la mật đa, (32) thị đại thần chú, (33) thị đại minh chú, (34) thị vô thượng chú, (35) thị vô đẳng đẳng chú, (36) năng trừ nhất thiết khổ, (37) chân thực bất hư. (38) Cố thuyết Bát nhã Ba la mật đa chú, (39) tức thuyết chú viết: (40) Yết đế yết đế, (41) ba la yết đế, (42) ba la tăng yết đế, (43) bồ đề tát bà ha.

SANSKRIT, AMOGHAVAJRA VERSION, after 774 (SA)
 Transcribed by Fumimasa-Bunga Fukui. See p. 68.

(0) prajñā pāramitā-hṛdaya-sūtraṃ (1) āryāvalokiteśvaro-bodhisattvo (2) gambhīrāṃ prajñā-pāramitā-caryāṃ caramāṇo (3) vyavalokayati sma: pañca skandhās tāṃś (4) ca svabhāva-śūnyaṃ paśyasti sma. (6) iha Śāriputra, (6x) rūpaṃ śūnyatā śūnyataiva rūpam. (7) rūpān na pṛthak śūnyatā, śūnyatāyā na pṛthag rūpam, (8) yad rūpaṃ sā śūnyatā yā śūnyatā sā rūpam. (9) evam eva vedanā-saṃjñā-saṃskāra-vijñānam, (10) iha Śāriputra sarva-dharmāḥ śūnyatā-lakṣaṇā, (11) anutpannā aniruddhā amalā avimalā anūnā aparipūrṇāḥ. (12) tasmāc Chāriputra śūnyatāyāṃ (13) na rūpaṃ na vedanā na saṃjñā na saṃskāra na vijñānam, (14) na cakṣuḥ-śrotra-ghrāṇa-jihvā-kāya-manāṃsi (15) na rūpa-śabda-gandha-rasa-spraṣṭavya dharmāḥ, (16) na cakṣur-dhātur yāvan na mano-vijñāna-dhātuḥ. (17) nāvidyā na vidyā

nāvidyā-kṣayo nāvidyā-kṣayo (18) yāvan na jarā-maraṇaṃ na jarā-maraṇa-
kṣayo (19) na duḥkha-samudaya-nirodha-mārgā, (20) [jñā] na jñānaṃ, na
prāptiś (21) ca tasmān nāprāpti-tvā (22) bodhisattvasyāṃ (23) prajñāpāramitām āśritya (24) viharaty acittāvaraṇaḥ. cittāvaraṇa- (25) nāstitvād
atrasto (26) viparyāsātikrāntaḥ (27) niṣṭhānirvāṇam. (28) tryadhva-
vyavasthitāḥ sarva-buddhāḥ (29) prajñā-pāramitām āśritya- (30) anuttarāṃ
samyak-[sam]bodhim abhisambuddhāḥ. (31) tasmāj jñā-tavyaṃ prajñāpāramitā (32) mahā-mantro (33) mahā-vidyā-mantraḥ (34) anuttara-
mantraḥ (35) asamasama-mantraḥ, (36) sarva-duḥkha-praśamanaḥ (37)
satyam amithyatvā. (38) prajñāpāramitām ukto mantraḥ, (39) tadyathā:
(40) (Oṃ) gate, gate, (41) pāragate, (42) pāra-saṃgate (43) bodhi svāhā.

CHINESE, AMOGHAVAJRA VERSION (CA)

Transcribed by Fumimasa-Bunga Fukui. See p. 68.

(0) 般若波羅蜜多心經 (1) 聖觀自在菩薩 (2) 深般若波羅蜜多行
行時 (3) 照見五蘊 (4) 彼自性空現 (6) 此舍利子 (6x) 色空空性是色
(7) 色不異空空亦不異色 (8) 是色彼空 是空 彼色 (9) 如是受想行識
(10) 此舍利子諸法空相 (11) 不生不滅不垢不淨不增不減 (12) 是故
舍利子空中 (13) 無色無受無想無行無識 (14) 無眼耳鼻舌身意 (15)
無色聲香味觸法 (16) 無眼界乃至無意識界 (17) 無明無明無明盡無
明盡 (18) 乃至無老死無老死盡 (19) 無苦集滅道 (20) 無智無得無證
(21) 以無所得故 (22) 菩提薩埵 (23) 般若波羅蜜多依於住 (24) 心無
罣礙心無 罣礙 (25) 無有恐怖 (26) 顛倒遠離 (27) 究竟涅槃 (28) 三
世所住諸佛 (29) 依般若波羅蜜多故 (30) 得無上等正覺 (31) 是故應
知般若波羅蜜多 (32) 大呪 (33) 大明呪 (34) 無上彼呪 (35) 無等呪
(36) 一切苦正息 (37) 眞實不虛 (38) 般若波羅蜜多 (39) 說呪曰 (40)
誐諦誐諦 (41) 播囉誐諦 (42) 播囉僧誐諦 (43) 冒地娑嚩賀 (44) 梵
本般若心經

CHINESE, AMOGHAVAJRA VERSION, transliteration of the above (CAtl)

(0) bo re bo luo mi duo xin jing (1) sheng guan zi zai pu sa (2) shen bo re
bo luo mi duo xing xing shi (3) zhao jian wu yun (4) bi zi xing kong xian
(6) ci She li zi (6x) se kong kong xing shi se (7) se bu yi kong kong yi bu yi
se (8) shi se bi kong shi kong bi se (9) ru shi shou xiang xing shi (10) ci She

li zi zhu fa kong xiang (11) bu sheng bu mie bu gou bu jing bu zeng bu jian
(12) shi gu She li zi kong zhong (13) wu se wu shou wu xiang wu xing wu
shi (14) wu yan er bi she shen yi (15) wu se sheng xiang wei chu fa (16) wu
yan jie nai zhi wu yi shi jie (17) wu ming wu ming wu ming jin wu ming jin
(18) nai zhi wu lao si wu lao si jin (19) wu ku ji mie dao (20) wu zhi wu de
wu zheng (21) yi wu suo de gu (22) pu ti sa duo (23) bo re bo luo mi duo yi
yu zhu (24) xin wu gua ai xin wu gua ai (25) wu you kong bu (26) dian dao
yuan li (27) jiu jing nie pan (28) san shi suo zhu zhu fo (29) yi bo re bo luo
mi duo gu (30) de wu shang deng zheng jue (31) shi gu ying zhi bo re bo luo
mi duo (32) da zhou (33) da ming zhou (34) wu shang bi zhou (35) wu deng
zhou (36) yi qie ku zheng xi (37) zhen shi bu xu (38) bo re bo luo mi duo
(39) shuo zhou yue (40) e'e di e'e di (41) bo luo e'e di (42) bo luo seng e'e di
(43) pu ti suo fu he (44) fan ben bo re xin jing

SANSKRIT, NEPALESE VERSION, after circa 1100 (SN)
Transcribed by Edward Conze. See p. 68.

(0x) oṃ namo bhagavatyai Ārya-Prajñāpāramitāyai!
(1) ārya-Avalokiteśvaro bodhisattvo (2) gaṃbhīrāṃ prajñāpāramitāyā-
caryāṃ caramāṇo (3) vyavalokayati sma: pañca-skandhās tāṃs (4) ca
svabhāva śūnyan paśyast sma. (6) iha Śāriputra (6x) rūpaṃ śūnyatā
śūnyataiva rūpaṃ, (7) rūpan na pṛthak śūnyatā, śūnyatāyā na pṛthag
rūpaṃ, (8) yad rūpaṃ sā śūnyatā yā śūnyatā tad rūpaṃ. (9) evam eva
vedanā-saṃjñā-saṃskāra-vijñānaṃ. (10) iha Śāriputra sarva-dharmāḥ
śūnyatā-lakṣaṇā, (11) anutpannā aniruddhā, amalā avimalā, anūnā
aparipūrṇāḥ. (12) tasmāc Chāriputra śūnyatāyāṃ (13) na rūpaṃ na vedanā
na saṃjñā na saṃskārāḥ na vijñānam, (14) na cakṣuḥ-śrotra-ghrāṇa-jihvā-
kāya-manāṃsi (15) na rūpa-śabda-gandha-rasa-spraṣṭavya-dharmāḥ. (16)
na cakṣur-dhātur yāvan na manovijñāna-dhātuḥ. (17) na-avidyā na-avidyā
kṣayo (18) yāvan na jarāmaraṇaṃ na jarāmaraṇakṣayo. (19) na duḥkha-
samudaya-nirodha-mārgā. (20) na jñānam na prāptir na-aprāptiḥ. (21)
tasmāc Chāriputra aprāptitvād (22) bodhisattvasya (23) prajñāpāramitāṃ
āśritya (24) viharaty acittāvaraṇaḥ. cittāvaraṇa- (25) nāstitvād
atrasto (26) viparyāsa-atikrānto (27) niṣṭhā-nirvāṇa-prāptaḥ. (28)
tryadhvavyavasthitāḥ sarva-buddhāḥ (29) prajñāpāramitām-āśritya- (30)
anuttarāṃ samyaksambodhim abhisambuddhāḥ. (31) tasmāj jñātavyam:
prajñāpāramitā (32) mahā-mantro (33) mahā-vidyā-mantro (34) 'nuttara-

mantro (35) 'samasama-mantraḥ, (36) sarva-duḥkha-praśamanaḥ, (37) satyam amithyatvāt. (38) prajñāpāramitāyām ukto mantraḥ. (39) tadyathā: (40) oṃ gate gate (41) pāragate (42) pārasaṃgate (43) bodhi svāhā. (44) iti prajñāpāramitā-hṛdayaṃ samāptam.

ENGLISH, F. Max Müller translation of the Horyu-ji version of the Hridaya, 1984 (EM). See p. 67.

(0) Pragñā-Pāramitā-Hridaya-Sūtra (0x) Adoration to the Omniscient! (1) The venerable Bodhisattva Avalokiteśvara, (2) performing his study in the deep Pragñāpāramitā (perfection of wisdom), (3) thought thus: 'There are the five Skandhas, (4) and these he considered as by their nature empty (phenomenal)' (6) 'O Śāriputra,' he said, (6x) form here is emptiness, and emptiness indeed is form. (7) Emptiness is not different from form, form is not different from emptiness. (8) What is form that is emptiness, what is emptiness that is form.' (9) 'The same applies to perception, name, conception, and knowledge.' (10) 'Here, O Śāriputra, all things have the character of emptiness, (11) they have no beginning, no end, they are faultless and not faultless, they are not imperfect and not perfect. (12) Therefore, O Śāriputra, in this emptiness (13) there is no form, no perception, no name, no concepts, no knowledge. (14) No eye, ear, nose, tongue, body, mind. (15) No form, sound, smell, taste, touch, objects.' (16) 'There is no eye,' &c., till we come to 'there is no mind.' (What is left out here are the eighteen Dhātus or aggregates, viz. eye, form, vision; ear, sound, hearing; nose, odour, smelling; tongue, flavour, tasting; body, touch, feeling; mind, objects, thought.) (17) 'There is no knowledge, no ignorance, no destruction of knowledge, no destruction of ignorance,' &c., till we come to (18) 'there is no decay and death, no destruction of decay and death; (19) there are not [the four truths, viz. that there] is pain, origin of pain, stoppage of pain, and the path to it. (20) There is no knowledge, no obtaining of [Nirvāna].' (23) 'A man who has approached the Pragñāpāramitā of (22) the Bodhisattva dwells (24) enveloped in consciousness. But when the envelopment of consciousness has been annihilated, (25) then he becomes free of all fear, (26) beyond the reach of change, (27) enjoying final Nirvāna. (28) All Buddhas of the past, present, and future, (29) after approaching the Pragñāpāramitā, (30) have awoke to the highest perfect knowledge.' (31) 'Therefore one ought to know the great verse of the Pragñāpāramitā,

(33) the verse of the great wisdom, (34) the unsurpassed verse, (35) the peerless verse, (36) which appeases all pain (37) — it is truth, because it is not false — (38) the verse proclaimed in the Pragñāpāramitā: (43) 'O wisdom, (40) gone, gone, (41) gone to the other shore, (42) landed at the other shore. (43) 'O wisdom Svaha!' (44) Thus ends the heart of the Pragñāpāramitā.

ENGLISH, D. T. Suzuki translation, 1953 (ES)
From *Manual of Zen Buddhism,* p. 26.

(0) Prajna-paramita-hridaya Sutra (1) When the Bodhisattva Avalo-kitesvara (2) was engaged in the practice of the deep Prajnaparamita, (3) he perceived: there are the five Skandhas; and these he saw (4) in their self-nature to be empty.(6) O, Sariputra, (6x) form is here emptiness, emptiness is form; (7) form is no other than emptiness, emptiness is no other than form; (8) what is form that is emptiness, what is emptiness that is form. (9) The same can be said of sensation, thought, confection, and consciousness. (10) O Sariputra, all things are here characterized with emptiness: (11) they are not born, they are not annihilated; they are not tainted, they are not immaculate; they do not increase, they do not decrease. (12) Therefore, O Sariputra, in emptiness (13) there is no form, no sensation, no thought, no confection, no consciousness; (14) no eye, ear, nose, tongue, body, mind; (15) no form, sound, odour, taste, touch, objects; (16) no Dhatu of vision, till we come to no Dhatu of consciousness; (17) there is no knowledge, no ignorance, no extinction of knowledge, no extinction of ignorance, (18) till we come to there is no old age and death, no extinction of old age and death; (19) there is no suffering, no accumulation, no annihilation, no path; (20) there is no knowledge, no attainment, [and] no realization, (21) because there is no attainment. (22) In the mind of the Bodhisattva (23) who dwells depending on the Prajnaparamita (24) there are no obstacles; and because there are no obstacles in his mind, (25) he has no fear (26) and, going beyond the perverted views (27) he reaches final Nirvana. (28) All the Buddhas of the past, present, and future, (29) depending on the Prajnaparamita, (30) attain to the highest perfect enlightenment. (31) Therefore, one ought to know that the Prajnaparamita is (32) the great Mantram, (33) the Mantram of great wisdom, (34) the highest Mantram, (35) the peerless Mantram, (36) which is capable of

allaying all pain; (37) it is truth because it is not falsehood; (38) this is the Mantram proclaimed in the Prajnaparamita. (39) It runs: (40) Gate, gate, (41) paragate, (42) parasamgate, (43) bodhi, svaha! (O Bodhi, gone, gone, gone to the other shore, landed at the other shore, Svaha!)

ENGLISH, Edward Conze translation, 1958 (EC)

(0) The *Heart Sutra* (0x) Homage to the Perfection of Wisdom, the lovely, the Holy! (1) Avalokita, The Holy Lord and Bodhisattva, (2) was moving in the deep course of the wisdom which has gone beyond. (3) He looked down from on high, he beheld but five heaps, and he saw that (4) in their own-being they were empty. (6) Here O Sariputra, (6x) form is emptiness and the very emptiness is form; (7) emptiness does not differ from form, form does not differ from emptiness; (8) whatever is form, that is emptiness; whatever is emptiness, that is form, (9) the same is true of feelings, perceptions, impulses, and consciousness. (10) Here, O Sariputra, all dharmas are marked with emptiness; (11) they are not produced or stopped, not defiled or immaculate, not deficient or complete. (12) Therefore, O Sariputra, in emptiness (13) there is no form, nor feeling, nor perception, nor impulse, nor consciousness; (14) No eye, ear, nose, tongue, body, mind: (15) No forms, sounds, smells, tastes, touchables or objects of mind; (16) No sight-organ element, and so forth, until we come to: No mind-consciousness element; (17) There is no ignorance, no extinction of ignorance, and so forth, (18) until we come to: there is no decay and death, no extinction of decay and death. (19) There is no suffering, no origination, no stopping, no path. (20) There is no cognition, no attainment and no non-attainment. (21) Therefore, O Sariputra, it is because of his non-attainmentness (22) that a Bodhisattva, (23) through having relied on the perfection of wisdom, (24) dwells without thought-coverings. In the absence of thought-coverings (25) he has not been made to tremble, (26) he has overcome what can upset, (27) and in the end he attains to Nirvana. (28) All those who appear as Buddhas in the three periods of time (30) fully awake to the utmost, right and perfect enlightenment (29) because they have relied on the perfection of wisdom. (31) Therefore one should know the prajñāpāramitā as (32) the great spell, (33) the spell of great knowledge, (34) the utmost spell, (35) the unequalled spell, (36) allayer of all suffering, (37) in truth — for what could go wrong? (38) By the

prajñāpāramitā has this spell been delivered. (39) It runs like this: (40) Gone, gone, (41) gone beyond, (42) gone altogether beyond, (43) O what an awakening, all-hail! (44) This completes the Heart of perfect wisdom.

ENGLISH, NEW VERSION, Kazuaki Tanahashi and Joan Halifax translation, 2007 (ETH). See also p. 3.

(0) The Sutra on the Heart of Realizing Wisdom Beyond Wisdom (1) Avalokiteśvara, who helps all to awaken, (2) moves in the deep course of realizing wisdom beyond wisdom, (3) sees that all five streams of body, heart, and mind (4) are without boundary, (5) and frees all from anguish. (6) O Sariputra, [who listens to the teachings of the Buddha], (7) form is not separate from boundlessness; boundlessness is not separate from form. (8) Form is boundlessness; boundlessness is form. (9) Feelings, perceptions, inclinations, and discernment are also like this. (10) O Sariputra, boundlessness is the nature of all things. (11) It neither arises nor perishes, neither stains nor purifies, neither increases nor decreases. (12) Boundlessness is (13) not limited by form, nor by feelings, perceptions, inclinations, or discernment. (14) It is free of the eyes, ears, nose, tongue, body, and mind; (15) free of sight, sound, smell, taste, touch, and any object of mind; (16) free of sensory realms, including the realm of the mind. (17) It is free of ignorance and the end of ignorance. (18) Boundlessness is free of old age and death, and free of the end of old age and death. (19) It is free of suffering, arising, cessation, and path, (20) and free of wisdom and attainment. (21) Being free of attainment, (22) those who help all to awaken (23) abide in the realization of wisdom beyond wisdom (24) and live with an unhindered mind. Without hindrance, (25) the mind has no fear. (26) Free from confusion, those who lead all to liberation (27) embody complete serenity. (28) All those in the past, present, and future, (29) who realize wisdom beyond wisdom, (30) manifest unsurpassable and thorough awakening. (31) Know that realizing wisdom beyond wisdom (32) is no other than this wondrous mantra, (33) luminous, (34) unequaled, (35) and supreme. (36) It relieves all suffering. (37) It is genuine and not illusory. (38) So set forth this mantra of realizing wisdom beyond wisdom. (39) Set forth this mantra that says: (40) *Gaté, gaté* (41) *paragaté,* (42) *parasamgaté,* (43) *bodhi! Svaha!*

Longer Texts

Sanskrit, Nepalese version, after circa 1100, transcription by Edward Conze. See p. 68.

(0x) Oṃ namo Bhagavatyai Ārya-prajñāpāramitāyai! Evaṃ mayā śrutam ekasmin samaye. Bhagavān Rājagṛhe viharati sma Gṛdhrakūṭa-parvate, mahatā bhikṣu-saṃghena sārdhaṃ mahatā ca bodhisattva-saṃghena. tena khalu punaḥ samayena Bhagavān gambhīra-avabhāsaṃ nāma dharmaparyāyaṃ bhāṣitvā samādhiṃ samāpannaḥ. tena ca samayena Ārya-avalokiteśvaro bodhisattvo mahāsattvo gambhīrāyāṃ prajñāpāramitāyāṃ caryāṃ caramāṇa evaṃ vyavalokayati sma: pañca-skandhās tāṃś ca svabhāva-śūnyān vyavalokayati. atha-āyuṣmāñc Chāriputro buddha-anubhāvena Ārya-avalokiteśvaraṃ bodhisattvaṃ mahāsattvam etad avocat: yaḥ kaścit kūlaputro vā kuladuhitā vā asyāṃ gambhīrāyāṃ prajñāpāramitāyāṃ caryāṃ cartukāmas tena kathaṃ śikṣitavyam? evam ukta Ārya-avalokiteśvaro bodhisattvo mahāsattvo āyuṣmantaṃ Śāriputram etad avocat: yaḥ kaścic Chāriputra kulaputro vā kuladuhitā vā asyāṃ gambhīrāyāṃ prajñāpāramitāyāṃ caryāṃ cartukāmas tenaivaṃ vyavalokitavyam. (1) Ārya-avalokiteśvaro bodhisattvo (2) gambhīraṃ prajñāpāramitā caryāṃ caramāṇo (3) vyavalokayati sma: pañca-skandhās tāṃś (4) ca svabhāva-śūnyan paśyati sma. (6) iha Śāriputra (6x) rūpaṃ śūnyatā śūnyataiva rūpaṃ, (7) rūpān na pṛthak śūnyatā śūnyatāyā na pṛthag rūpaṃ, (8) yad rūpaṃ sā śūnyatā yā śūnyatā tad rūpaṃ; (9) evam eva vedanā-saṃjñā-saṃskāra-vijñānam. (10) iha Śāriputra sarva-dharmāḥ śūnyatālakṣaṇā, (11) anutpannā aniruddhā, amalā avimalā, anūnā aparipūrṇāḥ. (12) tasmāc Chāriputra śūnyatāyāṃ (13) na rūpaṃ na vedanā na saṃjñā na saṃskārāḥ na vijñānam. (14) na cakṣuḥ-śrotra-ghrāṇa-jihvā-kāya-manāṃsi. (15) na rūpa-śabda-gandha-rasa-spraṣṭavya-dharmāḥ. (16) na cakṣur-dhātur yāvan na manovijñāna-dhātuḥ. (17) na-avidyā na-avidyā-kṣayo. (18) yāvan na jarā-maraṇaṃ na jarāmaraṇakṣayo. (19) na duḥkha-samudaya-nirodha-mārgā. (20) na jñānam, na prāptir na aprāptiḥ. (21) tasmāc (22) Chāriputra aprāptitvād bodhisattvasya (23) prajñāpāramitām āśritya (24) viharaty acittāvaraṇaḥ. cittāvaraṇa- (25) nāstitvād atrasto (26) viparyāsa-atikrānto (27) niṣṭhā-nirvāṇa-prāptaḥ. (28) tryadhva-vyavasthitāḥ sarva-buddhāḥ (29) prajñāpāramitām-āśritya- (30) anuttarāṃ samyaksambodhim abhisambuddhāḥ. (31) tasmāj jñātavyam:

prajñāpāramitā (32) mahā-mantro (33) mahā-vidyā-mantro (34) 'nuttara-
mantro (35) samasama-mantraḥ, (36) sarva-duḥkha-praśamanaḥ, (37)
satyam amithyatvāt. (38) prajñāpāramitāyām ukto mantraḥ. (39) tadyathā
(40) gate gate (41) pāragate (42) pārasaṃgate (43) bodhi svāhā. (43x)
Evam Śāriputra gambhīraṃ prajñāpāramitāyāṃ caryāyāṃ śikṣitavyaṃ
bodhisattvena. Atha khalu Bhagavān tasmāt samādher vyuttāya-
Ārya-avalokiteśvarāya bodhisattvāya mahāsattvāya sādhukāram adāt.
sādhu sādhu kulaputra, evam etat kulaputra evam etad, gambhīrāyāṃ
prajñāpāramitāyāṃ caryāṃ cartavyaṃ yathā tvayā nirdiṣṭam anumodyate
sarva-Tathāgatair arhadbhiḥ. idam avocad Bhagavān. āttamanā-āyuṣmāñc
Chāriputtra Ārya-avalokiteśvaro bodhisattvo mahāsattvas te ca bhikṣavas
te ca bodhisattvā mahāsattvāḥ sā ca sarvāvatī parṣat sa-deva-mānuṣa-asura-
garuḍa-gandharvaś ca loko Bhagavato bhāṣitam abhyanandann iti. (44) iti
ārya-prajñāpāramitā-hṛdayaṃ samāptam.

CHINESE VERSION, translated by Prajna, Liyan, et al., 790
(From *Taisho,* no. 253.)

(0) 般若 波羅蜜多心經 (0x) 如是我聞一時佛在王舍城耆闍崛山中
與大比丘衆及菩薩衆俱時佛世尊即入三昧名廣大甚深爾時衆中
有菩薩摩訶薩名 (1) 觀自在 (2) 行深般若 波羅蜜多時 (3) 照見五蘊
(4) 皆空 (5) 離 諸苦厄 (5x) 即時舍利弗承佛威力合掌恭F.M敬白觀
自在菩薩 摩訶薩言善男子若有欲學甚深般若波羅蜜多行者云何
修行如是問已爾時觀自在菩薩摩訶薩告具壽舍利弗言舍利子若
善男子善女人行甚深 般若波羅蜜多行時應觀五蘊性空 (6) 舍利子
(7) 色不異 空空不異色 (8) 色即是空空即是色 (9) 受想行識亦復如
是 (10) 舍利子是諸法空相 (11) 不生不滅不垢不淨不增不減 (12) 是
故空中 (13) 無色無受想行識 (14) 無眼耳鼻舌身意 (15) 無色聲香味
觸法 (16) 無眼界乃至無意識界 (17) 無無明亦無無明盡 (18) 乃至無
老死亦無老死盡 (19) 無苦集滅道 (20) 無智亦無得 (21) 以無所得故
(22) 菩提薩埵 (23) 依般若波羅蜜多故 (24) 心無罣礙無罣礙故 (25)
無有恐怖 (26) 遠離顛倒夢想 (27) 究竟涅槃 (28) 三世諸佛 (29) 依般
若 波羅蜜多故 (30) 得阿耨多羅三藐三菩提 (31) 故知般若 波羅蜜
多 (32) 是大神咒 (33) 是大明咒 (34) 是無上咒 (35) 是無等等咒 (36)
能除 一切苦 (37) 眞實不虛 (38) 故説般若波羅蜜多咒 (39) 即説咒
曰 (40) 蘗諦蘗諦 (41) 波羅蘗諦 (42) 波羅僧蘗諦 (43) 菩提娑婆訶
(43x) 如是舍利弗諸菩薩摩訶薩於甚深般若波羅蜜多行應如是行

如是說已即時世尊從廣大甚深三摩地起讚觀自在菩薩摩訶薩言
善哉善哉善男子如是如是如汝所說甚深般若波羅蜜多行應如是
行如是行時一切如來皆悉隨喜爾時世尊說是語已具壽舍利弗大
喜充遍 觀自在菩薩 摩訶薩亦大歡喜時彼衆說會天人阿修羅乾闥
婆等聞佛所說皆大歡喜信受奉行 (44) 般若波羅蜜多心經

CHINESE VERSION, translated by Prajna, Liyan, et al., transliteration of the above

(0) bo re bo luo mi duo xin jing (1x) ru shi wo wen yi shi fo zai wang she cheng qi she jue shan zhong yu da bi qiu zhong ji pu sa zhong ju shi fo shi zun ji ru san mei ming guang da shen shen er shi zhong zhong you pu sa mo he sa ming (1) guan zi zai (2) xing shen bo re bo luo mi duo shi (3) zhao jian wu yun (4) jie kong (5) li zhu ku e (5x) ji shi she li fu cheng fo wei li he zhang gong jing bai guan zi zai pu sa mo he sa yan shan nan zi ruo you yu xue shen shen bo re bo luo mi duo xing zhe yun he xiu xing ru shi wen yi er shi guan zi zai pu sa mo he sa gao ju shou she li fu yan she li zi ruo shan nan zi shan nü ren xing shen shen bo re bo luo mi duo xing shi ying guan wu yun xing kong (6) she li zi (7) se bu yi kong kong bu yi se (8) se ji shi kong. kong ji shi se (9) shou xiang xing shi yi fu ru shi (10) She li zi shi zhu fa kong xiang. (11) bu sheng bu mie bu gou bu jing, bu zeng bu jian (12) shi gu kong zhong (13) wu se, wu shou xiang xing shi (14) wu yan er bi she shen yi (15) wu se sheng xiang wei chu fa (16) wu yan jie nai zhi wu yi shi jie (17) wu wu ming yi wu wu ming jin (18) nai zhi wu lao si yi wu lao si jin. (19) wu ku ji mie dao (20) wu zhi yi wu de (21) yi wu suo de gu (22) pu ti sa duo (23) yi bo re bo luo mi duo gu (24) xin wu gua ai. wu gua ai gu (25) wu you kong bu (26) yuan li dian dao meng xiang (27) jiu jing nie pan (28) san shi zhu fo (29) yi bo re bo luo mi duo gu (30) de a nou duo luo san miao san pu ti (31) gu zhi bo re bo luo mi duo (32) shi da shen zhou (33) shi da ming zhou (34) shi wu shang zhou (35) shi wu deng deng zhou (36) neng chu yi qie ku (37) zhen shi bu xu (38) gu shuo bo re bo lo mi duo zhou (39) ji shuo zhou yue (40) jie di jie di (41) bo luo jie di (42) bo luo seng jie di (43) pu ti suo po he (43x) ru shi she li fu zhu pu sa mo he sa yu shen shen bo re bo luo mi duo xing ying ru shi xing ru shi shuo yi ji shi shi zun cong guang da shen shen shan mo di qi zan guan zi zai pu sa mo he sa yan shan zai shan zai shan nan zi ru shi ru shi ru ru suo shuo shen shen bo re bo luo mi duo xing ying ru shi xing ru shi xing shi yi qie ru lai jie xi sui xi er shi shi zun shuo shi yu yi

ju shou she li fu da xi chong bian guan zi zai pu sa mo he sa yi da huan xi shi
bi zhong shuo hui tian ren a xiu luo qian ta po deng wen fo suo shuo jie da
huan xi xin shou feng xing (44) bo re bo luo mi duo xin jing

TIBETAN VERSION
Transcribed by Christian P. B. Haskett for this book.

(0) bcom ldan 'das ma shes rab kyi pha rol tu phyin pa'i snying po bzhugs
so (0x1) bcom ldan 'das ma shes rab kyi pha rol tu phyin pa'i snying po
bzhugs so (0x2) smra bsam brjod med shes rab pha rol phyin ma skyes
mi 'gag nam mkha'i ngo bo nyid so so rang rig ye shes spyod yul ba dus
gsum rgyal ba'i yum la phyag 'tshal lo. (0x3) rgya gar skad du bha ga wa ti
pra dznyA pA ra mi tA hri da ya. (0x4) bod skad du, bcom ldan 'das ma
shes rab kyi pha rol tu phyin pa'i snying po. (0x5) bcom ldan 'das ma shes
rab kyi pha rol tu phyin pa la phyag 'tshal lo. (0x6) 'di skad bdag gis thos
pa dus gcig na. bCom lDan 'Das rgyal bo'i khab Bya rGod Phung Po'i Ri
na, dge slong gi dge 'dun chen po dang, byang chub sems dpa'i dge 'dun
chen po dang thabs gcig tu bzhugs te. de'i tshe, bCom lDan 'Das zab mo
snang ba zhes bya ba'i chos kyi rnam grangs kyi ting nge 'dzin la snyoms
par zhugs so. yang de'i tshe, (1) Byang Chub Sems dPa' Sems dPa' Chen
po 'Phags Pa sPyan Ras gZigs dBang Phyug shes rab kyi pha rol tu phyin
pa zab mo'i spyod pa nyid la rnam par blta zhing (3) phung po lnga po de
dag la yang rang bzhin gyis stong par rnam par lta'o. (0x7) de nas Sangs
rGyas kyi mthus Tshe dang lDan Pa ShA Ri'i Bus Byang Chub Sems dPa'
Sems dPa' Chen po 'Phags Pa sPyan Ras gZigs dBang Phyug la 'di skad ces
smras so. rigs kyi bu 'am rigs kyi bu mo gang la la shes rab kyi pha rol tu
phyin pa zab mo'i spyod pa spyad par 'dod pa des ji ltar bslab par bya. de
skad ces smras pa dang, Byang Chub Sems dPa Sems dPa' Chen po 'Phags
Pa sPyan Ras gZigs dBang Phyug gis Tshe Dang lDan Pa ShA Ra Dwa
Ti'i Bu la 'di skad ces smras so. ShA Ri'i Bu, rigs kyi bu 'am rigs kyi bu mo
gang la la shes rab kyi pha rol tu phyin pa zab mo'i spyod par 'dod pa des
'di ltar rnam par blta bar bya ste. (3) phung po lnga po de dag kyang (4)
rang bzhin gyis stong par yang dag par rjes su blta'o. (8) gzugs stong pa'o.
stong pa nyid gzugs so. (7) gzugs las stong pa nyid gzhan ma yin stong
pa nyid las kyang gzugs gzhan ma yin no. (9) de bzhin du tshor ba dang
'du shes dang 'du byed dang rnam par shes pa rnams stong pa'o. (10) shA
ri'i bu, de ltar chos thams cad stong pa nyid de. mtshan nyid med pa. (11)

ma skyes pa. ma 'gags pa. dri ma med pa. dri ma dang bral ba med pa. bri ma med cing. gang ba med pa'o. (12) ShA ri'i bu, de lta bas na, stong pa nyid la (13) gzugs med, tshor ba med, 'du shes med, 'du byed rnams med, rnam par shes pa med. (14) mig med, rna ba med, sna med, lce med, lus med, yid med. (15) gzugs med, sgra med, dri med, ro med, reg bya med, chos med do. (16) mig gi khams med pa nas yid kyi khams med. (16x) yid kyi rnam par shes pa'i khams kyi bar du yang med do. (17) ma rig pa med, ma rig pa zad pa med pa nas (18) rga shi med, rga shi zad pa'i bar du yang med do. (19) de bzhin du, sdug bsngal ba dang. kun 'byung ba dang. 'gog pa dang. lam med. (20) ye shes med, thob pa med, ma thob pa yang med do. (22) ShA Ri'i Bu. (21) de lta bas na. (22x) byang chub sems dpa' rnams ni thob pa med pa'i phyir. (23) shes rab kyi pha rol tu phyin pa 'di la brten cing gnas te. (24, 25) sems la sgrib pa med pas skrag pa med de. (26) phyin ci log las shin tu 'das nas, (27) mya ngan las 'das pa'i mthar phyin to. (28) dus gsum du rnam par bzhugs pa'i sangs rgyas thams cad kyang (29) shes rab kyi pha rol tu phyin pa 'di la brten nas bla na med pa (30) yang dag par rdzogs pa'i byang chub tu mngon par rdzogs par sangs rgyas so. (31) de lta bas na, shes rab kyi pha rol tu phyin pa'i sngags. (32) rig pa chen po'i sngags. (33) bla na med pa'i sngags. (34) mi mnyam pa dang (35) mnyam par byed pa'i sngags. (36) sdug bsngal thams cad rab tu zhi bar byed pa'i sngags. (37) mi brdzun pas na bden par shes par bya ste. (38) shes rab kyi pha rol tu phyin pa'i sngags smras pa. (39) ta dya thA. (40) ga te ga te. (41) pa ra ga te. (42) pa ra saṃ ga te. (43) bo dhi svA hA. (43x) ShA Ri'i Bu, byang chub sems dpa' sems dpa' chen pos de ltar shes rab kyi pha rol tu phyin pa zab mo la bslab par bya'o. de nas bCom lDan 'Das ting nge 'dzin de las bzhengs nas. Byang Chub Sems dPa Sems dPa' Chen po 'Phags Pa sPyan Ras gZigs dBang Phyug la legs so zhes bya ba byin te, legs so legs so. rigs kyi bu de de bzhin no. de de bzhin te. ji ltar khyod kyis bstan pa de bzhin du shes rab kyi pha rol tu phyin pa la spyad par bya ste, de bzhin gshegs pa rnams kyang rjes su yi rang ngo. bCom lDan 'Das kyis de skad ces dka' stsal nas, Tshe Dang lDan Pa ShA Ri'i Bu dang, Byang Chub Sems dPa Sems dPa' Chen po 'Phags Pa sPyan Ras gZigs dBang Phyug dang, thams cad dang ldan pa'i 'khor de dag dang, lha dang, mi dang, lha ma yin dang, dri zar bcas pa'i 'jig rten yi rangs te, bCom lDan 'Das kyis gsungs pa la mngon par bstod do. (44) bcom ldan 'das ma shes rab kyi pha rol tu phyin pa'i snying po zhes bya ba theg pa chen po'i mdo rdzogs so.

ENGLISH, TIBETAN VERSION

Translation of the above by Christian P. B. Haskett.

(0) bcom ldan 'das ma shes rab kyi pha rol tu phyin pa'i snying po bzhugs so (0x1) [prefatory matter] Here sits the Bhagavatī Prajñāpāramitā hṛdaya. (0x2) [introductory verse]

> Inexpressible, Inconceivable, Ineffable Perfection of Wisdom
> Unborn, Unobstructed, the Essence of Space
> Realm of Self-aware Primordial Wisdom
> Mother of the Victors of the Three Times, to You I prostrate.

(0x3) [Transliterated Sanskrit title] In the language of India, bhagavatī prajñāpāramitā hṛdaya (0x4) [Translated Tibetan title] In the language of Tibet, the Blessed One, Heart of the Perfection of Wisdom.
(0x5) [Introductory verse of veneration]

> Reverence to you
> O Blessed One
> Perfection of Wisdom.

(0x6) [Prefatory Matter] Thus did I hear once: The Bhagavan was staying on Vulture Peak in Rājagṛha, together with a great assembly of monks and a great assembly of bodhisattvas. At that time, the Bhagavan was absorbed in the deep concentration on the expression of the dharma known as "The Profound Illumination." (1) And at that time, the Bodhisattva Mahāsattva, the Noble Avalokiteśvara (2) looked at the activities of the Profound Perfection of Wisdom (3) and saw that the five aggregates (4) were devoid of self-nature. (0x7) Then, by the power of the Buddha, the Elder Śāriputra spoke to the Bodhisattva Mahāsattva, the Noble Avalokiteśvara: "How should a Noble Son or Noble Daughter train, who wishes to engage in the profound activities of the Perfection of Wisdom?" The Bodhisattva Mahāsattva, the Noble Avalokiteśvara, said to Sāradvatiputra these words: "O, Śāriputra, a Noble Son or Daughter who wishes to engage in the profound activities of the Perfection of Wisdom should consider thusly, and should regard the five aggregates as devoid of self-nature. (8) Form is empty. Emptiness is form. (7) Emptiness is not other than form, nor is form other than emptiness. (9) Similarly, sensations, conceptions, formations, and consciousnesses are empty. (10) Śāriputra, in that way all phenomenon are emptiness. They have no characteristics. (11) They are not born. They do not cease. There is no defilement. There is no lack of defilement. There is no taking away, and there is no filling. (12) O Śāriputra, therefore, in emptiness there is (13) no form, no sensation, no conception, no formations, no consciousness. (14) There is no eye, no nose, no ear, no tongue, no body, no mind. (15) There is no form, no sound, no scent, no taste, no touch, and no phenomenon. (16) There is no visual sphere, and on through to no mental sphere, (16x) up to: there being no sphere of mental consciousness either. (17) There is no ignorance, nor is there anything from elimination of ignorance to (18) there being no aging and death, up to: there being no end to aging and death either. (19) Similarly, there is no suffering, source, cessation, or path. (20) There is no primordial wisdom, there is no attainment, and there is no non-attainment. (22) O Śāriputra, (21) Therefore (22x) Because for bodhisattvas there is no attainment, (23) then remaining in reliance on the Perfection of Wisdom, (24, 25) Because there is no obstruction to the mind, there is no fear. (26) Having completely gone beyond perversity (27) They have reached the end, nirvana. (28) All the Buddhas who reside in the three times, too, (29) having relied on the Perfection of Wisdom, (30) have completely awakened into enlightenment, total and complete, the unsurpassable. (31) Therefore, there is the mantra of the Perfection of Wisdom. (32) It is the mantra of great awareness. (33) It is the unsurpassable mantra. (34, 35) It is the mantra that is the equal of the unequalled. (36) It is the mantra which pacifies all suffering. (37) Because it is not false, it should be known as true. (38, 39) The mantra of the Perfection of Wisdom is spoken: (40) ga te ga te. (41) pa ra ga te. (42) pa ra saṃ ga te. (43) bodhi svāhā. (43x) O Śāriputra, the Mahāsattva Bodhisattva should train in the profound Perfection of Wisdom in just that way." Then, the Blessed One, having risen from his meditation, spoke to the Mahāsattva Bodhisattva Avalokiteśvara and giving his endorsement, said, "Excellent! Excellent! O Noble son, it is just that way. It being just that way, One should engage in the Perfection of Wisdom just as you have taught, and even the tathāgatas will rejoice." The Blessed One having uttered these words, the Elder Śāriputra, the Mahāsattva Bodhisattva Ārya Avalokiteśvara, the entire retinue, and the whole world including gods, humans, demi-gods, and gandharvas, all rejoiced. (44) This concludes the Blessed One, the Mahāyāna Sūtra called the Heart of the Perfection of Wisdom.

MONGOLIAN VERSION

Transcribed by Erdenebaatar Erdene-Ochir for this book.

(0)Bilgïin zürxän xämääx sudar orshwoï (0x) Iïn xämään miniï sonsson nägän cagt Yalj Tögs Nögqsön bäär xaany xarsh Xajir *Shuvuud Cogcolson* uuland ayagxa täximlägïin ix xuwraguud xïigääd bodisadwa naryn ix xuwraguud lugaa xamt nägänää suun bülgää. Tär cagt Yalj Tögs Nögqsön Gün nariïnyg üzäxüï xämäägdäx nomyn züïl toony samadid tägsh orshwoï. Mön tär cagt (1) bodisadwa maxasadwa xutagt Nüdäär Üzägq Ärhät q bilgïin qanadad xürsän gün nariïn yawdlyg tiïn üzääd (2) tädgäär tawan cogcyg q mon canaraar xooson xämään tiïn bogood üzwäï. (2x) Tändääs Burxany xüqäär nasnaa tögöldör Shaaryn xöwgüün bäär bodisadwa mahūsadwa xutagt Nüdäär Üzägq Ärxätäd iïn xämään ögüülwäï, "Yazguurtany xöwgüün ba yazguurtany oxin xän zarimuud bilgïin qanadad xürsniï gün yawdlaar yawsugaï xämään xüsägch täd bäär yamar mät suralcax buï?" Tiïn xämään ögüülsänd bodisadwa mahūsadwa xutagt Nudäär Üzägq Ärxät bäär nasanaa tögöldör Shaaryn höwgüünd iïn xämään ögüülwäï, "Shaaryn xöwgüün ää! Yazguurtany xöwgüün ba yazguurtany oxin xän zarimuud bilgïin qanadad xürsniï gün yawdlaar yawsugaï xämään xüsägq täd bäär änä mät tiïn üzäx bögööd (3) tädgäär tawan cogcyg q (4) mön qanaraar xooson xämään ünäxäär dagan üzäx boloï. (8) Dürs xooson boloï. Xooson dürs boloï. Dürsnääs q xooson angid bus boloi. Xoosnoos q dürs angid bus boloi. (9) Tüünqlän mädräxüï xïigääd xuraan mädäxüï ba xuraan üïldäxüï, tiïn mädäxüïnüüd xooson boloï. (10) Shaaryn xöwgüün ää! Tär mätiïn tuld xamag nom xooson bögööd bilig qanar ügüï, (11) töröx ügüï, türdäx ügüï, xir ügüï, xirääs xagacsan ügüï, buurax ügüï, nämäx ügüï boloï. (12) Shaaryn xöwgüün ää! Tär mätiïn tuld xoosond (13) dürs ügüï, mädräxüï ügüï, xuraan mädäxüï ügüï, xuraan üïldäxüïnüüd ügüï, tiïn mädäxüï ügüï, (14) nüd ügüï, qix ügüï, xamar ügüï, xäl ügüï, bie ügüï, sätgäl ügüï, (15) dürs ügüï, duu ügüï, ünär ügüï, amt ügüï, xürälcäxüï ügüï, nom ügüï boloï. (16) Nüdniï oron ügüïgääs sätgäliïn oron ügüï. (16x) Sätgäliïn tiïn mädäxüïn orond xürtäl ügüï boloï. (17) Munxag ügüï, munxag baragdaxuï ügüïgääs (18) ötlöxüï üxäxüï ügüï, ötlöxüï üxäxüï baragdaxuïd q xürtäl ügüï boloï. (19) Tüünqlän zowlon ba büxän garax xïigääd türdäxüï ba mör ügüï. (20) Bälgä bilig ügüï, oloxuï ügüï, ül oloxuï bäär q ügüï boloi. (22) Shaaryn xöwgüün ää! (21) Tär mätiïn tuld, (22x) bodisadwa nar oloxuï ügüïn tul (23) bilgïin

qanadad xürsän gün üünd shütän orshood, (24 & 25) sätgäld tüitgär
ügüï bolood aïx ügüï buyuu. (26) Qanx buruugaas mashid nöxqij, (27)
nirwaany äcäst xürwäï. (28) Gurwan cag dor ilt suusan xamag burxan
bäär (29) bilgiïn qanadad xürsän gün üünd shütäj däär ügüï (30) ünäxäär
tuulsan bodi dor ilt tögsgön burxan bolwoï. (31) Tär mätiin tuld bilgiïn
qanadad xürsnïï tarni, (32) ix uxaany tarni, (33) tänsäl ügüï tarni, (34) sac
bus lugaa (35) sacuu tarni, (36) xamag zowlong mashid amirluulagq tarni,
(37) xudal busyn tuld ünän xämään mädääd (38) bilgiïn qanadad xürsnïï
tarnïïg ögüülwäï. (39) Dadyata, Um (40) gadä gadä (41) baara gadä (42)
baara sam gadä (43) bodi suuxaa. (43x) Shaaryn xöwgüün ää! Bodisadwa,
maxasadwa nar bäär tär mät gün bilgiïn qanadad xürsänd suralcax
boloï." Tändääs Yalj Tögs Nögqsön tär samadigaas bosoj, bodisadwa
maxasadwa xutagt Nüdäär Üzägq Ärhätäd "Saïn" xämään ögööd "Saïn
saïn. Yazguurtany xöwgüün tär tüünqlän boloï. Tär tüünqlän bögööd qinïï
yamar mät üzüülsen tüünqlänxüü gün bilgiïn qanadad xürsänd yawagdax
buï. Tüünqlän irsänüüd bäär dagan bayasalcaxuï boloï." Yalj Tögs Nögqsön
tiin xämään zarlig bolsond nasnaa tögöldör Shaaryn xöwgüün xiïgääd
bodisadwa maxasadwa xutagt Nüdäär Üzägq Ärhät ba xamag lugaa
tögöldörüüd tädgäär ba tängär xümüün ba asuri, gandari sält ertönc daxin
dagan bayasalcaad Yalj Tögs Nögqsön bäär nomlosnyg ilt mägtwäï. (44)
Yalj Tögs Nögqsönïï ix bilgiïn qanadad xürsnïï zürxän xämääx sudar
tögsöw. Ölziï orshix boltugaï.

Appendix 2: Identical Expressions
in the Chinese Texts

THE LIST IN THE following pages shows how ancient Chinese translators adopted expressions from earlier translators' works, and added their
own expressions. The dominance of the letter "K" shows the overwhelming
influence of Kumarajiva in all *Heart Sutra* translations.

(...): Original expression or slightly different from an earlier
version

K: Identical to expression in the *Large Prajna Paramita Sutra*
translated by Kumarajiva

D: Identical to expression in *Dazhidu Lun*

α: Identical to expression in the α version of the *Heart Sutra*

X: Identical to expression in the Xuanzhuang version of the
Heart Sutra

P, DC, Z, C, DP: Prajna, et al; Dharmachandra; Zhihuilun;
Chosgrub; Danapala, respectively

Segments	Large Sutra Kumarajiva	Dazhidu Lun Kumarajiva	Shorter Text α	Shorter Text Xuanzhuang
0			(α)	(X)
0X				
1			(α)	(X)
2			(α)	(X)
3			(α)	(X)
4			(α)	(X)
5			(α)	α
5X				
6	(K)	K	K	(X)
6X	(K)	K	K	
7	(K)	(D)	D	K
8	(K)	K	K	K
9	(K)	K	K	K
9X				
10	(K)	K	K	(X)
11	(K)	K	K	K
11X	(K)	K	K	
12	(K)	K		K
13	(K)	K	K	K
14	(K)	K	K	K
15	(K)	K	K	K
16	(K)	K	K	K
17	(K)	K	K	K
18	(K)	K	K	K
19	(K)	K	K	K
20	(K)	K	K	K
20X				

Longer Text Prajna, et al.	Longer Text Dharmachandra	Longer Text Zhihuilun	Longer Text Chosgrub	Longer Text Danapala
X	(DC)	X	X	(DP)
(P)	(DC)	(Z)	(C)	(DP)
(P)	(DC)	(Z)	(C)	(DP)
X	X	(Z)	X	(DP)
X	X	X	(C)	(DP)
X	(DC)	DC	(C)	(DP)
(P)		P		
(P)		(Z)	(C)	
X		X	(C)	X
		(Z)	(C)	(DP)
K	K	K	K	(DP)
K	K	(Z)	K	(DP)
K	K	K	(C)	K
	(DC)			
X	X	(Z)	(C)	(DP)
K	K	K	(C)	(DP)
K	K	K	(C)	K
K	K	K	(C)	K
K	K	K	(C)	K
K	K	K	(C)	K
K	K	K	K	(DP)
K	K	K	K	(DP)
K	K	(Z)	K	K
K	K	K	K	K
K	K	(Z)	(C)	(DP)
			(C)	(DP)

Segments	*Large Sutra* Kumarajiva	*Dazhidu Lun* Kumarajiva	Shorter Text α	Shorter Text Xuanzhuang
21			(α)	α
22			(α)	(X)
23			(α)	(X)
24			(α)	α
25			(α)	α
26			(α)	(X)
27			(α)	α
28			(α)	α
29			(α)	(X)
30			(α)	α
30X				
31			(α)	(X)
32				(X)
33			(α)	α
34			(α)	(X)
35			(α)	(X)
36			(α)	α
37			(α)	α
38			(α)	(X)
39			(α)	α
40			(α)	(X)
41			(α)	(X)
42			(α)	(X)
43			(α)	α
43X				
44			(α)	(X)

Longer Text Prajna, et al.	Longer Text Dharmachandra	Longer Text Zhihuilun	Longer Text Chosgrub	Longer Text Danapala
α	α	α	α	(DP)
X	X	X	(C)	(DP)
X	X	(Z)	(C)	(DP)
X	X	(Z)	(C)	(DP)
α	α	α	α	α
X	X	X	(C)	(DP)
α	α	(Z)	α	(DP)
α	α	α	(C)	(DP)
X	X	X	X	(DP)
α	α	α	(C)	α
		(Z)	(C)	
X	X	X	(C)	(DP)
X	X	(Z)	(C)	(DP)
α	α	(Z)	α	(DP)
X	X	(Z)	X	(DP)
X	X	(Z)	X	(DP)
α	α	α	(C)	(DP)
α	α	α	(C)	(DP)
X	X	(Z)	(C)	(DP)
α	X	(Z)	(C)	(DP)
(P)	X	(Z)	(C)	(DP)
(P)	X	(Z)	(C)	(DP)
(P)	X	(Z)	(C)	(DP)
(P)	α	(Z)	α	(DP)
(P)	(DC)	(Z)	(C)	(DP)
(P)	(DC)	X	X	(DP)

Appendix 3: Names in Ideography

As one romanized syllable or set of syllables correspond to a number of ideographs with different meanings, it is difficult to guess or identify ideographs of names from their alphabetic spellings. The list presented here shows the reader how proper nouns cited in this book are represented in their ideographic form.

Amoghavajra	不空
Anguo Jingjiao	安國淨覺
Asangha	無着
Avatamsaka Sutra	華嚴經
Awakening of Faith in Mahayana	大乘起信論
Baekje	百濟
Biography of High Monks in Great Tang Who Searched for Dharma in the West	大唐西遊求法高僧傳
Biography of the Tripitaka Dharma Master of the Da Ci'en Monastery of Great Tang	大唐大慈恩寺三藏法師傳
Bodhiruchi	菩提流支
Busan	釜山
Chang'an	長安
Chengshi School	成實宗
Chiko	智光
Chitatsu	智達
Chitsu	智通
Chosgrub	法成

Chronology of Buddha Ancestors	佛祖統紀
Chu Suiliang	褚遂良
Collected Outstanding Sayings from Zen Monasteries	禪苑集英語錄
Collection of Categorized Books	群書類従
Complete Catalogue of Japanese Books	国書総目録
Consciousness Only	唯識
Crazy Cloud Person (Ikkyu)	狂雲子
Cuiwei Palace	翠微宮
Dabianzheng Guanzhi (Amoghavajra)	大辯正廣智
Da Ci'en Si	大慈恩寺
Dadian Fatong	大顛寶通
Dai Thua Dang	大乘燈
Dajian Huineng, Sixth Ancestor	大鑑慧能
Daman Hongren, Fifth Ancestor	大満弘忍
Danapala	施護
Daoxuan	道宣
Da Xingshan Monastery	大興善寺
Dharmachandra	法月
Dharmapala	護法
Diamond Sutra	金剛經
Documents of the Shoso-in Treasury	正倉院文書
Dosho	道昭
Dunhuang	敦煌
Eihei Dogen	永平道元
Eloquent Commentary on the Prajna Paramita Heart Sutra	般若波羅蜜多心經華言
Emperor Dai	代宗
Emperor Gao	高宗
Emperor Gomizuno'o	後水尾天皇
Emperor Gonara	後奈良天皇

Emperor Hyeon	顯宗
Emperor Qianlong	乾隆帝
Emperor Se	世宗
Emperor Sushun	崇峻天皇
Emperor Tai	太宗
Emperor Wen	文帝
Emperor Yang	煬帝
Essential Meaning of Prajna	理趣分
Fabao	法寶
Faxiang School	法相宗
Furong Daokai	芙蓉道楷
Gikaku	義覺
Goryeo	高麗
Goryeo Tripitaka	高麗版大藏經
Great Prajna Paramita Sutra	大般若般波羅蜜多經
Great Sutra	大經
Guang Hongming-ji	廣弘明集
Gyoin Hashimoto	橋本凝胤
Haein Monastery	海印寺
Hakuin	白隱
Hejian	荷堅
Hokiichi Hanawa	塙保己一
Hongfu Monastery	弘福寺
Horyu Monastery	法隆寺
Huairen	懷仁
Huayuan School	華嚴宗
Huijing	慧浄
Huili	慧立
Ikkyu	一休
Illustrated Prajna Heart Sutra	般若心經圖繪
Imperial Model	帝範
Introduction to the Sacred Scriptures of the Great Tang	大唐聖敎序

Japanese Book of Miraculous Stories	日本霊異記
Jiguo Monastery	紀国寺
Jin Dynasty	金朝
Journey to the West	西遊記
Jushe School	俱舍宗
Kaifeng	開封
Kaiyuan Era Catalogue of Shakyamuni's Teachings	開元釋教録
King Harshavandhana	戒月王
Kofuku-ji	興福寺
Koin Takada	高田好胤
Kuiji	窺基
Kukai	空海
Kumarajiva	鳩摩羅什
Kusha School	俱舍宗
Lady Aoi	葵上
Lanxi Daolong	蘭渓道隆
Liang	梁
Li Shimin (Emperor Tai)	李世民
Liyan	利言
Li Yuan	李淵
Lokakshema	支縷迦纖
Lu Guang	呂光
Luoyang	洛陽
Madhiyamika Treatise	中論
Maha Prajna Paramita	摩訶般若波羅蜜多
Maha Prajna Paramita Great Dharani Sutra	摩訶般若波羅蜜多大明呪經
Maha Prajna Paramita Heart Sutra	摩訶般若波羅蜜多心經
Maha Prajna Paramita Sutra	大般若波羅蜜多經
Maitribharda	慈賢
Minh Chau Huong Hai	明珠香海
Mogao Cave group	莫高窟

Mount Fang	房山
Mount Koya	高野山
Nagarjuna	龍樹
Nalanda Monastery	那蘭陀寺
Nanyang Huizhong	南陽慧忠
"One Thousand Character Text"	千字文
Poisonous Commentary on the Heart Sutra	般若心經毒語
Praise to the Heart Sutra	般若心經贊
Prajna	般若
Prajnacakra	智慧輪
Prajna Paramita Following the Heart Sutra	般若波羅蜜多随心經
Prajna Paramita Mantra Sutra	般若波羅蜜咒經
Puguang	普光
Queen Y Lan	倚蘭皇后
Recorded Sayings of Dhyana Masuter Huong Hai	香海禪師語錄
Record of the Translated Tripitaka	出三藏記集
Record of the Western Region Compiled during the Great Tang Dynasty	大唐西域記
Rinzai School	臨濟宗
Rough Notes on the Prajna Paramita Heart Sutra	若波羅蜜多心經疏
Sacred Mother of Buddhas Prajna Paramita Heart Sutra	聖佛母般若波羅蜜多經
Samadhi Nirmacana Scripture	解深密經
Secret Key to the Heart Sutra	心經秘鍵
Sengyou	僧祐
Sengzao	僧肇
Shakyamuni Buddha	釋迦牟尼佛
Shentai	神泰
Shikshananda	實叉難陀
Shilabhadra	戒賢

Shingon School	眞言宗
Showa Catalogue of Dharma Treasures	昭和法寶録
Shu	蜀
Shu version	蜀版
Silla	新羅
Sino-Sanskrit Version Prajna Paramita Heart Sutra	梵本般若多心經
Soto School	曹洞宗
Stages of Yogachara	瑜伽師地論
Stories Now and Then	今昔物語
Subtle Praise to the Prajna Paramita Heart Sutra	般若波羅蜜多心經幽賛
Suki	守其
Sui Dynasty	随朝
Sutra of Great Incantations	大陀羅尼經
Taisho Canon	大正大藏經
Tale of Genji	源氏物語
Thanh Dam	清潭
Three Treatise School	三論宗
Tianshan Mountains	天山山脈
Tiantai School	天臺宗
Tojung	道證
Torei	東嶺
Treasury of the True Dharma Eye	正法眼藏
Treatise on Completion of Consciousness Only	成唯識論
Treatise on Realization of Great Wisdom (*Dazhidu Lun*)	大智度論
Tripitaka	大藏經
Tu Turong	慈祥
Unfolding the Secret	解深密經
Universal Treasury of Wisdom Prajna Paramita Heart Sutra	普遍智藏般若波羅蜜多心經
Vasubandhu	世親

Wang Xizhi	王羲之
Wang Xuanmo	王玄謨
Wang Yuanlu	王圓籙
Wonch'uk	圓測
Xiaoyao Garden	逍遥園
Ximing Villa	西明閣
Xixia	西夏
Xuanzang	玄奘
Yakushi-ji	薬師寺
Yancong	彦悰
Yaoxing	姚興
Yijing	義浄
Yogachara	瑜伽行
Yulin Cave Group	榆林窟
Yumen Barrier	玉門関
Yu Shinan	虞世南
Zanning	贊寧
Zen School	禅宗
Zhihuilun	智慧輪
Zhipan	志磐
Zhiqian	支謙
Zhiren	知仁
Zhisheng	智昇
Zhongnan Mountain	終南山
Zizhou Zhishen	資州智詵
Zou (Dynasty)	周
Zou Xingsi	周興嗣

Notes

PREFACE AND ACKNOWLEDGMENTS

1. Edward Conze, *The Prajnaparamita Literature* (The Hague: Mouton, 1960; Tokyo: The Reiyukai, 1978), 11.

CHAPTER 2. ENCOUNTERING THE ENIGMA

1. D. T. Suzuki. *Essays in Zen Buddhism: 1–3 Series* (London: Rider & Co., 1973), 27.
2. Karl Brunnhölzl, *The Heart Attack Sutra: A New Commentary on the Heart Sutra* (Ithaca, N.Y.: Snow Lion Publications, 2012), 7.

CHAPTER 3. INSPIRATION OF THE SUTRA

1. Jon Kabat-Zinn, "Selected Scientific Papers on Mindfulness and MBSR," in the Appendix: Reading List for *Full Catastrophe Living: Using the Wisdom of Your Body and Mind to Face Stress, Pain, and Illness* (New York: Delacorte Press, 1990), 452. Jon Kabat-Zinn and Richard J. Davidson, eds., with Zara Houshmand, *The Mind's Own Physician: A Scientific Dialogue with the Dalai Lama on the Healing Power of Meditation* (Oakland, Calif.: New Harbinger Publications, 2011).
2. Kazuaki Tanahashi, ed., *Treasury of the True Dharma Eye: Zen Master Dogen's Shobo Genzo* (Boston: Shambhala Publications, 2010), 332.
3. Ibid.
4. Ibid., 5.
5. Ibid., 29.
6. Ibid.
7. About scientific studies on efficacy of prayer for healing, see Larry Dossey, *Healing Words: The Power of Prayer and the Practice of Medicine* (San Francisco: HarperSanFrancisco, 1993), 169.
8. Tanahashi, ibid., 287
9. Ibid., 25

CHAPTER 4. PILGRIMAGE TO THE WEST

1. *Biography of the Tripitaka Dharma Master of the Da Ci'en Monastery of the Great Tang Dynasty,* * *Taisho,* no. 2053. I have also referred to the accounts of Eryu (Huili*)

and Genso (Yancong*), in Kazutoshi Nagasawa, trans., *Genjo Sanzo: Saiiki,·Indo Kiko* (Tripitaka Master Xuanzang: Central Asia and India Journal) (Tokyo: Kodansha, 1998). For additional descriptions of Xuanzang's life, see Samuel Beal, trans., *The Life of Hiuen-tsiang* (London, 1888, 1914), or the translation by Li Yunghsi, *The Life of Hsüan-tsang* (Peking: The Chinese Buddhist Association, 1959).

The Silk Road Journey with Xuanzang by Sally Hovey Wriggins (Boulder, Col.: Westview Press, 2004) provides an excellent account of Xuanzang's journey. In this book I have largely followed her choice of best-known versions of place names.

2. *Hongguang Mingji** by Sengzao* states that Xuanzang departed in 627. Eryu (Huili) and Genso, *Genjo Sanzo*, 54.

3. This text exists only in the form of a Chinese translation by Xuanzang.

CHAPTER 5. A TINY TEXT BY A GIANT TRANSLATOR

1. *Records of the Western Regions Compiled during the Great Tang Dynasty,** *Taisho,* no. 2087.

2. The stone monument to record this introduction was erected at Xuanzang's Da Ci'en Monastery* later in 656, three years after Tai's death. The calligraphy was done by Chu Suiliang,* the court calligrapher.

3. This story was recorded in Fascicle 8 of the *Kaiyuan Era Catalog of Shakyamuni's Teachings* (Kaiyuan Shijiao Lu),* compiled by Zhisheng in 730. *Taisho,* no. 2154, vol. 55, 555c.

4. This text, *Great Prajna Paramita Sutra,** *Taisho,* no. 220, occupies volumes 5 through 7, three out of the eighty-five volumes of literature in the one-hundred-volume *Taisho Shinshu Daizokyo* (abbreviated in this book as *Taisho*), the most extensive Buddhist canon in the Chinese language.

CHAPTER 6. TALISMAN OF TALISMANS

1. *Japanese Book of Miraculous Stories* (Nihon Ryoi Ki),* vol. 1, sec. 14.

2. Ibid., vol. 2, sec. 15.

3. Fumimasa-Bunga Fukui, *Comprehensive Study of the Heart Sutra* (Hannya Shingyo no Sogoteki Kenkyu), 49.

4. *Complete Collection of the National Treasures and Important Cultural Properties* (Kokuho Juyo Bunkazai Taizen) (Tokyo: Mainichi Shinbunsha, 1997), 1:626.

5. Shinko Mochizuki, ed., *Mochizuki's Great Encyclopedia of Buddhism* (Mochizuki Bukkyo Daijiten) (Tokyo: Sekai Seiten Kanko Kyokai, 1954–63) 9:456.

6. *Great Dictionary of Classical Japanese Literature* (Nihon Koten Bungaku Daijiten), 5:113.

CHAPTER 7. IN PRINT FOR ONE THOUSAND YEARS

1. Roger S. Keyes, *Ehon: The Artist and the Book in Japan* (New York: The New York Public Library; Seattle: University of Washington Press, 2006), 1.

2. Frances Wood and Mark Barnard, *The Diamond Sutra: The Story of the World's Earliest Dated Printed Book* (London: British Library Board, 2010), 6.

3. Shuyu Kanaoka et al., *Great Encyclopedia of Buddhist Culture* (Bukkyo Bunka Daijiten) (Tokyo Kosei Publications, 1989), 98.

4. Genmyo Ono, ed. *Great Dictionary of Explanations on Buddhist Books* (Bussho Kaisetsu Daijiten) (Tokyo: Daito Publications, 1936), 12:691.

5. Fukui, ibid., 441.

6. Given the prominent status of the *Heart Sutra,* as I will discuss in the chapter "Chinese Enthusiasm," I see no reason for its exclusion from any of these versions of the *Tripitaka.*

7. Lewis R. Lancaster, with Sung-bae Park. *The Korean Buddhist Canon: A Descriptive Catalogue* (Berkeley, Los Angeles, London: University of California Press, 1979), 15. Ahn Kai-hyon," Publication of Buddhist Scriptures in the Goryeo Period" in *Buddhist Culture in Korea,* Chun Shin-yong, general ed. (Seoul: International Cultural Foundation), 87.

8. Ibid. The numbers of blocks and scriptures vary according to scholars.

9. See Lancaster, 16.

CHAPTER 8. AN ANCIENT TOWER RESURRECTED

1. Tsunekazu Nishioka, et al. *Yomigaeru Yakushi-ji Saito* (The Yakushi-ji West Pagoda Resurrected, Tokyo: Soshisha, 1981), 127.

2. Ibid., 195.

CHAPTER 9. THE EARLIEST MAHAYANA SCRIPTURE

1. Many contemporary Japanese scholars support the dates ca. 448–ca. 368 B.C.E., based on the northern textual tradition. According to Paul Harrison, professor of Buddhist studies at Stanford University, in his 2013 e-mail communication to me, "Many scholars now believe the dates 566–486 to be too early. Some put the Buddha's death nearer the end of the fifth century, i.e., 400 B.C.E. In any case, there is no concensus on this issue now."

2. Kazuaki Tanahashi and Peter Levitt, trans. and retold. *A Flock of Fools: Ancient Buddhist Tales of Wisdom and Laughter from the One Hundred Parable Sutra* (New York, Grove Press, 2004), 13.

3. Edward Conze, *The Prajnaparamita Literature* (The Hague: Mouton, 1960; Tokyo: The Reiyukai, 1978), 9. *The Thirty Years of Buddhist Studies* (Oxford: Bruno Cassirer Publishers, 1967), 123.

CHAPTER 10. *PRAJNA PARAMITA* AS THE BASIS FOR THE *HEART SUTRA*

1. Raghu Vira and Lokesh Chandra, eds., *Gilgit Buddhist Manuscripts: Revised and Enlarged Compact Facsimile Edition* (*Bibliotheca Indo-Buddhica* Series No. 150) (Delhi: Sri Satguru Publications, 1995), vol. 1, plates 215–216.

2. Jan Nattier, "The *Heart Sutra*: A Chinese Apocryphal Text?" *The Journal of the International Association of Buddhist Studies,* vol. 15, no. 2 (1992), 204, note 15.

Chapter 11. Versions of the Chinese *Heart Sutra*

1. Fukui, ibid., 11.
2. *Taisho,* no. 250.
3. *Taisho,* no. 251.
4. Fukui, ibid., 69.
5. *Taisho,* no. 252.
6. *Taisho,* no. 253.
7. *Taisho,* no. 255.
8. *Taisho,* no. 254.
9. *Taisho,* no. 257.
10. Fukui, ibid., 12.
11. The "inclusion" of the so-called Zhiqian translation of the *Heart Sutra* in Sengyou's list is discussed by Jan Nattier. Her observation is introduced in chapter 13.
12. Wood and Barnard, ibid., 20.
13. Fukui, ibid., 25.

Chapter 12. Versions of the *Hridaya*

1. Masayoshi Kaneko believes that the material on which this manuscript is written is not a palm leaf, and that this was created in China. Shuyo Takubo and Shoko Kanayama, *Bonji Shittan* (Sanskrit and Siddham Scripts; Tokyo: Hirakawa Publications, 1981), 58.
2. F. Max Müller, ed., *Buddhist Texts from Japan* (Oxford: Clarendon Press, 1881).
3. *Mikkyo Kenkyu* (Study of Esoteric Buddhism), vol. 70. Cf. Nakamura Hajime and Kino Kazuyoshi, *Hannya Shingyo / Kongo Hannya Kyo* (Prajna Heart Sutra and Diamond Sutra; Tokyo: Iwanami Shoten, 1959, 2001), 172.
4. Takubo and Kanayama, ibid., 42, 180.
5. Ibid., 56.
6. The word *ushnisha* refers to a fleshy protuberance on the crown, one of the thirty-two marks of the Buddha.
7. Takubo and Kanaoka, ibid., 168.
8. Müller, *Buddhist Texts from Japan.*
9. Shuyu Kanaoka, *Hannya Shingyo* (Prajna Paramita Heart Sutra; Tokyo: Kodansha, 2001), 17, 166.
10. *Taisho,* no. 256; Stein, no. 700 (London: The British Library).
11. Fukui, ibid., 95. (The quotation is translated by Tanahashi.)
12. Conze, *Thirty Years of Buddhist Studies,* 154.
13. Fukui, ibid., 63, 64.
14. Donald S. Lopez, Jr., *The Heart Sutra Explained: Indian and Tibetan Commentaries* (Albany: State University of New York Press, 1988), 5.

Chapter 13. A Chinese Apocryphal Text?

1. Nattier, ibid. Dr. Nattier is formerly Professor at the International Research Institute for Advanced Buddhology, Soka University, Tokyo. I have changed the Chinese

transliteration she used into the pinyin system, and altered word divisions in the titles of sutras in order to maintain the stylistic consistency of the present book.

2. It is known as the *Maha Prajna Paramita Sutra** or *Large Sutra* from its Chinese title, but its Sanskrit title can be translated as "25,000-line Prajna Paramita" and does not include the word "sutra."

3. For example, Nattier demonstrates that the Sanskrit *25,000-line Prajna Paramita*, "*na ... utpadyate, na nirudhyate ...*" ([It] does not originate, is not extinguished ...) → Chinese *Large Sutra* and Chinese *Heart Sutra*, "*bu sheng bu mie*" → Sanskrit *Heart Sutra*, "*anutpanna aniruddh>*" ([They] are non-originated, non-extinct . . .). Between these two Sanskrit texts, the grammar differs — verbs vs. adjectives, singulars vs. plurals. This is segment 11 in my division. (See appendix 1.) For more comparison of these two Sanskrit texts, see Nattier, ibid., 163.

4. Nattier, ibid., 172.

5. The *Heart Sutra* mantra is found in the third fascicle of the *Sutra of a Collection of Dharanis, Taisho,* No. 901, 18:807.

6. Nattier cites the source of this story as Arthur Waley, *The Real Tripitaka and Other Pieces* (London: Allen & Unwin, 1952), 53. Nattier, ibid., n61.

7. Nattier, ibid., 182. And see John McRae, "Ch'an Commentaries on the *Heart Sutra*: Preliminary Inferences on the Permutation of Chinese Buddhism," *The Journal of the International Association of Buddhist Studies,* 11:88 (1988).

8. Nattier, ibid., 183.

9. Ibid., n71 cites Fukui, ibid., 177.

10. Nattier, ibid., 187. Compare segment 7 in these texts in appendix 1.

11. Ibid., 188.

12. Ibid., 189.

13. Ibid., 189

14. Ibid., 191.

15. Ibid., 190.

16. Ibid., 194.

17. Ibid., 199.

CHAPTER 14. THOUGHTS ON THE APOCRYPHON THEORY

1. Fukui, ibid., 549. The quotation is translated by Tanahashi.

2. Ibid. The quotation is translated by Tanahashi.

3. Ibid., 561. The quotation is translated by Tanahashi.

4. Red Pine, *The Heart Sutra* (Washington, D.C.: Shoemaker & Hoard, 2004), 23.

5. See above, 69, for the line from Amoghavajra's* bilingual *Heart Sutra* (fig. 7).

6. According to Nattier: "While the *Large Sutra* had been translated into Chinese by the end of the third century C.E., the *Heart Sutra* makes its appearance much later, in the fifth century C.E. at the earliest and quite possibly not until the seventh." (Ibid., 166.)

7. Ibid., 191: "If these lines were not removed by Xuanzang himself, then, they must have been extracted at some time prior to his encounter with the text." She seems to be implying that the Xuanzang version came after the so-called Kumarajiva version of the *Heart Sutra*. These are segments 6x and 11x in my division.

8. The reason for this conjecture is that if the "Kuramajiva" version had come later than the "Xuanzang" version, the two sections that were taken out in the "Xuanzang" version would have been put back in the "Kumarajiva" version.

9. It corresponds to segment 32 of my division.

10. Segment 6x, right before segment 7, of my division.

11. Fukui, ibid., 78.

12. Ibid., 562.

13. Nattier, ibid., 189.

14. Xuanzang's successor Kuiji* wrote another account: Later, when Xuanzang was doing walking meditation around the sutra storehouse at the Nalanda Monastery, India, that monk reappeared and identified himself as Avalokiteshvara, gave him blessings for a safe return home, and disappeared. (Fukui, ibid., 79.) The text that includes this introduction mentions the posthumous name of Amoghavajra.* This means it was copied after his death in 774.

15. Nattier, ibid., 196.

16. Kuiji's* text was carved on the stone wall at the Da Xingshan Monastery* in the west of the capital (Fukui, ibid., 78).

CHAPTER 15. ROLES OF ANCIENT CHINESE TRANSLATORS

1. According to *Eulogy to Dharma Master Kumarajiva** by one of his top students, Sengzao,* included in *Hongming Mingji.**

2. *Great Dictionary of Buddhist Culture*, 320. *Satyasiddhi* is a treatise by Harivaran (250–350), discussing "All is *shunyata*." *Three Treatises* consists of two treatises attributed to Nagarjuna and one to Aryadeva.

3. For example, compare segment 9 of his text with that of the preceding texts.

4. Identical in the Kumarajiva translation of the *Large Sutra* and the Xuanzang version of the Chinese *Heart Sutra* are segments 7–9 and 11–20. In addition, segments 6 and 10 are similar except for the different ideographs of Shariputra's name. See appendix 2, "Identical Expressions in the Chinese Texts."

5. This identical line in the two texts is pointed out by Nattier, ibid., 171. See segment 7 in my division. Note that *Dazhidu Lun* has a different expression on this segment.

6. Nattier, ibid., 184.

7. They are segments 5, 8, 9, 11, 13–21, 24, 25, 27, 28, 30, 33, 36, 37, 39, and 43. Eleven out of the twenty-three shared segments between the α and Xuanzang versions are identical with those in Kumarajiva's *Large Sutra*. See appendix 2, "Identical Expressions in the Chinese Texts."

8. They are segments 6 and 40–42.

9. In segments 2, 23, 31, and 38.

10. Xuanzang eliminated characters from segments 6x, 11x, and 22. He added characters in segments 2, 4, 22, 23, 29, 31, and 38.

11. See segment 0 in the part "Terms and Concepts" (p. 140).

12. See the discussion of *mantra* in segment 33 in "Terms and Concepts" (p. 195)

13. Identical in the translation of the longer text and the Xuanzang translation are: segments 6–39.

CHAPTER 16. EMERGENCE AND EXPANSION OF THE *HEART SUTRA*

1. See Nattier, ibid., 177.
2. The first longer text of the *Hridaya* we know of is a translation into Chinese by Dharmachandra, who arrived in China in 732; it is titled "Treasury of Universal Wisdom Prajna Paramita Heart Sutra."

CHAPTER 17. CHINESE ENTHUSIASM

1. Hongfu Monastery is where Xuanzang first engaged in translation from 645 until 648, when he moved to Da Ci'en Monastery.* See Fukui, *Hannya Shingyo no Sogoteki Kenkyu* 27, for the text of the carving related to the *Heart Sutra*. Also, Shunkei Iijima, ed., *Shodo Jiten* [Great Encyclopedia of Calligraphy] (Tokyo: Tokyodo Shuppan, 1995), 59.
2. Fukui, *Hannya Shingyo no Sogoteki Kenkyu*, 365.
3. *Taisho*, no. 1710. This text is also translated as "Comprehensive Commentary on the Heart Sutra." See the Selected Bibliography for details.
4. Taisho, ibid., 33-524a.
5. John R. McRae, "Ch'an Commentaries," 91.
6. Ibid., 92.
7. Ibid.
8. Ibid., 87.

CHAPTER 18. THE PAN-ASIAN EXPERIENCE

1. *Taisho,* no. 1711.
2. Eunsu Cho, "Wonch'uk's Place in the East Asian Buddhist Tradition," *Currents and Countercurrents*, ed. Robert E. Buswell, Jr. (Honolulu: University of Hawai'i Press, 2005), 198.
3. Yijing (635–713), *Da Tang xiyu qiufa gaoseng zhuan* (Biography of High Monks in the Great Tang Who Searched for Dharma in the West*), *Taisho*, vol. 51, no. 2066, 4, 8; Zanning (919–1001), *Song gaoseng zhuan* (Biography of High Monks in the Song), *Taisho*, vol. 50, no. 2061, 727.
4. Suggested by my Vietnamese researcher, Quang Huyen.
5. *Thien uyen tap anh ngu luc* (Collected Outstanding Sayings from Zen Monasteries*), 19a–21b.
6. This is included in *Recorded Sayings of Dhyana Master Huong Hai,* *ed. Tu Turong.* Soc Thien Pagoda, 1833.
7. *The History of Buddhism in Vietnam*, ed. Nguyen Tai Thu (The Council for Research in Values and Philosophy, 2008), 247.
8. My brief references to some of the Indian and Tibetan commentaries in this chapter owe much to the great scholarship of Donald S. Lopez in *Heart Sutra Explained*.
9. Ibid., 3.
10. Ibid., 8, 71. I have applied my own rewording to the translated line by Lopez.

11. Ibid., 130. This line represents Lopez's summary of a statement by Atisha.

12. Shu'yu Kanaoka, *Hannya Shin Gyo* [Prajna Paramita Heart Sutra] (Tokyo: Kodansha, 2001), 208.

13. Lopez, 68, 112.

14. This information is based on my 2013 correspondence with Tempa Dukte Lama from Humla, Nepal, and Changa Dorji of the Royal University of Bhutan.

15. Lopez, 14.

16. Ibid., 143.

17. Ibid., 148.

18. James Gentry, "Representation of Efficacy: The Ritual Expulsion of Mongol Armies in the Consolidation and Expansion of the Tsang (Gtsang) Dynasty," in *Tibetan Ritual,* ed. José Ignacio Cabezón (Oxford: Oxford University Press, 2010), 150.

19. Vesna Wallace, "Texts as Deities: Mongols' Rituals of Worshipping Sutras and Rituals of Accomplishing Various Goals by Means of Sutras," ibid., 219. (I have changed the Sanskrit names of the sutras into their English translations.)

20. Ibid., 218, 220.

21. Patrick Hanan, ed., *Treasures of the Yenching* (Cambridge, Mass.: Harvard-Yenching Library, Harvard University, 2003), 112.

CHAPTER 19. JAPANESE INTERPRETATIONS

1. Tanahashi, ibid., 28.

2. This quotation is my own translation from *Illustrated Prajna Heart Sutra* (Hannya Shingyo Zue) (Kyoto: Zen Bunka Kenkyu-jo, 1995), 1.

3. This quotation is my own translation from *Complete Works of Priest Hakuin* (Hakuin Osho Zenshu), vol. 2, ed. Mitsumura Goto (Tokyo: Ryukinsha, 1935), 8. See also *Zen Words for the Heart: Hakuin's Commentary on the Heart Sutra,* trans. Norman Waddell (Boston: Shambhala Publications, 1996).

CHAPTER 20. SCRIPTWISE

1. Takubo and Kanayama, *Sanskrit Letters and Shiddham* (Bonji Shittan) (Tokyo: Hirakawa Shuppan, 1981), 25.

2. Ibid., 40–57.

3. Akira Suganuma, *New Basics for Sanskrit* (Shin Sansukuritto no Kiso) (Tokyo: Hirakawa Shuppan, 1994), 1–13.

4. Anshuman Pandey, "Proposal to Encode the Siddham Script in ISO/IEC 10646," www.unicode.org/L2/L2012/12234r-n4294-siddham.pdf.

5. Peter B. Golden, *Central Asia in World History* (New York: Oxford University Press, 2011), 47.

6. Abdurishid Yakup, *Prajnaparamita Literature in Old Uyghur* (Thurnhout, Belgium: Brepols Publishers, 2010), 223.

7. Akira Nakanishi, *Writing Systems of the World* (Rutland, Vt.: Charles E. Tuttle Co., 1980), 96.

8. Prods Oktor Skjœrvø, "The Khotanese Hrdayasutra," in *A Green Leaf: Papers in Honour of Professor Jes P. Asmussen,* ed. W. Sundermann et al. *(*Leiden: E. J. Brill: 1988), 157.

9. Yakup, *Prajnaparamita Literature,* 223; see also figs. 79–88.

10. Nakanishi, *Writing Systems of the World,* 90.

11. Takubo and Kanayama, *Bonji Shittan,* 97.

12. Andrew Robinson, *The Story of Writing* (London: Thames and Hudson, 1995), 16.

13. Ibid., 11.

14. Gordon J. Hamilton, *The Origins of the West Semitic Alphabet in Egyptian Scripts* (Washington, D.C.: The Catholic Biblical Association of America, 2006), 16.

15. Geoffrey Sampson, *Writing Systems: A Linguistic Introduction* (Stanford, Calif.: Stanford University Press, 1985), 99.

16. A chart on the inside back cover of the the *The American Heritage Dictionary of the English Language,* 4th ed., displays the genealogical relationships of languages in this family.

17. Sampson, 150.

18. Andrew Dalby, *Dictionary of Languages* (New York: Columbia University Press, 1998).

19. Nankei Tachibana, *Hoppo Kiko* (Journal in the North), in Mochizuki, *Mochizuki Bukkyo Daijiten,* 1085.

20. Sampson, 120.

CHAPTER 21. RITUALS IN THE WESTERN WORLD

1. *Garuda* (Berkeley: Shambhala, 1973), 3:40.

2. I will discuss the similarity and difference between *dharani* and *mantra* on p. 194.

3. D. T. Suzuki, *Manual of Zen Buddhism,* 26.

4. Edward Conze, *Buddhist Wisdom Books: Containing the Diamond Sutra and the Heart Sutra* (London: Allen & Unwin, 1958), 77.

CHAPTER 22. SCIENTIFIC THINKING

1. Hideo Itokawa, *Hannya Shingyo to Saishin Uchuron: Uchu no Meikyu e no Chosen: Saisentan Kagaku no Kabe wo Uchiyabutta Shogeki no Kagi* [Prajna *Heart Sutra* and the Newest Cosmology: Challenge to the Maze of Cosmos; Shocking Key that Broke through the Barrier of the Most Advanced Science](Tokyo: Sheisun Shuppansha, 1994), 33. For further discussion of the relationship between the *Heart Sutra* and quantum physics, see *Heart Sutra: Ancient Buddhist Wisdom in the Light of Quantum Reality* by Mu Soeng.

2. This is an excerpt of my interview with Dr. Hut in my home in Berkeley, California, in April 2013.

3. Neil D. Theise, "From the Bottom Up," *Tricycle: The Buddhist Review,* Summer 2006, 24.

4. Ibid.

5. This is a summary of a communication by Dr. Kaszniak on May 16, 2007.

6. Ibid.

7. This is also from my interview with Dr. Hut in April 2013.

PART SIX. TERMS AND CONCEPTS

1. For semantic study of Sanskrit words, I rely primarily on Monier Monier-Williams, *A Sanskrit-English Dictionary* (Oxford, Clarendon Press, 1899) [hereafter abbreviated SED].

2. For comparative linguistic study of Sanskrit words, I largely rely on SED as well as Julius Pokorny, *Indogermanisches Etymologiscshes Wörterbuch* [Indo-Germanic Etymological Dictionary], vol. 1 (Bern: Francke, 1959; hereafter abbreviated IEW). I also use Calvert Watkins, ed., *The American Heritage Dictionary of Indo-European Roots,* 2000 (hereafter abbreviated AHDIER). And I have also benefited from Isao Suzuki, *Eigo to Hannya Shingyo wo Musubu Gogen no Hashi* [An Etymological Bridge between English and Prajnaparamitahridaya], (Chubu Nihon Kyoiku Bunka Kai, 1981).

3. On the grammatical analysis of Sanskrit in the *Heart Sutra,* I have benefited from Shuyo Takubo, *Kaisetsu Hannya Shingyo* [*Heart Sutra* commentary] (Tokyo: Hirakawa Shuppanasha, 1983).

4. Franklin Edgerton, *Buddhist Hybrid Sanskrit Grammar and Dictionary,* vol. 1 (Delhi: Motilal Banarsidass, 1953), 1.

5. Conze, *Thirty Years,* 153; Fukui, *Hannyashin-gyo,* 174. I will discuss "dharani" later at section 32 of this part.

6. *Zhongguo Meishu Quanji* [Complete Collection of Chinese Fine Art], vol. 2 (Beijing: Renmin Meishu Chuba She, 1986), Calligraphy and Seals, 153.

7. Fukui, 39.

8. Pokorny, IEW, 708; AHDIER, 52.

9. Monier-Williams, SED, 652; Pokorny, IEW, 810; AHDIER, 65.

10. Pokorny, IEW, 376; AHDIER, 32.

11. Nakamura and Kino, *Hannya Shingyo,* 17.

12. Yuichi Kajiyama, *Hannya Kyo* [Prajna Sutra] (Tokyo: Chuokoron-sha, 1976), 100.

13. Dogen, "Manifestation of Great Prajna," in Tanahashi, ed., *Treasury of the True Dharma Eye* (Boston: Shambhala Publications, 2013), 25.

14. Monier-Williams, SED, 1302; Pokorny, IEW, 579; AHDIER, 41.

15. AHDIER, 89.

16. *Suttanipāta* is a notable exception.

17. Monier-Williams, SED, 152.

18. Nakamura and Kino, *Hannya Shingyo,* 18. Also, according to Nobumi Iyanaga, *Kannon Hen'yo Tan* [The Story of Avalokiteshvara's Transformation], (Kyoto: Hozokan, 2002), 335, the name Avalokitashvara is seen in an ancient manuscript of the *Lotus Sutra* unearthed in Central Asia. On discussion of the origin of the deity's name, Iyanaga cites M. Th. de Mallmann, *Introduction à l'Étude d'Avalokiteshvara* [*Annales du Musée Guimet, Bibliothèque d'Études,* vol. 57] (Paris: P.U.F., 1967), 59–82. See also Mircea Eliade et al., eds., *The Encyclopedia of Religion* (New York: Macmillan, 1987), 11, under the entry "Avalokiteshvara."

19. *Taisho,* no. 2087, 2–11, 932. See also Iyanaga, *Kannon Hen'yo Tan,* 335.

20. Shuyo Takubo, *Shingon Darani no Kaisetsu* [Commentaries on Mantra and Dharani Treasury] (Tokyo: Shingon-shu Buzan-ha Shumu-cho, 1960), 120. Also, Toshihiko Kimura and Chitai Takenaka, *Zenshu no Darani* [Dharanis in the Zen school], (Tokyo: Daito Shuppansha, 1998), 138. Joan Halifax and I translated this esoteric Sanskrit text following Takubo and Takenaka's interpretations: "Homage to the Three Treasures. Homage to noble Avalokiteshvara, noble Bodhisattva Mahasattva, who embodies great compassion. Om. Homage to you who protect all of those who are fearful. Being one with you, the blue-necked noble Avalokiteshvara, I bring forth your radiant heart that grants all wishes, overcomes obstacles, and purifies delusion. Here is the mantra: Om. You are luminous with shining wisdom. You transcend the world. O Lion King, great bodhisattva. Remember, remember, this heart. Act, act. Realize, realize. Continue, continue. Victor, great victor. Maintain, maintain. Embodiment of Freedom. Arise, arise, the immaculate one, the undefiled being. Advance, advance. You are supreme on this earth. You remove the harm of greed. You remove the harm of hatred. You remove the harm of delusion. Lion King, remove, remove all defilements. The universal lotus grows from your navel. Act, act. Cease, cease. Flow, flow. Awaken, awaken. Compassionate One, enlighten, enlighten. Blue-Necked One, you bring joy to those who wish to see clearly. *Svaha.* You have succeeded. *Svaha.* You have greatly succeeded. *Svaha.* You have mastered the practice. *Svaha.* Blue-Necked One. *Svaha.* Boar-Faced One, Lion-Faced One. *Svaha.* You hold the lotus. *Svaha.* You hold the blade wheel. *Svaha.* You liberate through the sound of the conch. *Svaha.* You hold a great staff. *Svaha.* You are the conqueror of darkness abiding near the left shoulder. *Svaha.* You wear a tiger skin. *Svaha.* Homage to the Three Treasures. Homage to noble Avalokiteshvara. *Svaha.* Realize all phrases of this mantra. *Svaha.*"

21. Iyanaga, *Kannon Hen'yo Tan,* 317.

22. Pokorny, IEW, 340; AHDIER, 24.

23. Bernie Glassman, *Infinite Circle: Teaching in Zen* (Boston: Shambhala Publications, 2002), 17.

24. Pokorny, IEW, 808; AHDIER, 64.

25. Myo Dennis Lahey, one of my Sanskrit consultants, prefers *skandhān,* the accusative plural case of *skandha,* in this sentence, as the object of the verb *avalok.*

26. Thich Nhat Hanh, *Heart of Understanding* (Berkeley: Parallax Press, 1988), 9.

27. Pokorny, IEW, 882; AHDIER, 87.

28. Monier-Williams, SED, 760. See also Pokorny, IEW, 146; AHDIER, 11.

29. Eliade, *Encyclopedia of Religion,* 14:153 (the section "Śūnyam and Śūniyatā").

30. Charles Seife, *Zero: The Biography of a Dangerous Idea* (New York: Penguin Books, 2000).

31. See their translations in the "Texts for Comparison" in the appendices.

32. Monier-Williams, SED, 632; Pokorny, IEW, 842; AHDIER, 62.

33. Monier-Williams, SED, 523; Pokorny, IEW, 756; AHDIER, 57.

34. Monier-Williams, SED, 434; Pokorny, IEW, 1086; AHDIER, 92.

35. Monier-Williams, SED, 1015; Pokorny, IEW, 1124; AHDIER, 96.

36. Monier-Williams, SED, 1152; Pokorny, IEW, 902; AHDIER, 75.

37. Conze, *Buddhist Wisdom,* 82.

38. Pokorny, IEW, 720; AHDIER, 53.

39. Nakamura and Kino, *Hannya Shingyo,* 185.

40. Myo Dennis Lahey points out that it is an error and should be *saṃskārā.*

41. Pokorny, IEW, 726; AHDIER, 54.

42. Chögyam Trungpa, *The Profound Treasury of the Ocean of Dharma,* vol. 2 (Boston: Shambhala Publications, 2013), 123.

43. Pokorny, IEW, 390; AHDIER, 27.

44. Pokorny, IEW, 735; AHDIER, 55.

45. Monier-Williams, SED, 483.

46. Red Pine, *Heart Sutra,* 119.

47. Pokorny, IEW, 5; AHDIER, 4.

48. Pokorny, IEW, 1095; AHDIER, 93.

49. Fukui, *Hannyashin-gyo,* 49.

50. Monier-Williams, SED, 1262; Pokorny, IEW, 1004; AHDIER, 84.

51. Pokorny, IEW, 6; AHDIER, 95.

52. Monier-Williams, SED, 457; Pokorny, IEW, 1090; AHDIER, 93.

53. Pokorny, IEW, 1103; AHDIER, 94.

54. Tenzin Gyatso, *Essence of the Heart Sutra: The Dalai Lama's Heart of Wisdom Teachings,* trans. and ed. Geshe Thupten Jinpa (Somerville, Mass.: Wisdom Publications, 2002), 129.

55. Pokorny, IEW, 726; AHDIER, 54.

56. Edward Conze, *The Large Sutra on Perfect Wisdom: With the Divisions of the Abhisamayālaṅkāra* (Berkeley and Los Angeles: University of California Press, 1975), 488.

57. Suzuki, *Essays in Zen Buddhism,* 216.

58. Nakamura and Kino, *Hannya Shingyo,* 36; also Edgerton, *Buddhist Hybrid,* 566.

59. Pokorny, IEW, 1135; AHDIER, 97.

60. Monier-Williams, SED, 347; Pokorny, IEW, 463; AHDIER, 33.

61. Monier-Williams, SED, 352; Pokorny, IEW, 463; AHDIER, 33.

62. Monier-Williams, SED, 1284.

Selected Bibliography

English

Bokar Rinpoche and Khenpo Donyo. *Profound Wisdom of the Heart Sutra and other Teachings*. Translated from the French by Christian Buchet. San Francisco: ClearPoint Press, 1994.

Brunnhölzl, Karl. *The Heart Attack Sutra: A New Commentary on the Heart Sutra*. Ithaca, NY: Snow Lion Publications, 2012.

Chang, Garma C. C. *The Buddhist Teaching of Totality: The Philosophy of Hwa Yen Buddhism*. London: Allen & Unwin, 1972.

Conze, Edward. *Buddhist Wisdom Books: The Diamond Sutra and The Heart Sutra*. London: Allen & Unwin, 1958.

———. *The Prajnaparamita Literature*. The Hague: Mouton, 1960.

———. *Thirty Years of Buddhist Studies*. Oxford: Bruno Cassirer Publishers, 1967.

———, trans. and ed. *The Large Sutra on Perfect Wisdom: With the Divisions of the Abhisamayalankara*. Berkeley: University of California Press, 1975.

Cook, Francis. "Fa-tsang's Brief Commentary on the Prajnaparamita-hrdaya-sutra," in *Mahayana Buddhist Meditation: Theory and Practice,* edited by Minoru Kiyota, 167–206. Honolulu: University of Hawaii Press, 1978.

Eckel, M. David. "Indian Commentaries on the *Heart Sutra:* The Politics of Interpretation." *Journal of the International Association of Buddhist Studies* 10, no. 2 (1987): 69–79.

Evans-Wentz, W. Y. *Tibetan Yoga and Secret Doctrines*. New York: Oxford University Press, 1935.

Fox, Douglas A. *The Heart of Buddhist Wisdom: A Translation of the Heart Sutra, with Historical Introduction and Commentary*. Studies in Asian Thought and Religion 3. Lewiston, N.Y.: The Edwin Mellen Press, 1985.

Glassman, Bernie. *Infinite Circle: Teachings in Zen*. Boston: Shambhala Publications, 2002.

Gyatso, Geshe Kelsang. *Heart of Wisdom: A Commentary to the Heart Sutra*. London: Tharpa Publications, 1986.

Hakuin. *Zen Words for the Heart: Hakuin's Commentary on The Heart Sutra*. Translated by Norman Waddell. Boston: Shambhala Publications, 1996.

Hasegawa, Seikan. *The Cave of Poison Grass: Essays on the Hannya Sutra.* Arlington, Va.: Great Ocean Publishers, 1975.

Hua, Hsuan. *The Heart of Prajna Paramita Sutra. With "Verses without a Stand" and Prose Commentary.* Translated by Buddhist Text Translation Society. San Francisco: Buddhist Text Translation Society, 1980.

K'ueichi. *Comprehensive Commentary on the Heart Sutra.* Translated from the Chinese of K'uei-chi by Heng-ching Shih. BDK Series, 66. Berkeley: Numata Center for Buddhist Translation and Research, 2001.

Kukai. *Major Works. With an Account of His Life and a Study of His Thought.* Translated by Yoshito S. Hakeda. New York: Columbia University Press, 1972.

Leggett, Trevor. *The Tiger's Cave.* London: Rider & Company, 1964.

———. *Zen and the Ways.* Boulder, Colo.: Shambhala Publications, 1978.

Loori, John Daido. *Mountain Record of Zen Talks.* Boston: Shambhala Publications, 1988.

Lopez, Donald S., Jr. *The Heart Sutra Explained: Indian and Tibetan Commentaries.* Albany, N.Y.: State University of New York Press, 1988.

———. *Elaborations on Emptiness: Uses of the Heart Sutra.* Princeton: Princeton University Press, 1998.

Luk, Charles (Lu K'uan Yu). *Ch'an and Zen Teaching:* London, Rider & Company, 1961.

Maha Prajna Paramita Hridaya Sutra: Heart of the Great Wisdom Paramita Sutra. Translated with commentary by Gyomay M. Kubose. Chicago: The Dharma House, 1975.

McRae, John R. "Ch'an Commentaries on the *Heart Sutra:* Preliminary Inferences on the Permutation of Chinese Buddhism," *Journal of the International Association of Buddhist Studies* 11, no. 2 (1988): 87–115.

Mu Soeng Sunim. *Heart Sutra: Ancient Buddhist Wisdom in the Light of Quantum Reality.* Cumberland, R.I.: Primary Point Press, 1991.

Müller, F. Max, and Bunyiu Nanjio, ed. "The Ancient Palm-leaves Containing the Prajnaparamita-hridaya-sutra and the Ushnisha-vigaya-dharani." *Anecdota Oxoniensia,* Aryan Series, vol. 1, part 3. Oxford: Clarendon Press, 1884.

Müller, Max F., ed. *Buddhist Mahayayana Texts. The Sacred Books of the East,* vol. 49. Oxford: Oxford University Press, 1894.

Nattier, Jan. "The *Heart Sutra:* A Chinese Apocryphal Text?" *Journal of the International Association of Buddhist Studies* 15, no. 2 (1992): 153–223.

Nhat Hanh, Thich. *The Heart of Understanding.* Edited by Peter Levitt. Berkeley, Calif.: Parallax Press, 1988.

Osho. *The Heart Sutra: Discourses on the Prajnaparamita Hridayam Sutra of Gautama the Buddha.* Shaftesbury, UK: Element Books, 1994.

Prajnaparamita and Related Systems: Studies in Honor of Edward Conze. Edited by Lewis Lancaster. Berkeley: Buddhist Studies Series 1. Berkeley: University of California, 1977.

Red Pine, trans. with commentary. *The Heart Sutra: The Womb of Buddhas.* Washington, DC: Shoemaker & Hoard, 2004.

Rinchen, Geshe Sonam. *The Heart Sutra: An Oral Teaching.* Translated and edited by Ruth Sonam. Ithaca, NY: Snow Lion Press, 2003.

Suzuki, Daisetz T. *Manual of Zen Buddhism.* London: Rider, 1950.

Swearer, Donald K., ed. *Secrets of the Lotus*. New York: The Macmillan Company, 1971.

Tenzin Gyatso, the Fourteenth Dalai Lama. *Essence of the Heart Sutra: The Dalai Lama's Heart of Wisdom Teachings*. Translated and edited by Geshe Thupten Jinpa. Somerville, Mass.: Wisdom Publications, 2002.

Trungpa, Chögyam. *Cutting Through Spiritual Materialism*. Boston: Shambhala Publications, 1973.

Vira, Raghu and Lokesh Chandra, eds. *Gilgit Buddhist Manuscripts,* rev. and enl. compact facsimile ed. [Bibliotheca Indo-Buddhica Series no. 150]. Delhi: Sri Satguru Publications, 1995), vol. 1, plates 215–16.

Wei Wu Wei. *Open Secrets*. Hong Kong: Hong Kong University Press, 1965.

Japanese

Fujita, Hironori. *Hannya Shingyo "Ku" no Seiko Hosoku* [The Prajna Heart Sutra: The Emptiness Laws of Success]. Tokyo: Yamashita Shuppan, 1996.

Fujiyoshi, Jikai. *Hannya Shingyo to Chado* [Prajna *Heart Sutra* and Tea Ceremony]. Tokyo: Daito Shuppansha, 1993.

Fukui, Fumimasa-Bunga, *Hannya Shingyo no Sogoteki Kenkyu* [Comprehensive Study of the Heart Sutra]. Tokyo: Shunjusha, 2000.

Hannya Shingyo Uranai [Prajna *Heart Sutra* Fortune-Telling]. Tokyo: Shogakukan Publications, 2000.

Hasegawa, Yozo. *"Hannya Shingyo" no Kenkyu: Kore wa Daizange no Kyoten de Aru.* [Study of the Prajna *Heart Sutra*: This Is a Scripture of Great Repentance]. Tokyo: Kobunsha, 1989.

Hiro, Sachiya. *Hannya Shingyo Jissenho: Nayami ga Mirumiru Kaiketsusuru* [Prajna *Heart Sutra* Way of Practice: Worries Are Instantly Resolved]. Tokyo: Shogagukan, 2000.

————. *Hannya Shingyo Nihyaku Rokujunimoji no Uchu* [Prajna *Heart Sutra*: A Universe of 262 Characters]. Tokyo: Shogagukan, 1998.

Itokawa, Hideo. *Hannya Shingyo to Saishin Uchuron: Uchu no Meikyu e no Chosen: Saisentan Kagaku no Kabe wo Uchiyabutta Shogeki no Kagi* [The Prajna *Heart Sutra* and the Newest Cosmology: Challenge to the Maze of the Cosmos; Shocking Key That Broke through the Barrier of the Most Advanced Science]. Tokyo: Seishun Shuppansha, 1994.

Iyanaga, Nobumi. *Kannon Hen'yotan* [Story of Avalokiteshvara's Transformation]. Kyoto: Hozokan, 2002.

Kajiyama, Yuichi. *Hannya Kyo* [Prajna Sutra]. Tokyo: Chuokoron-sha, 1976.

Kanaoka, Shuyu. *Hannya Shingyo* [Prajna Paramita Heart Sutra]. Tokyo: Kodansha, 2001.

Kimura, Toshihiko, and Tomoyasu Takenaka. *Zenshu no Darani* [Dharanis in the Zen School]. Tokyo: Daito Shuppansha, 1998.

Kiriyama, Yasuo. *Hannya Shingyo Meisoho* [The Prajna *Heart Sutra* Way of Meditation]. Tokyo: Hirakawa Shuppansha, 1994.

Konno, Ken'ichi. *Hannya Shingyo wa Shitte Ita: Sentan Kagaku no Shikaku* [The Prajna *Heart Sutra* Knew It: The Dead Angle of Cutting-Edge Science]. Tokyo: Tokuma Shoten, 2000.

Kubo, Shunryo. *Hannya Shingyo 90 no Chie: 276 Ji ni Kome rare ta Ikikata no Shinzui* [90 Wisdoms of the Prajna *Heart Sutra*: The Essence of Living Condensed in 276 Ideographs]. Tokyo: Mikasa Shobo, 1985.

—–—. *Hannya Shingyo: Jinsei wo Tsuyoku Ikiru 101 no Hinto* [Prajna *Heart Sutra*: 101 Suggestions for a Powerful Life]. Tokyo: Mikasa Shobo, 1993.

Matsumoto, Yukio. *Hannya Shingyo 100 no Seiko Hosoku: Gammo ga Jitsugensuru Kiseki no Godairiki* [The Prajna *Heart Sutra*'s One Hundred Laws for Success: Five Miraculous Great Powers for Actualizing Wishes). Tokyo: Uiguru, 1986.

Muraoka, Tasaburo. *Hannya Shingyo to Seisho* [The Prajna *Heart Sutra* and the Bibles]. Kyoto: Uchuronsha, 1980.

Nakamura, Hajime, and Kazuyoshi Kino. *Hannya Shingyo / Kongohanna-kyo* [The Prajna Paramita Heart Sutra and the Diamond Sutra]. Tokyo: Iwanami Shoten, 1959, 2001.

Nakano, Yudo. *Hannya Shingyo no Kakumei: Tohigan no Shugyo wo Toku* [Revolution of the Prajna *Heart Sutra*: Expounding the Practice of Arriving at the Other Shore]. Tokyo: Genshu Shuppansha, 1993.

Nhat Hanh, Thich. *Tikku Natto Han no Hannya Shingyo* [Thich Nhat Hanh's Prajna *Heart Sutra*]. Translation by Kazuaki Tanahashi of *The Heart of Understanding*. Tokyo: Sojinsha, 1995. Originally published as *The Heart of Understanding*. Berkeley Press, 1988.

Osuga, Katsumi. *Hannya Shingyo de Tsukamu Ki no Gokui* [The Ultimate Secret for Grasping Ki with the *Prajna Heart Sutra*]. Tokyo: Purejidento-sha, 1993.

Setouchi, Jakucho, Umehara Takeshi, et al. *Hannya Shingyo no Kokoro: Torawarenai Ikikata wo Motomete* [Heart of the Prajna *Heart Sutra*: In Search of an Unbound Way of Living]. Tokyo: Purejidento-sha, 2000.

Suzuki, Isao. *Eigo to Hannya Shingyo wo Musubu Gogen no Hashi* [An Etymological Bridge between English and the *Prajnaparamita-hridaya*]. Nagoya: Chunichi Bunka, 1981.

Takubo, Shuyo. *Kaisetsu Hannya Shingyo* (Prajna *Heart Sutra* Commentary). Tokyo: Hirakawa Shuppansha, 1983.

Index of Names

Index of Terms and Syllables

Sanskrit words and syllables in the shorter-text *Hridaya* are shown in citation forms. A simplified Sanskrit spelling is followed by that with diacritical marks; for example: *shunyata/śūnyatā*.

Chinese and Japanese words in the shorter-text *Heart Sutra* are shown respectively with their principal meanings; for example: *bu/fu* (not).